ISBN 978-1-331-41951-8
PIBN 10187565

1 MONTH OF FREE READING

at

www.ForgottenBooks.com

By purchasing this book you are eligible for one month membership to ForgottenBooks.com, giving you unlimited access to our entire collection of over 1,000,000 titles via our web site and mobile apps.

To claim your free month visit:

www.forgottenbooks.com/free187565

English
Français
Deutsche
Italiano
Español
Português

www.forgottenbooks.com

Mythology Photography **Fiction**
Fishing Christianity **Art** Cooking
Essays Buddhism Freemasonry
Medicine **Biology** Music **Ancient
Egypt** Evolution Carpentry Physics
Dance Geology **Mathematics** Fitness
Shakespeare **Folklore** Yoga Marketing
Confidence Immortality Biographies
Poetry **Psychology** Witchcraft
Electronics Chemistry History **Law**
Accounting **Philosophy** Anthropology
Alchemy Drama Quantum Mechanics
Atheism Sexual Health **Ancient History**
Entrepreneurship Languages Sport
Paleontology Needlework Islam
Metaphysics Investment Archaeology
Parenting Statistics Criminology
Motivational

Phillipps, Samuel March

FAMOUS CASES

OF

CIRCUMSTANCIAL EVIDENCE.

WITH AN INTRODUCTION

ON THE

THEORY OF PRESUMPTIVE PROOF.

BY

S. M. PHILLIPS,

AUTHOR OF "PHILIIPS ON EVIDENCE."

(Fourth Edition Enlarged and Revised.)

JERSEY CITY:

FREDERICK D. LINN & CO.

1879.

CONTENTS.

CONTENTS.

APPENDIX.

THE THEORY

OF

PRESUMPTIVE PROOF.

THERE is no branch of legal knowledge which is of more general utility, than that which regards the rules of evidence. The first point in every trial, is to establish the facts of the case; for he who fails in his proof, fails in every thing. Although the jurists hold the law to be always fixed and certain, yet the discovery of the fact, they say, may deceive the most skillful. No work has as yet appeared in the English language on the theory of evidence; and the nature of circumstantial evidence has been still less inquired into. The object of the present Essay is to inquire into some of the more general principles of legal proof, and particularly into that species of proof which is founded on presumptions, and is known to the English lawyer by the name of circumstantial evidence.

Evidence and proof are often confounded, as implying the same idea; but they differ, as cause and effect. Proof is the legal credence which the law gives to any statement, by witnesses or writings; evidence is the legal process by which that proof is made. Hence, we say, that the law admits of no proof but such as is made agreeably to its own principles.

The principles of evidence are founded on our observations on human conduct, on common life, and living manners: they are not just because they are rules of law; but they are rules of law because they are just and reasonable.

It has been found, from common observation, that certain circumstances warrant certain presumptions. Thus, that a mother shall feel an affection for her child,—that a man shall be influenced by his interest,—that youth shall be susceptible of the passion of love,—are laws of our general nature, and grounds of evidence in every country. Of the two women who contended for their right to the child, she was declared to be the mother who would not consent to its being divided betwixt them. When _Lothario_ tells us that he stole alone, at night, into the chamber of his mistress, "hot with the Tuscan grape, and high in blood!" _Cœtera quis nescit?_

As the principles of evidence are founded on the observations of what we have seen, or believed to have been passing in real life, they will accordingly be suited to the state of the society in which we live, or to the manners and habits of the times. The following passage, in the excellent memoirs of _Philip de Comines,_ I believe to be perfectly true, because it is confirmed by other accounts of the general state of manners at the period when he wrote.

Louis XI. distributed, he asserts, for corrupt purposes, sixteen thousand crowns among the King of England's officers that were about his person, particularly to the chancellor, the master of the rolls, the lord chancellor, &c.*

The truth of this narrative has never been called in question, because it is given by an historian of great gravity and character, and is illustrated by the manners of the age; yet although the author says that his design in writing of these transactions, is to show the method and conduct of all human affairs, by the reading of which such persons as are employed in the negotiation of great matters, may be instructed how to manage their administrations, we should find it difficult to give credence to such facts, if related of any modern lord high chancellor or officer of state of the court of England. Thus, the same presumptive evidence that is good as to the court of Edward IV. and the era of 1477, is altogether extravagant if applied to the court of George III. and the beginning of the 19th century.

* V. 2. p. 7.

The oration of Cicero for Cluentius, exhibits evidence of judicial corruption which can only be credited from our general knowledge of Roman manners at the era of the facts which he describes.

The King of Siam gave credence to everything which a European ambassador told him, as to the circumstances and condition of Europe. until he came to acquaint him, that the rivers and sea were occasionally made so hard, by the cold, that people could walk on them; but this story he totally disbelieved and rejected, as entirely repugnant to every thing which he had either seen or heard; and the ground of his disbelief was perfectly rational.

A similar principle sways our belief in respect to the acts of individuals, as arising in the society and period in which we live. We always refer the credibility of the case to what has fallen within our own observation and experience of men and things. We readily give credence to acts of common occurrence, and are slow in yielding our assent to the existence of new and unlooked for events. When a wretch, at no distant period, in affluent circumstances, was accused of having stolen some sheets of paper in a shop, the judges admitted him to bail against evidence, because the charge was altogether unlikely in one of his condition in life. From these instances, we may safely infer that the principles for our believing or disbelieving any fact, are rather governed by the manners and habits of society, than by any positive rule. The writers on the general law of evidence, such as Mascardus and Menochius, have accordingly declared that all proof is arbitrary, and depends on the feelings of the judges.

There are two species of presumptive proof: the first is the presumption of the law, and the second the presumption of the judge, juryman, or trier.

The presumption of the law is that conclusion which the law attaches to a certain species of guilt. Thus, that he whc has deliberately and willfully killed another, has done so from malice, is a presumption of the law. But how far he who has been found with the sword in his hand by the body of the man just killed, did or did not give the mortal stroke, is a presumption to be made by the jury, and is not determinable by any positive rule of law.

The presumption of the law, Montesquieu observes, is preferable to that of man. The French law considers every act of a merchant, during the ten days preceding his bankruptcy, as fraudulent; this is the presumption of the law.

The modern French code has wisely decreed, that when the law, on account of circumstances, shall have deemed certain acts fraudulent, proof shall not be admitted that they were done without fraud. And in our own, as in every other system of legislation, a variety of qualities are presumed as to different persons and things, against which no proof shall be allowed. Certainty is the great object of legislation, and nothing could be established but by the determination of some thing as already fixed.

All proof is in reference to some fact already known and admitted,—what is doubtful must be proved in reference to what is true.

The following rules, by Quintilian, proceed upon this principle, but they are, perhaps, rather curious than useful:— *One thing is, because another is not:* it is day, therefore it is not night. *One thing is, therefore another is:* the sun is risen, therefore it is day. *One thing is not, therefore another is :* it is not night, therefore it is day. *One thing is not, therefore another is not :* he is not rational, therefore not a man.

Evidence is divided into positive and presumptive. Positive evidence is where the witness swears distinctly to the commission of the act or crime which forms the subject of the trial. Presumptive evidence is that conclusion which the jury draw for themselves, from circumstances or minor facts, as sworn to by the witnesses.

Presumptions are consequences drawn from a fact that is known to serve for the discovery of the truth of a fact that is uncertain, and which one seeks to prove. But no presumption can be made but on a fact already known and ascertained. Thus, if the stains of blood on the coat of one tried for murder, are to be presumed as evidence of his guilt, the fact of the stains being occasioned by blood must be first distinctly ascertained; the one presumption cannot be made to aid the other.

The stains are not to be presumed from blood because he is presumed to have been the murderer; nor, on the other hand, is he to be believed the murderer, because the stains are believed to be from blood; for this is reasoning in a circle, and returning back to the point whence the argument commenced. In laws, the arguments should be drawn from one reality to another, and not from reality to figure, or from figure to reality.

Whilst dwelling on the general head of proof, it may be proper to inquire in what does proof naturally consist. Is one witness, according to the principles of natural reason, sufficient to give legal credence, or are two witnesses necessary?

The Roman or civil law has required two witnesses to each separate fact.

But this principle did not, perhaps, arise from the dictates of legal prudence, but was borrowed from a text of Scripture: "In the mouth of two or three shall the truth be established." The text was meant merely to carry reference to certain circumstances incident to the Christian religion. But the principles of religion are happily founded on higher evidence than is necessary to guide men in the business of common life.

The incidents of commerce, and the daily intercourse of mankind require not only that moral certainty which we are warranted, from general observations, to confide in. It were superfluous to show how difficult it must be, nay, how impossible, often, to prove a crime by two witnesses. The absurdity and inconveniency of the rule has been attended with that effect which will always attend an inconvenient law ; a variety of shifts have been invented to evade it. One witness is held sufficient to a fact of a general nature, and half proofs have been established.

If the rules of evidence are founded on the principles of human nature ; if, like other rules, their fitness is to be judged of by their practical utility, it must be admitted that a proof by one witness, or by circumstances, in certain cases, is good and reasonable.

It is true, that by the English law of high treason, that is, by the 25th of Edward the Third, two witnesses are required to convict a prisoner of the charge : that is to say, one witness to one fact, and another to a different fact, of the same species of treason, shall be held to be two witnesses within the meaning of the statute. But this law was passed for the security of the subject, and to guard against the over-bearing influence of the crown in state prosecutions ; and it is no doubt in reference to crimes against the state, that Montesquieu has made the following observation :—" Those laws which condemn a man to death, on the deposition of a single witness, are fatal to liberty. In right reason there should be two ; because a witness who affirms, and the accused who denies. make an equal balance, and a third must incline the scale."*—Besides, the observation is made by a writer speaking in reference no doubt to the *civil law,* where there is no jury to estimate the weight due to the evidence. In the present Essay, it is not meant to inquire, what crimes should be liable to the punishment of death, and what not ; it is only proposed to inquire, what degree of proof is sufficient to satisfy the mind of the commission of the act. The principle in law is clear, that the guilt is neither increased nor diminished by the fullness or defect of the proof.

When, it will be asked, shall a proof be said to complete ? The answer must be,—when the judges are satisfied ; if the

---

* Spirit of Laws, b 12, c. 3.

process be regular. For what is implied by the term to prove?

The jurists acquaint us, that to prove is to convince the judge.

Probare est fidem facere judici. And this is the meaning assigned to the term by the English language. The common saying, as used in argument, where a fact is disputed,—*I will prove this to you,—I will convince you of this,—I will satisfy you on this head,*—sufficiently show, that to prove, only implies, to convince another of the truth of our assertions.

The proof must be held to be complete, on the part of the prosecutor, when he produces the best evidence which the case will afford, and such as shall induce the judges to believe the commission of the fact, until it is refuted by opposite evidence on the part of the defendant :* one story is good, until another is told. Where the evidence is believed, and is sufficient to account for the fact, no other proof is necessary.

Hypothetical reasonings are susceptible of the highest degree of evidence, when the *hypothesis* explains many *phenomena,* and contradicts none ; and, when every other *hypothesis* is inconsistent with some of the *phenomena.* And this is the principle on which the philosophy of Sir Isaac Newton, as to the motion of the heavenly bodies, is founded.

Where there is no reason, *not* to believe ; that, alone, is a reason for believing the evidence of our senses.

The senses are ever true, but the understanding often reasons ill. It is not proper to reject a probable opinion, without establishing a better in the room of it.

But these remarks are, after all, but barren generalities ; and the observation of the great writers on this subject, will too often be found to be just,—that all proof is arbitrary, and cannot be reduced to positive rules. It happens, sometimes,

---

* Indeed, the proof is complete, on the part of the prosecution, when the best evidence has been produced. That is to say, the proof should be made to rest there, whatever the probable effect of the evidence or the court may or may not be.

that the most probable things are false; for, if they were always separated from falsehood, they would be certain, and not probable. Or, as rendered by some other translators,—

The most probable things, sometimes prove false; because, if they were exempt from falsity, they would not be probable, but certain.*

It is likely several things may happen, which are not likely.

The ancient Romans were so sensible of the uncertainty of evidence, and the difficulty of always ascertaining the guilt of the prisoner, that their form of judgment (or verdict of the jury as we should style it), merely expressed, that he appeared to have done it, _fecisse videtur._

It is not the fact, always, that constitutes the guilt, but the opinion of the judge. "What have the laws ordered in such a case?" was asked of an advocate ot Byzantium: "What I please," was the answer.†

The end of a proof, is to establish the matter in debate· In every case, whether by direct proof, or by that of circumstantial evidence, the jury ought always to be fully satisfied of the guilt of the prisoner, before they return such a verdict. It is immaterial what the proof is, if it is not believed, and brings conviction to the mind of the jury.

It has been, of late years, a favorite theme, to descant upon the certainty of circumstantial evidence. The practice of the law, like other things, has its prejudices; and the name of an eminent man, the success of a particular trial, will sometimes give sanction to a false theory.

Circumstances, it is said, cannot lie. This is very true but witnesses can. And from whom do you obtain circumstances, but from witnesses? Thus, you are liable to two deceptions: first, in the tale told by the witness; and, secondly, in your own application of those circumstances. Where a fact is positively sworn to, as seen by the witness, the conclusion

---

* Aristotle, Vide Bayle Dict. Agathon.
† Travels of Anacharsis, v. 4 p. 400.

or inference to be drawn from it, is generally obvious. But, where the inference is to be drawn from a long train of circumstances, it is a matter of judgment; it is an exercise of the understanding; and, as all men do not understand alike, very opposite conclusions are sometimes drawn from the same shades of probability.

When the ancient prudence of the law denied to a prisoner the benefit of counsel, on a capital charge, to plead for him, it was understood that the proof should be so clear, as to be self-evident to the jury. It was understood that the judge should be counsel for the prisoner; that is to say, that he should see that the process was fair and regular, and that no undue advantages were taken; but that process is vitiated in its vital part, when a false principle is introduced.

"A presumption, which necessarily arises from circumstances, is very often more convincing, and more satisfactory, than any other kind of evidence; it is not within the reach and compass of human abilities to invent a train of circumstances, which shall be so connected together as to amount to a proof of guilt, without affording opportunities of contradicting a great part, if not all, of these circumstances." (*Charge of Mr. Justice Bullen, on the trial of Captain Donnellan.*)

I deny the position. I maintain, that the theory is repugnant to the received principles of jurisprudence; as known to the best foreign writers on the law of evidence. I maintain that it is not warranted by experience,—the greatest proof of every rule, the proof of proofs. And I may further assert, that it is new to the practice of the English law.

First, I shall show, that the theory is repugnant to the received principles of jurisprudence, as known to the best foreign writers, on the law of evidence.

The first to whom I shall refer is Mascardus, a writer of great eminence on the general theory of proof; regarding which, he has published four volumes.

" Proof by evidence of the thing, is superior to every other;

and of all different kinds, none is so great as that which is made by witnesses deposing to what they have seen."*

"Proof by presumption and conjectures," he observes in another place, "cannot be called a true and proper proof."†

The work of Menochius is entirely dedicated to the doctrine of presumptions or circumstantial evidence; and although he displays the partiality for this species of proof, which is natural to one who has dedicated his attention to a particular subject' yet, in the very first chapter of his work, he observes, that "the proof or credence which arises from the testimony of witnesses, is superior to any other."‡

I shall not think it necessary to load this Essay with quotations from other writers on the civil law; the above two possess the most eminent authority of any on the subject of evidence. But the same opinion is expressed by every other author, whom I have had occasion to consult: no one has maintained the absurd position, that circumstances cannot lie; or, that conjectural proof is superior to that of ocular demonstration.

Secondly. I maintain, that it is not warranted by experience,—the great test of every rule.

It might appear invidious, to carry reference to cases of modern occurrence, where fatal mistakes have been discovered of persons too hastily convicted on mere circumstantial evidence; the history of the judicial proceedings in this and every other country will afford too many illustrations.

Some cases of this kind will be found well illustrated in Lord Chief Justice Hale's Pleas of the Crown, vol. 2, p. 289.

Various instances occur, of the fatal error being too late

---

* Probatio per evidentiam rei omnibus est potentior, et inter omnes ejus generis major est illa, quæ fit per testes de visu. (Macardus de Probationibus, v. 1, q. 3, n. 8.

† Probatio per presumtiones et conjecturas dici non potest vera et propria probatio.

‡ Probatio seu fides quæ testibus fit, cœteris excellet. (Menochius ue Præsumptionibus, l. 1, q. 1.)

discovered; but who can say, how many instances have occurred, where the mistake has never been discovered?

It has often happened, that the real murderer has confessed the fact for which the innocent man has suffered; but, as real murderers do not always confess when innocent men suffer, it is impossible to say to what length this dangerous doctrine may have been carried.

Thirdly. I have further to observe, that this principle is new to the practice of the English law.

That great collection of criminal cases, which bears the name of the State Trials, contains a great fund of criminal knowledge.

The opinions of the judges, however, as expressed in state prosecutions, are not always to be regarded as law, until we reach the period of the revolution.

New enactments of the legislature have changed some part of the law, and the improving experience of time has altered others. The first notice to be found of this principle, in sound and wholesome times, is on the trial of Miss Blandy, for poisoning her father,—before Mr. Baron LEGGE, in 1752.

The judge, in summing up the evidence to the jury, declares that circumstances are more convincing and satisfactory than any other kind of evidence; because "*facts*," he says, "*cannot lie.*"*

That facts cannot lie, is sound logic, no doubt. Men only lie. But as we only know facts through the medium of witnesses, the truth of the fact depends always upon the truth of the witness; so that, although he furnishes us with a thousand facts, it is of no consequence, if he himself is unsound.

The next occasion on which this doctrine appears, is on the celebrated trial of Captain Donnellan, in 1781, before Mr. Justice BULLER, in the passage already quoted. But he has altered the position a little, by shifting the criterion from facts

---

* State Trials, v. 10, p. 32.

to circumstances. Facts, before, were the standard of truth; circumstances are now made to be so. For circumstances cannot lie. But what else are circumstances but facts, or *minor* facts; and I must take the liberty to say, that circumstances are still more liable to deceive, or to lead to deception, than even facts. A fact being more an object of sight, is easier apprehended by the senses than a circumstance; which, from its triviality, often escapes the attention altogether, is misapprehended, or assigned to a wrong cause.

The trial in question, will afford a most unparalleled illustration of the truth of this observation; it will show the fallibility of circumstances, and the very opposite conclusions which different men will draw from the same appearances.

I shall here give the general shape of the case—

> If shape it might be called, which shape had none,
> Or substance might be called, which shadow seemed.

Sir Theodosius Boughton, a young man of a delicate constitution, had sent to a country apothecary's shop for a draught of medicine. Different vials appear to have been in his chamber, at the time he took the draught; which was intended to be a composition of rhubarb, jalap, and lavender water.

He was suddenly seized with convulsions in his stomach, and foaming at the mouth; and expired before he could give any explanation. On rinsing one of the vials, the sediment gave the effluvia of laurel water, which is known to be a strong poison. Convulsions, foaming at the mouth, and sudden death, are the natural effects of that liquid.

But every man who dies in that way, is not, therefore, poisoned. The apoplexy will produce the same effects and appearances: of which disease, the father of the young man was known to have died. No evidence whatever was produced as to the existence of the laurel water.

Captain Donnellan, the brother-in-law of Sir Theodosius,

was living in his house at the time of the accident. He was the next heir to the estate, and, accordingly, the person who had the most immediate interest in his death. He certainly betrayed some uneasiness on the event, and appearances indicated that he was afraid of being suspected as the author of the mischief. But, if it was natural that he should be suspected, if the *cui bono* points out the actor of a nefarious deed, it was not unnatural that he should find himself placed in circumstances of peculiar delicacy, and manifest embarrassment and confusion in his conduct.

Captain Donnellan was brought to trial, on a charge of poisoning Sir Theodosius Boughton.

The leading point in every case of this sort, is—did the deceased die of poison? For, if he did not, there is an end of the whole. Where there was no poison, there was no poisoner.

But this was altogether a question to be decided by the opinion of medical men. From what then did they form their opinion? From any of those broad marks, respecting which all men judge alike. No; there was nothing of the kind to guide their judgment. The whole cause turned on circumstances, from first to last. Presumptions were formed on conjectures; and conjectures supposed from circumstances never proved. Four physicians inspected the body, on dissection, the eleventh day after the death. They gave their opinion to the jury, and described the circumstances on which that opinion was founded; those four said, they believed him to have died of poison.

The circumstances on which they had given their opinion, were stated, at the trial, to Doctor John Hunter, the most eminent physician of the age. He declared he could not discover, in any of those circumstances, nor in all of them united, any sign of the deceased having died from poison, nor any symptoms beyond those incident to a man dying suddenly.

Q. from the court to Mr. Hunter. Then, in your judgment, upon the appearance the gentlemen have described, no inference can be drawn from thence that Sir Theodosius

Boughton died of poison?—*A.* Certainly not: it does not give the least suspicion.

In questions of science, and above all, in those of medical science, the faith to be reposed in any opinion, will be regulated by the professional eminence of the person giving it. One man's sight being generally as good as that of another, as to a mere matter of fact; as whether he saw, or did not see such a thing, the learned and the ignorant are upon a par, and one witness to a fact is just as good as another. But the case is very different as to a matter of science; for one man's judgment will outweigh that of many. Upon a point of law or equity, we would not put the opinion of a country attorney, or of four country attorneys, against that of a chief justice, Doctor John Hunter stood, at that time, at the very head of his profession; his opinion gave the law to that profession, both in England and in every country in Europe. Had the profession been to estimate his opinion, and not the jury, a very different verdict would have been given. The case referred peculiarly to to Doctor Hunter's line of study,—that of dissection, and the appearances incident to a body on sudden and convulsive death. He pronounced, that the dissection had been irregularly made, and in a way not to afford the true criterion to judge by. And, where the process is irregular, when the experiment is defective, the conclusion must always be vague and doubtful.

The gentlemen composing the jury did not perhaps know the eminence of Mr. Hunter's character; nor, consequently, the weight due to his opinion. But the judge, on the bench, no doubt knew this; and in balancing the evidence, and in summing up, it was clearly his duty to have stated the great weight to be attached to Mr. Hunter's observations. He stated nothing of all this; but took them numerically, "four medical men to one."

Thus, from an irregular dissection, a positive conclusion was admitted.

It is a rule of law, and above all in cases of life and death, that the want of any one circumstance will prevent the effect of the whole. Thus, if the dissection were irregular, the opinion formed in reference to that dissection was a mere nothing. As well may you suppose that proposition itself to be true, which you wish to prove, as that other, whereby you hope to prove it.

Post hoc, ergo propter hoc —a species of argument which often leads to fallacy.

Because the fact immediately followed; therefore it was occasioned by that which it followed. He died immediately after taking the medicine; therefore, he was killed by the medicine.

The present question is, was the process on the trial according to law? Was the conclusion arrived at by regular and legal forms? The grounds on which the legal inference is to be drawn, must always of themselves be clear and certain; there is no presumption upon a presumption; there is no inference from a fact not known.

When the judgment of the law is passed in reference to a certain thing, the existence of that thing should be first clearly made to appear.

The fact of poisoning ought to have been established beyond a shadow of doubt, before any person was convicted as the poisoner.

But the jury, it will be said, were satisfied on this point. Had the evidence been duly summed up by the judge; had they been told, as they ought to have been, that in experimental philosophy, such as tracing the effects of a particular poison, in tracing the causes, so many and so complicated that lead to death, if the experiment is defective, if the process is vitiated in one instance, the result is also vitiated and defective. Every practitioner in philosophy is sensible and aware of this truth; and wherever he finds that he has erred in his experiment, he sets the case aside, as affording no satisfactory result, and renews his process in another subject.

But, unfortunately, it is a matter of pride, in some men

to be always certain in their opinion, and to appear beyond the influence of doubt. Very different was the practice of that modest and eminent man who gave his evidence on this trial: he was accustomed to the fallaciousness of appearances, —to the danger of hasty inferences from imperfect proofs, and refused to give his assent to an opinion, without facts being first produced to support it. " If I knew," said Mr. Hunter, " that the draught was poison, I should say, most probably, that the symptoms arose from that; but when I don't know that that draught was poison, when I consider that a number of other things might occasion his death, I cannot answer positively to it."

During the whole course of this celebrated trial, there was not a single fact established by evidence, except the death, and convulsive appearances at the moment. These appearances, Mr. Hunter declared, offered no suspicion whatever of poison, and were generally incident to sudden death, in what might be called a state of health ; not only there was no fact proved, but there was not one single circumstance proved. One circumstance was supposed from another, equally suppositious, and from two fictions united a third was produced. The existence of the laurel water was thus made out: the sediment found in the vial, from which the unfortunate young man had drunk, was supposed to smell like bitter almonds; for, as the smell of laurel water was not then known to Lady Boughton, she could not trace the resemblance further; bitter almonds were supposed to smell like laurel water.

It is here to be observed, that the smell attached to the vial was momentary, for it was washed out almost immediately, and could not be twice experienced. But what so uncertain as the sense of smell ? Of all the human senses, it is the most uncertain, the most variable, and fallacious. It is often different to different men, and different in the same person, at one hour, from what it is at the next; a cold, a slight indisposition, the state of the stomach, a sudden exposure to the air, will extenuate or destroy this impression.

But this train of proof was altogether at variance with principles. In law, as already observed, the arguments should be drawn from one reality to another; but here, the argument turned upon the breath, the smell of a woman, distracted at the moment, with the loss of her son, and ready to ascribe that evil to the first thing that came in her way.

All proof must begin at a fixed point. The law never admits of an inference from an inference. Two imperfect things cannot make one perfect. That which is weak, may be made stronger; but that which has no substance, cannot be corroborated. The question is never what a thing is like; but the witness must swear to his belief, as to what it is. A simile is no argument. Upon the principle, that comparison of hands is no evidence, in a criminal trial, comparison of smells must be held to be equally defective. Besides, there are a variety of articles that resemble bitter almonds in the smell, and many of these altogether innoxious.

In circumstantial evidence, the circumstance and the presumption are too often confounded; as they seem to have been throughout this trial. The circumstance is always a fact; the presumption is the inference drawn from that fact. It is hence called presumptive proof; because it proceeds merely on presumption or opinion. But the circumstance itself is never to be presumed, but must be substantively proved. An argument ought to consist in something that is itself admitted; for who can prove one doubtful thing by another. If it was not laurel water, that Sir Theodosius drank, the proof fails as to the effect; and, certainly, some of the usual proofs, some of the common *indicia* or marks of things, should have been established. Where did the prisoner procure it? From whom did he obtain it? Where, and what time,—and by whom, or how did he administer it?* Nothing of this kind was proved.

The whole proof, as to laurel water, rested upon the com-

* Venenum arguis: ubi emi? a quo? quanti? per quem dedi? quo conscio? Quintilian, l. 5, c. 8, s. 37

parison of the smell. Question to Doctor Parsons, " You
ground your opinion upon the description of its smell by Lady
Boughton?" Answer. "Yes, we can ground our opinion upon
nothing else but that, and the subsequent effects."

But the judgment of the cause from its effects, Mr. Hunter
has already shown to be equally conjectural as that formed
from its resemblance in smell.

The proof proceeds. He was supposed to be poisoned,
because it was believed to be laurel water; and it was believed
to be laurel water, because he was supposed to be poisoned.
We will not say that both these suppositions might not have
been true; yet still they were but conjectures, unsupported by
any proof, and formed against all the rules of law.

But the accused, it is said, furnished the proof against himself, by his own distrust of his innocence. He no doubt betrayed great apprehensions of being charged with the murder;
but are innocent men never afraid of being thought guilty?

We readily recognize all the general truisms, and common-
place observations, as to the confidence of innocence, and the
consciousness of guilt; but, we find, from history, that innocence loses its confidence, when oppressed with prejudice; and
that men have been convicted of crimes, which they never
committed, from the very means which they have taken to
clear themselves.

" An uncle who had the bringing up of his niece, to whom
he was heir at law, correcting her for some offense, she was
heard to say, ' Good uncle, do not kill me;' after which time
she could not be found; whereupon the uncle was committed
upon suspicion of murder, and admonished, by the justices of
the assize, to find out the child by the next assizes; against
which time he could not find her, but brought another child,
as like her in years and person as he could find, and apparelled her like the true child; but on examination she was
found not to be the true child. Upon these presumptions
(which were considered to be as strong as facts that appear in
the broad face of day), he was found guilty and executed;

but the truth was, the child, being beaten, ran away, and was received by a stranger; and afterwards, when she came of age to have her land, came and demanded it, and was directly proved to be the true child.*

The above case was referred to by Lord MANSFIELD, in his speech in the Douglass cause, as an illustration that forgery, and falsehood itself, has been sometimes used to defend even an innocent cause. "It was no uncommon thing," he observed, "for a man to defend a good cause by foul means, or false pretenses."

Captain Donnellan was liable to suspicion, and to great suspicion, on the general relations of the subject, independent of particular circumstances, and would have been suspected by all the world, had he been never so innocent.

In the first place, it was a well-known fact, that he had been obliged either to quit the army (to which he originally belonged), or had been cashiered by the sentence of a court-martial.

Secondly, he was of all other men the person who was to have gained by the death of Sir Theodosius Boughton; to whose estate and property he succeeded as his brother-in-law. No other human being had an interest in the case. Such is the disposition in human nature (founded perhaps on a too just knowledge of our feelings and principles of action), that first suspicion always points to the person who is to gain by it, as the author of any mischief of which the real perpetrator is not known. The *cui bono* was not invented by Cassius Severus, to whom it is ascribed,—but every man is alike the *rock of the accused,* in this respect.

If, therefore, it was natural, on general grounds, that Mr. Donnellan should be so suspected, it was also natural for him to be sensible that he would be so, and consequently, to be alarmed, distracted, and uneasy.

But it will be said, that, granting all this, he displayed

---

* Hale's Pleas of the Crown, v. 2, p. 290.

more uneasiness than was even natural to one in his situation. It is a delicate thing to answer this question,—it is a nice thing to fix the standard of human feelings,—and to say what degree of perturbation a man, already branded with guilt and conviction, shall feel when placed under circumstances which make him to be suspected of a capital crime.

Lawyers, and those accustomed to see and advise with persons in that unfortunate predicament, only can tell the terrible apprehensions that every man feels at the idea of being a second time brought to a public trial; it is altogether a new view of human nature, and we seldom estimate, rightly, feel ings which we have never experienced, nor expect to ex perience in our own persons, nor have witnessed in that of other persons;—

" To thee no reason,—
" Who good has only known, and evil has not proved."

They who have been accustomed to carry on criminal prosecutions, must be fully aware of the influence which a former trial and conviction is calculated to have on almost any accusation; but in no case can that influence be greater than where the trial turns on presumptive proof. For here it is often the feelings, the prejudices, and opinion of the the jury, that supply the want of evidence.

Suspicion is to be distinguished from proof,—a thousand suspicions do not form one proof. We understand, in common language, by the term suspicion, the imagining of something ill, without proof. It may, therefore, form a proper ground of accusation, but never of conviction: it seems to arise from the general semblance of things, and often from the morals of the individual, rather than from any distinct act. Thus, in the civil law, a guardian is regarded as suspected, whose morals render him so.

A suspicion, is on a thing, and a necessary inference another: a suspicion is an impression on another man's mind, —an inference is made from the fact itself.

There certainly was no overt act proved against the prisoner during the whole course of this trial; it was not proved that he gave the poison, or saw it given, or had such in his possession. Many things, no doubt, in his demeanor and conversation, gave strong suspicions against him; but, if the civil law positively forbids a man being condemned on suspicion, can that be justified by ours?

" The wisdom and goodness of our law appears in nothing more remarkably, than in the perspicuity, certainty, and clearness of the evidence it requires to fix a crime upon any man, whereby his life, his liberty, or his property can be concerned: herein we glory and pride ourselves, and are justly the envy of all our neighbor nations. Our law, in such cases, requires evidence so clear and convincing, that every bystander, the instant he hears it, must be fully satisfied of the truth and certainty of it. It admits of no surmises, innuendoes, forced consequences, or harsh constructions, nor anything else to be offered as evidence, but what is real and substantial, according to the rules of natural justice and equity."*

We have been the more full in our observations on this trial, because it has been so often quoted with a sort of triumph, as forming a model and illustration of the nature of circumstantial evidence. It is an illustration, indeed, of how little evidence one man has been convicted on; but it is an illustration of nothing else.

We can never bring ourselves to believe, that it is necessary to forfeit the life of a man on bare suspicion, on presumptions without proof, and on inferences unsupported by evidence.

A rule of conduct, to be good, must be so on general grounds, and in reference to the state of society in which we

---

* Lord Cowper's speech on the Bishop of Rochester's trial.

are placed; and, happily, the wholesome state of British morals does not require that men should be convicted on any evidence but that which is established by law, and warranted by sound reason.

The mischief of a nice conviction does not rest with the particular case; precedents are grounds of law by the English practice, and indeed the most general ground of our law of evidence.

We have, in more than one instance, witnessed the doctrine of circumstantial evidence being hastily applied by loose analogies and incidents, foreign to the intrinsic conditions of the subject. But we do not feel ourselves at liberty to hurt the tenderness due to living reputation, by recurrence to recent instances; we adopt the more agreeable duty of bearing testimony to the wise maxim of an eminent magistrate: "Nothing can be more dangerous or unjust, in matters of this nature," says Mr. Chief Justice HYDE, speaking of homicide, "than to establish material distinctions upon points which do not enter into the intrinsic merits of the case." (*East's Pleas of the Crown*, p. 241.)

The evidence of circumstances on every criminal trial, should be confined as much as possible to the actual commission of the fact.

The intention, indeed, must always precede the act, and is chiefly to be judged of by the antecedent circumstances. But then each of these circumstances should be regarded as a fact to be proved and established by evidence; and, unless so established, ought never to form a ground of conviction. We must once more revert to the trial for illustration. On passing sentence, Mr. Justice BULLER conveyed the following opinion as to the motives:—"Probably the greatness of his fortune caused the greatness of your offense; and I am fully satisfied, on the evidence given against you, that avarice was your motive, and hypocrisy served you with the means."

But where or how was this proved by evidence on the trial? The speech of a judge is to be taken out of the evidence adduced on the trial;—if it is not so limited, it may be difficult to fix its bounds.

In a criminal trial, and more especially in the trial for a capital offense, everything is supposed to be governed by fixed and known rules. There is here no room for the discretion of a judge; the proof by which the prisoner is to be tried is as fixed as the law which condemns the crime; at least, the principles of that proof are to be stated by the judge to the jury, as known and received maxims of reason, handed down by a long train of precedents, or fixed by statutory enactment. "Whatever the rules in Westminister Hall are, it is not therefore reason because it is a rule; but because it is reason, and reason approved of by long experience, therefore it is a rule." (*State Trials*, vol. 4, p. 291.) The opinion of Mr. Justice BULLER might have been very just, but if it was not regularly formed, it was extra-judicial and of dangerous example.

It is an observation warranted by the history of our crimi nal law, that all the instances by which innocent men have lost their lives, have arisen from precedents against guilty men;* but laws were meant to protect the innocent, as well as to punish the guilty.

The following observation, by Lord BACON, suggests the caution with which men should give their assent to any proposition founded on a mere similarity of circumstances:— "The mind," he observes, "has this property,—that it readily supposes a greater order and conformity in things than it finds; and although many things in nature are singular, and extremely dissimilar, yet the mind is still imagining parallel correspondence and relations betwixt them which have no existence.

"Nor does this folly," he adds, "prevail only in abstract tenets, but also in simple notions." (*Novum organum, s. 2, aphorim* 45.)

---

* Omnia mala exampla, ex bonis initiis orta sun.

Every one may prove the justice of these remarks, by his reflections on what he sees every day occurring in common life.

Weak men are always the first to assent and to admit of loose analogies, imperfect resemblances, and inferences without proof,—whilst men of stronger minds, and more reflection, look out for distinctions; they search for discriminations in subjects nearly similar, and are slow in yielding their assent to first impressions. Judgment consists in distinguishing things which are nearly alike, without exactly being so.

In the general prejudice, which at present prevails for circumstantial evidence, the mind, I am afraid, is rather disposed to look out for analogies and resemblances, than for discrimination.

In almost every trial, it is the interest of the accuser to accumulate his proofs, whilst the safety of the prisoner consists in considering these, separate and apart; this practice, therefore, has a tendency rather to convict than to acquit.

We should lament to advance any thing that might tend to weaken the facility of detecting crimes; but that facility may be increased by establishing certain rules for the determination of proof.

Without presuming to state a body of general rules, we may be allowed to show where some obvious principles have been violated. All instruction proceeds safest by negatives and exclusives to what is positive and affirmative. And it was this principle which led us to dwell so particularly on the above case. We conceive one great error has arisen trom the popular saying, that circumstances cannot lie; from the idea that circumstantial evidence is equivalent to direct proof.

And, perhaps, from the vanity of forming resemblances, where (if that passion in the judicial character is ever allowable), the vanity should rather be in perceiving distinctions.

Nothing is more dangerous in the mouth of a judge, than popular brocards, barren generalities, and loose unsettled maxims, which carry away the attention of the jury from the intrinsic evidence of the case itself, and prevent the free exercise of their own understandings. It is not every jury-man that can understand a general theory, but every man ot sense can compare what he hears at the trial, with similar circumstances, as falling under his own experience, and so estimate for himself the credibility of the evidence.

I deprecate an argumentative judge, reasoning a jury into a belief of guilt or innocence, rather than leaving them to judge from their own feelings; from those feelings which God and nature have bestowed on them, as the safeguard of inno-cence, and the true measure of human conduct.

The following observation, in the charge so often alluded to, deserves particular remark:—"It is not within the reach and compass of human abilities to invent a train of circum-stances which shall be so connected together as to amount to a proof, without affording opportunities of contradicting a great part, if not all, of these circumstances."

This is one of those general sayings which, coming from high authority, is allowed to pass without examination, and, from being often repeated, no one thinks to doubt of its truth No other remark, however, was ever more refuted by experi-ence. If the observation was just, we should find it illus-trated by practice; but we know that there are infinitely more instances of mistaken convictions on circumstantial evidence, than by any other species of proof whatever " Reducing general words to particular facts, clears the sophistry of them."*

I beg here to dwell, a little more minutely, on the hard-ship of requiring a prisoner to controvert a train of circum-stantial evidence. For, how can a prisoner, altogether innocent of the charge, controvert circumstances, or an account of events, with which he is unacquainted. A man, charged with the commission of a crime, at a period long an-

---

* Remarks on College's trial, by Sir J. Hawles. State Trials, vol. 3 p 621.

terior to the trial, if innocent, and at a distance from the place, at the time of its occurrence, can only establish his innocence by one of two methods:—first, by showing a con-. tradiction in the circumstances of the proof itself; or, secondly, by establishing an *alibi*,—that is, by showing that he was at a different place at the time.* In regard to the first mode of refuting the charge: if he is ignorant of the facts, if he is unaccustomed to the nature of legal argument, he may not easily confute the chain of circumstances. A premeditated story is always so made up as to bear the appearance of consistency. Men will believe a probable falsehood rather than a singular truth; and, in regard to the proof of an *alibi*, if the prisoner does not happen to recollect the day, or cannot, perhaps, recall to mind where he chanced to be on that day, he is left without a defense. The proof of a negative is always difficult, often impossible.

But what is the situation of a person charged with a capital crime? Suspicions of this sort generally fall upon the needy and unfortunate. He is brought from a jail, where he has been perhaps long confined, distracted and agitated with his situation; he has none to assist him or suggest to him what course to pursue; and no counsel is allowed to plead for him, and assert his innocency of the facts charged. A long train of circumstances are offered by the witnesses, of the whole of which he is ignorant, and, therefore, unprepared to ask the necessary questions, or to point out to the jury the incongruity of the story advanced:—his very attempt to do so, unsuccessfully (that is to say, if he makes observations on the evidence, which are not explanatory or correct), will be held an argument of his guilt. But the facts have been sworn to, and his personal appearance is perhaps against him; and his character,—it may be, suffering under prejudice. If a weak magistrate happens to sit on the bench (and weak men

---

* The character of the witnesses is, no doubt, always a matter of the most important consideration.

sometimes find their way to the bench, as well as to other places); if the judge is infirm, or his attention exhausted by the fatigue of a long trial; and if, in summing up, he loses sight of the chain of incidents, assumes a fact as established before it is so,—endeavors to prove facts by other facts, which are not proved themselves,—forgets the attention which is due to the character of the witnesses, and has allowed the counsel for the prosecution, in his opening speech, to prejudice and inflame the minds of the jury!—

It were superfluous to ask what the result of such a trial must naturally be. We hope, and believe, that such a concurrence of incidents, hostile to justice, is very uncommon.

But to return to the proposition in the charge: can it ever be admitted that the number of circumstances alleged against a prisoner, facilitates the refutation? Surely the difficulty of defense is increased by the multiplicity of proof that it has to contend with! The attention is distracted; and the very embarrassment incident to the occasion, is alone sufficient to bereave any common man of his faculties.

The civil law has foreseen the embarrassments, which a prisoner must always be under, from a variety of witnesses being produced against him; and has, therefore, left it to the discretion of the judge to moderate their number. It might as well be said, that a prisoner has an advantage in the multiplicity of witnesses opposed to him, because if false he can always refute some of them.

But, if you break the chain of circumstances, it will be said, in one link, the whole structure falls to the ground. This, no doubt, ought to be the consequence. But is the fact so? Does experience warrant the observation? Are we to suppose that all those who have been irregularly convicted, made no defense, and broke no part of the chain? They must naturally have offered something to the consideration of the jury. Yet still, we see, that the general effect of the whole, the multiplicity of the circumstances, pointing against

C

the prisoner, has been thought sufficient to warrant conviction.

It happens, not unfrequently, that a prisoner is not apprized of the evidence intended to be produced against him. If the case is altogether false on the part of the prosecution, the difficulty of defense is increased. For a man can only refute a false story, by being acquainted with some part of it. The true case must always be opposed to the false one. Thus, in the case of two men who were tried some few years ago, for the murder of Mr. Steele, on Hounslow Heath, a long detail of the circumstances attending the occasion, was given in evidence against them. But if they were not, as they asserted, present on the occasion, and knew nothing of either Mr. Steele or the murder, how was it possible for them to refute or disprove the circumstances?

The accusation was not brought until some years after the murder. They could not bring to recollection where they were on that day, and so failed in establishing an alibi.

A different man has been since brought to trial for that very murder. It is true that the judges did not allow the evidence to be entered upon, because they thought that it was insufficient on the statement of the counsel in his opening speech.

It should be always kept in mind, that circumstantial evidence is merely supplemental; and is only resorted to from the want of original and direct proof. And it never can be said that what is secondary, is equal to that which is original, —the thing substituted equal to that which it is meant to supply.

And this distinction seems fully recognized by Lord Chief Baron GILBERT. "When the fact itself cannot be proved, that which comes nearest to the proof of the fact, is the proof of the circumstances that necessarily and usually attend such facts, and called presumptions; and not proof, for they stand instead of the proofs of the fact till the contrary be proved." (*Gilbert's Law of Evidence*, vol. 1, p. 142.)

A regard to the peace and good order of society, certainly requires that crimes shall be liable to be proved by circumstantial evidence. But a regard to the well being of society likewise demands, that the mode of proof should be regulated by some fixed rules. If the nature of the thing admits of but few rules, for that very reason, those few should be the more distinctly observed. This principle is excellently illustrated by the deep Gravina, who somewhere observes (for the book is not at hand for reference), that as the military state admits of but few laws, those few should be the more distinctly observed, as they could only have been introduced into an army or camp from a strong sense of their necessity.

Legal proceedings would be vague and uncertain, judges would become arbitrary, and innocence would be exposed to the resentment of witnesses, if some general and fixed rules were not observed for the discovery of truth.

Of these the following are perhaps the chief:—

1. *The actual commission of the crime itself (the corpus delicti) shall be clearly established.*

2. *Each circumstance shall be distinctly proved.*

3. *The circumstance relied on, shall be such as is necessary or usually incident to the fact charged.*

4. *When the number of circumstances depend on the testimony of one witness, that number shall not increase the strength of the proof.* For, as the whole depends on the veracity of the witness, when that fails the whole fails.

5. *Direct evidence shall not be held refuted from being opposed to circumstances incongruous with that evidence.* Because a certain degree of incongruity is incident to every man's conduct.

6. *The judge, in summing up, shall assume no fact or circumstance as proved; but shall state the whole hypothetically and conditionally; leaving it entirely to the jury, to determine how far the case is made out to their satisfaction.*

7. *The difficulty of proving the negative shall in all cases be allowed due weight.* But the silence of the prisoner as to

facts, which, if innocent, he might have explained, shall be held an argument against him. This, of course, proceeds upon the supposition, that he stood fully apprized, before his trial, of all that was intended to be produced.

8. *The counsel for the prisoner shall be allowed to object freely to the production of any evidence, as not proper to go to the jury, or as not being of legal credence.* On Captain Donnellan's trial, the counsel do not appear to have always availed themselves of this privilege.

The liberty of objecting to any piece of evidence, ought, on every occasion, to be strenuously exerted; as supplying, in a great measure, the right of making the defense.

9. *The jury shall be as fully convinced of the guilt of the prisoner, from the combination of the circumstances, as if direct proof had been brought.*

It should always be considered, whether the connection betwixt the circumstances and the crime is necessary, or only casual and contingent; and whether, therefore, the circumstances necessarily involve the guilt of the prisoner, or only probably so; whether these circumstances might not all exist, and yet the accused be innocent.

It seems desirable, that some inchoate act, approaching to the crime, should be proved on the prisoner; and that he should not be convicted on general appearances,—such as from being found in a certain situation. The improper conviction seem chiefly to have been owing to a neglect of this rule. Strong appearances, but without any act proved against the prisoner, have too often turned out unfounded.

It is sometimes said, in summing up by the judge, that the evidence is the best that the nature of the case can be supposed to afford; but this, certainly, is no reason for the 'ury being satisfied with it. In the first place, the nature of the case is only to be known by the evidence. The case of an innocent man must always be of a nature to afford very little evidence; but the jury, let the case be what it will, must be distinctly persuaded of the guilt of the prisoner, before they return such a verdict. Agreeably to the common law, where the facts have gone regularly before a jury, and there is no misdirection from the judge in summing up, the proof is complete. When the jury is satisfied, the law is satisfied. No principle can be at once more calculated to facilitate the detection of crimes, to ensure the safety of innocence, and to maintain the general peace of society.

10. *Where the body of the act is distinctly sworn to, a variation in the circumstances does not destroy the proof.* "If several independent witnesses, of fair character, should agree in all the parts of a story (in testifying, for instance, that a murder or a robbery was committed at a particular time, in a particular place, and by a certain individual), every court of justice in the world would admit the fact, notwithstanding the abstract possibility of the whole being false. Again, if several honest men should agree in saying that they saw the king of France beheaded, though they should disagree as to the figure of the guillotine, or the size of his executioner, as to the king's head being bound or loose, as to his being composed or agitated in ascending the scaffold, yet every court of justice in the world would think that such difference, respecting the circumstances of the fact, did not invalidate the evidence respecting the fact itself.

" When you speak of the whole of a story, you cannot mean every particular circumstance connected with the history, but not essential to it; you must mean the pith and marrow of a story; for it would be impossible to establish the truth of any fact (of Admirals Byng or Keppel, for example, having neglected or not neglected their duty), if a disagreement in the evidence of witnesses, in minute points, should be considered as annihilating the weight of the evidence in points of importance. In a word, the relation of a fact differs essentially from the demonstration of a theorem; if one step is left out, one link in the chain of ideas constituting a demonstration is omitted, the conclusion will be destroyed; but a fact may be established notwithstanding a disagreement of witnesses in certain trifling particulars of their evidence respecting it."*

The following rule is the converse of the preceding one :

11. *Where the leading fact or crime is only to be collected from circumstances, a material variation in these will defeat the effect of the whole.*

For, as each particular is to have an effect on the general conclusion, a variation in the circumstances may give a different color to the whole transaction.

A system of propositions is only true, because each of the propositions, of which it is composed, is true.

12. *There being no repugnance in the chain of circumstances, is a proof that a thing may be ; not that it is: though there being a repugnance, is a proof that it cannot be.* Whatever does not involve a contradiction, is possible; whatever involves one, is impossible.

13. *The absence of the proof, naturally to be expected, is a strong argument against the existence of any fact alleged.* This applies particularly to cases where violence is charged.

"It is an undoubted truth" (Lord MANSFIELD observed in the Douglass cause), "that judges, in forming their opinion of events, and in deciding upon the truth or falsehood of controverted facts, must be guided by the rules of probability; and, as mathematical or absolute certainty is seldom to be attained in human affairs, reason and public utility require that judges, and all mankind, in forming their opinion of the truth of facts, should be regulated by the superior number of the probabilities on the one side or the other,

---

* Apology for the Bible, p. 344.

We shall search in vain our State Trials, for a happier illustration of the principle than the above, from the elegant pen of Doctor Watson. "Literary men," it has been observed, "have marked superiority over lawyears, whenever they assume their profession."

Quæ argumenta ad quem modum probandæ cuique rei sufficiant, nullo certo modo satis definiri potest.

Ex sententia animi tui te æstimare oportet, quid aut credas, aut parum probatum tibi opinaris (ff. lib. 22, tit. 5, s. 3).

whether the amount of these probabilities be expressed in words and arguments, or by figures and numbers."

Applied to the affairs of civil life in reference to which the observation was made, the proposition is excellent; but the rule does not hold in criminal cases. The impression on the mind of the jury, in a criminal case, must be, not that the prisoner is probably guilty, but that he really and absolutely is so;—where they doubt, they are to acquit.

It is often said, in respect to evidence of this sort, if you break the chain of circumstances, the whole falls to the ground. It is material, always, to be apprised of the meaning of terms, before we argue as to their effect. What is the import of the term? In what does this interruption consist? The Douglass cause turned entirely on circumstantial evidence; yet neither the speeches of the judges, nor the singularly acute letters of Mr. Stewart, on the subject of the trial, afford any solution of the term. The chain appears, on both sides of the question, repeatedly broken, and as often renewed; the want of the fact is supplied by argument, and the argument invalidated by the want of the fact, in endless prolixity.

We hazard an explanation of it with great diffidence:— the chain of circumstances is broken, whenever there is such a defect in the thread of the narrative as cannot be accounted for; or, such a contradiction in the statement, as is irreconcilable with probability.

We will not add to the number of the above rules, lest we might appear to aim at forming a technical system for the belief or disbelief of facts, independent of the free exercise of the understanding over the circumstances of the case.

We must never bind ourselves down to believe or disbelieve, on general grounds, abstracted from the condition of times, persons, motives, and all the variety of relations of which the particular case happens to consist. Irregular, capricious, and shifting as man is, in all his actions, we can never establish absolute grounds for judging of these.

Famous Cases

of

Circumstantial Evidence.

I.

The Old Woman of the Place St. Michel.

THERE lived in Paris, more than a century ago, an old dame who kept a shop in a house not far distant from the Place St. Michel. She was reputed rich, and was supposed to keep her money in the house. Her only servant was a boy who had lived with her for several years ; he slept in the house, but high up in the fourth story, or rather loft, which could only be reached by a staircase, such as was common in those days, outside the house wall, the old lady sleeping in a room on the ground floor at the back of the shop. It was the boy's duty to lock the shop door at night and retain possession of the key. One morning the neighbors found the shop door open much earlier than usual, and as there was no one to be seen in the shop, some of them, suspecting that all was not right, went in. There were no marks betokening a violent entry of the premises, but the old lady was discovered dead in her bed, having received many wounds, such wounds, to all appearance, having been inflicted with a knife; and a knife covered with blood was found lying in the middle of the shop floor. One hand of the corpse yet grasped a thick lock of hair, and in the other was a neck-handkerchief. It was proved beyond doubt that the knife and the neck-handkerchief belonged to the boy who had been so long her servant, and the lock of hair also matched his exactly. He was arrested, charged with the crime, and (probably under torture) confessed it, and suffered capital punishment as a murderer. He was innocent, notwithstanding. Not very long after his execution another boy, a servant in a neighboring wine-shop, being taken into custody for another offense, and seized with the pangs of remorse, confessed to the murder of the old dame. He had long been familiarly acquainted with the shop boy, who had suffered innocently, and had been in the habit of dressing his hair. He had managed by degrees to save up enough of the lad's hair from the comb he made use of to make into a tolerably stout lock, and this he had put into the hand of the dead woman. He had stolen one of the boy's neck-handkerchiefs, and also his knife, and by taking an impression in wax of the key, had been able to construct another by which to gain entrance to the shop. At the first glance, the evidence in this case seems at once clear, natural and spontaneous; but the very completeness of the evidentiary facts ought to have aroused suspicion; and there is no doubt that had a rigid investigation been set on foot, the innocence of the accused would have been established.

II.

Case of John Jennings.

A CASE of fabricated evidence of a sufficiently remarkable kind occurred near Hull, in the year 1742. A gentleman traveling to that place was stopped late in the evening, about seven miles from the town, by a masked highwayman, who robbed him of a purse containing twenty guineas. The highwayman galloped off by a side road, and the traveler, in no way injured, save in purse, continued his journey. It was now growing late, and, being excited and alarmed by what had happened, he naturally looked out for a place of shelter, and, instead of riding on to Hull, stopped at the first inn he came to, which was the "Bell Inn," kept by Mr. James Brunell. He went into the kitchen to give directions for his supper, and there he related to several persons the fact of his having been robbed, to which he added the further information, that when he traveled he always gave his gold a peculiar mark, and that every guinea in the purse taken from him was thus marked. He hoped, therefore, that the robber would yet be detected. Supper being ready, he withdrew. The gentleman had not long finished his supper, when Mr. Brunell came into the parlor where he was, and, after the usual inquiries of landlords as to the desires of the guest, observed, "Sir, I understand you have been robbed in this neighborhood this evening?" "Yes," said the traveler, "I have." "And your money was marked?" continued the landlord. "It was so," was the reply. "A circumstance has arisen," resumed Mr. Brunell, "which leads me to think I can point out the robber. Pray, at what time in the evening were you stopped." "It was just setting in to be dark," replied the traveler. "The time confirms my suspicions," said the landlord; and he then informed the gentleman that he had a waiter, one John Jennings, who had of late been so very full of money, and so very extravagant, that he (the landlord) had been surprised at it, and had determined to part with him, his conduct being every way suspicious; that long before dark that day, he had sent out Jennings to change a guinea for him; that the man had only come back since the arrival of the traveler, saying he could not get change; and that, seeing Jennings to be in liquor, he had sent him off to bed, deter-

mined to discharge him in the morning. Mr. Brunell
continued to say, that when the guinea was brought
back to him, it struck him that it was not the same
he had sent out for change, there being on the
returned one a mark which he was very sure was
not upon the other; but he should probably have
thought no more of the matter, Jennings having
frequently had gold in his pocket of late, had not the
people in the kitchen told him what the traveler had
related respecting the robbery, and the circumstance
of the guineas being marked. He (Mr. Brunell) had
not been present when this relation was made, and,
unluckily, before he heard of it from the people in
the kitchen, he had paid away the guinea to a man
who lived at some distance, and who had now gone
home. "The circumstance, however," said the landlord, in conclusion, "struck me so very strongly,
that I could not refrain, as an honest man, from
coming and giving you information of it."

Mr. Brunell was duly thanked for his disclosure.
There appeared from it the strongest reasons for
suspecting Jennings; and if, on searching him, any
others of the marked guineas should be found, and
the gentleman could identify them, there would then
remain no doubt in the matter. It was now agreed
to go up to his room. Jennings was fast asleep; his

pockets were searched, and from one of them was drawn forth a purse containing exactly nineteen guineas. Suspicion now became certainty; for the traveler declared the purse and guineas to be identically those of which he had been robbed. Assistance was called; Jennings was awakened, dragged out of bed, and charged with the robbery. He denied it firmly; but the circumstances against him were too strong, and he was not believed. He was secured that night, and next day was taken before a justice of the peace. The gentleman and Mr. Brunell deposed to the facts upon oath; and Jennings, having no proofs, nothing but mere assertions of innocence, which could not be credited, was committed to take his trial at the next assizes.

So strong seemed the case against him, that most of the man's friends advised him to plead guilty, and throw himself on the mercy of the court. This advice he rejected, and when arraigned, pleaded not guilty. The prosecutor swore to the fact of the robbery; though, as it took place in the dusk, and the highwayman wore a mask, he could not swear to the person of the prisoner, but thought him of the same stature nearly as the man who robbed him. To the purse and guineas, when they were produced in court, he swore—as to the purse, positively, and as

to the marked guineas, to the best of his belief; and
he testified to their having been taken from the
pocket of the prisoner.

The prisoner's master, Mr. Brunell, deposed as to
the sending of Jennings for the change of a guinea,
and to the waiter's having brought him back a
marked one instead of the one he had given him
unmarked. He also gave evidence as to the discovery of the purse and guineas on the prisoner. To
consummate the proof, the man to whom Mr. Brunell
had paid the guinea, as mentioned, came forward
and produced the coin, testifying at the same time,
that he had received it on the evening of the robbery, from the prisoner's master, in payment of a
debt; and the prosecutor, on comparing it with the
other nineteen, swore to its being, to the best of his
belief, one of the twenty marked coins taken from
him by the highwayman, and of which the other
nineteen were found on Jennings.

The judge summed up the evidence, pointing out
all the concurring circumstances against the prisoner; and the jury, convinced by this strong accumula-
tion of testimony, without going out of court, brought
in a verdict of guilty. Jennings was executed some
time afterwards, at Hull, repeatedly declaring his
innocence up to the moment of his execution.

Within a twelvemonth afterwards, Brunell, the master of Jennings, was himself taken up for a robbery committed on a guest in his house, and the fact being proved on trial, he was convicted and ordered for execution. The approach of death brought on repentance and confession. Brunell not only acknowledged he had been guilty of many highway robberies, but owned that he had committed the very one for which Jennings suffered. The account which he gave was, that after robbing the traveler, he had reached home before him by swifter riding, and by a nearer way. That he found a man at home waiting for him, to whom he owed a little bill, and to whom, not having enough of other money in his pocket, he gave away one of the guineas which he had just obtained by robbery. Presently came in the robbed gentleman, who, whilst Brunell, not knowing of his arrival, was in the stable, told his tale, as before related, in the kitchen. The gentleman had scarcely left the kitchen before Brunell entered it, and there, to his consternation, heard of the facts, and of the guineas being marked. He became dreadfully alarmed. The guinea which he had paid away he dared not ask back again ; and as the affair of the robbery, as well as the circumstance of the marked guineas, would soon become publicly known, he saw nothing before him but detection, disgrace, and death. In this dilemma, the thought of accusing and sacrificing poor Jennings occurred to him. The state of intoxication in which Jennings was, gave him an opportunity of concealing the purse of money in the waiter's pocket. The rest the reader knows.

III.

Case of James Harris.

JAMES HARRIS kept a public house within eighteen miles of York, having in his service a man named Morgan, who, to his other occupations, added that of gardener. It happened that one Grey, a blacksmith, journeying on foot to Edinburgh, supped and slept at this public house. Next morning Morgan deposed before a magistrate, that his master strangled Grey in his bed—that he actually saw him commit the murder—that he in vain endeavored to prevent it, his master insisting that the man was in a fit, and that he was merely endeavoring to assist him. Morgan further swore, that, affecting to believe this, he left the room ; but after retiring, looked through the keyhole, and saw the murderer rifling the pockets of the deceased. Harris, as well he might, vehemently denied the accusation, and, haplessly for himself, threatened a prosecution for perjury. As no mark of violence was visible on the body, Harris was on the point of being discharged, when the maid-servant demanded to be heard. She swore that from a wash house window, as she was descending the stairs, she saw her master take some gold from his pocket, and having carefully wrapped it up, bury it under a tree in the garden, the position of which she indicated. Upon this, Harris turned pale, and the earth under the tree having been searched by a constable, thirty pounds in gold was found wrapped up in a paper. Harris then admitted that he had buried the money for security's sake, but answered in so confused and hesitating manner, that he was committed. He was tried at York for the murder. The man, the maid, the constable, and the magistrate, were all examined, and no suspicion attaching to their testimony, a verdict of guilty was at once pronounced. He died protesting his innocence, and ere long his innocence became manifest to all men. The real facts were as follows. In a quarrel between Harris and his servant, Morgan received a blow, and vowed revenge. Soon afterwards, Grey's arrival furnished the opportunity. The part which the servant maid played in the business is explained by the fact that she and the gardener were sweethearts. Seeing her master one day apparently hiding something under a tree, she apprised Morgan, who, on digging, found five guineas concealed there. On this, they agreed to purloin the hoard, when it should amount to a sum sufficient to enable them to set up in business. But

Harris's threat of a prosecution for perjury so terrified the girl, that she resolved to save her lover by the sacrifice both of the money and of her master's life. A subsequent quarrel, the not unusual consequence of guilt like theirs, betrayed the truth They died of jail fever, on the day previous to that appointed for their trial. It was afterwards ascertained that Grey had had two apoplectic fits, and had never been in possession of five pounds at a time in his life.

In this melancholy case, it will be observed that the victim of circumstantial evidence himself unconsciously prepared the principal fact which told against him.

IV.

Case of Soren Qvist.

THE most striking case of circumstantial evidence, in which the testimony against the accused was altogether fabricated by the accuser, is one taken from the Danish records, and which, from its impressiveness, has been made the subject of remark by both Danish and German writers. The unhappy fate of the clergyman, Soren Qvist, is familiar to his countrymen, though many generations have passed away since the events which are about to be related.

Soren was the pastor of the little village of Veilby, situated a few miles from Grenaee, in the Jutland peninsula. He was a man of excellent moral character, generous, hospitable, and diligent in the performance of his sacred duties ; but he was also a man of constitutionally violent temper, which he lacked the ability to restrain, and was consequently subject at times to fierce outbreaks of wrath, which were a scourge to his household when they occurred, and a humiliation to himself. Like most Danish clergymen of that day, he was a tiller of the soil, as well as a preacher of the word ; and from the produce of his tithes, and the cultivation of his farm, realized a comfortable competence. He was a widower with two children—a daughter who kept house for him, and a son holding an officer's commission in the army. At Ingvorstrup, a village not far from Veilby, dwelt a cattle-farmer, one Morten Burns, who, by means anything but honest and honorable, had acquired considerable property, and who was in ill repute as a reckless self-seeker, and oppressor of the poor. This man Morten thought fit to pay court to the pastor's daughter, but his suit was rejected by both parent and child ; and either the refusal, or the manner of it, so irritated the suitor that he swore secretly to be revenged on both.

Some months later, when the short-lived suit had been forgotten, the pastor, being in want of a farm servant, engaged Niels Burns, a poor brother of the rich Morten, the discarded lover. Niels soon showed himself to be an utterly worthless fellow, lazy, impudent, and overbearing ; and the result was a constant recurrence of quarrels and mutual recriminations between him and his master. Sören on more than one occasion gave the fellow a thrashing, which did not at all tend to improve the relations between

them. These relations, however, were destined to
come to a speedy close. The pastor had set Niels
to dig a piece of ground in the garden, but on coming out he found him not digging, but leisurely
resting on his spade and cracking nuts which he
had plucked, his work being left undone. The
pastor scolded him angrily; the man retorted that
it was no business of his to dig in the garden; at
which Sören struck him twice in the face, and the
fellow, throwing down the spade, retaliated with a
volley of abuse. Thereupon the old man lost all
self-control, and seizing the spade, he dealt the fellow
several blows with it. Niels fell to the earth like one
dead; but when his master in great alarm raised him
up he broke away, leaped through the hedge, and
made off into the neighboring wood. From that time
he was seen no more, and all inquiries after him
proved vain. The above was the pastor's account
of the facts.

Ere long strange rumors began to circulate in
the neighborhood, and, as a matter of course, they
reached the pastor's ears. Morten Burns was known
to have said that "he would make the parson produce his brother even if he had to dig him out of
the earth." Sören was intensely pained at the
calumny implied, and instituted at his own expense

a quiet search after the missing man—a search which failed altogether. Even before that failure was known, Morten Burns, in fulfillment of his threat, applied to the district magistrate, taking with him as witnesses one Larsen, a cottager, and a laborer's widow and daughter, on the strength of whose testimony he declared his suspicion that the pastor had slain his brother. The magistrate represented to him the risk he ran in making so serious a charge against the clergyman, and advised him to weigh the matter well before it was too late. But Morten persisted in his design, and the statements of the witnesses were taken down. The widow Karsten deposed, that on the very day when Niels Bruns was said to have fled from the parsonage, she and her daughter Else had passed by the pastor's garden about the hour of noon. When they were nearly in front of the hedge which encloses it on the eastern side, they heard some one calling Else. It was Niels, who was on the other side of the hazel bushes, and who now bent back the branches, and asked Else if she would have some nuts. She took a handful, and then asked him what he was doing there? He answered, that the pastor had ordered him to dig, but that the job did not suit him, and he preferred cracking nuts. Just then they heard a door in the house open, and Niels said, "Now, listen, and you shall hear a preachment." Directly after they heard (they could not see, because the hedge was too high and too thick) how the two quarreled, and how the one paid the other in kind. At last they heard the pastor cry, "I will beat thee, dog, until thou liest dead at my feet!" Whereupon there were sounds as of blows, and then they heard Niels calling the pastor a rogue and a hangman. To this the pastor made no reply; but they heard two blows, and they saw the iron blade of a spade and part of the handle swing twice above the hedgerow, but in whose hands they could not discern. After this all was quiet in the garden, and, somewhat alarmed and excited, the widow and her daughter hurried on their way.

Larsen disposed that on the evening of the day following that of the disappearance of Niels, as he was returning home very late from Tolstrup, and was passing along the footpath which flanks the southern side of the pastor's garden, he heard from within the garden the sound of some one digging the earth. At first he was rather startled; but seeing that it was clear moonlight, he determined to find out who it was that was working in the garden at that late hour; whereupon he slipped off his

wooden shoes, climbed up the hedge, and parted
the tops of the hazel bushes so as to enable himself
to see. Then he saw the pastor in the green dressing-
gown he usually wore, and with a white night-cap
on his head, busied in leveling the earth with a
spade; but more than this he did not see, for the
pastor turned suddenly round as if some sound
had struck his ear, and witness being afraid of detection, let himself down, and ran away.

When the witnesses had thus disposed, Morten
demanded that the parson should be arrested.
Wishing to avoid such a scandal if possible, the
magistrate, who was a friend of Sören's, proposed
that they should go together to the parsonage,
where they would probably receive a satisfactory
explanation of the facts deposed to. Morten consented to this, and the party set ont. On approaching the house they saw Sören coming to meet them
—when Morten ran forward, and bluntly accused
him of murdering his brother, adding that he was
come with the magistrate to make search for the
body. The pastor made him no reply, but courte-
ously greeting the magistrate, gave directions to
the farm servants, who now gathered round, to aid
by all the means in their power the search about
to be made. Morten led the way into the garden,

and after looking round for some time, pointed to a certain spot and called upon the men to dig there. The men fell to work, and Morten joined them, working with a show of frantic eagerness. When they had dug to a little depth the ground proved so hard that it was evident it had not been broken up for a long while. Sören had looked on quite at ease, and now he said to Morten, "Slanderer, what have you got for your pains?" Instead of replying, Morten turned to Larsen, and asked him where it was that he had seen the parson digging. Larsen pointed to a heap of cabbage stalks, dried haulms, and other refuse, and said he thought that was the place. The rubbish was soon removed, and the men began digging at the soil beneath. They had not dug long, when one of them cried out, "Heaven preserve us!" and as all present crowded to look, the crown of a hat was visible above the earth. "That is Niel's hat!" cried Morten, "I know it well—here is a security we shall find him! Dig away!" he shouted with fierce energy, and was almost as eagerly obeyed. Soon an arm appeared, and in a few minutes the entire corpse was disinterred. There could be no doubt that it was the missing man. The face could not be recognized, for decomposition had commenced, and the features had been injured by blows; but all his clothes, even unto his shirt with his name on it, were identified by his fellow servants; even a leaden ring in the left ear of the corpse was recognized as one which Niels had worn for years.

There was no alternative but to arrest the pastor on the spot—indeed, he willingly surrendered himself, merely protesting his innocence. "Appearances are against me," he said; "surely this must be the work of Satan and his ministry; but He still lives who will at his pleasure make my innocence manifest. Take me to prison; in solitude and in chains I will await what He in his wisdom shall decree."

The pastor was removed to the goal at Grenaee the same night, and on the following day came the judicial examination. The first three witnesses confirmed their former statements on oath. Moreover, there now appeared three additional witnesses, viz: the pastor's two farm servants and the dairymaid. The two former explained how on the day of the murder they had been sitting near the open window in the servant's room, and had heard distinctly how the pastor and the man Neils were quarreling, and how the former had cried out, "I will slay thee, dog! thou shalt lie dead at my feet!" They added that they had twice before heard the pastor

threaten Niels with the like. The dairymaid deposed that on the night when Larsen saw the pastor in the garden, she was lying awake in bed,
and heard the door leading from the passage into
the garden creak ; and that when she rose and
peeped out, she saw the pastor, in his dressing-
gown and night-cap, go out into the garden. What
he did there she saw not ; but about an hour afterwards she again heard the creaking of the door.

When asked what he had to say in his defense, the pastor replied solemnly, "So help me
God, I will say nothing but the truth. I struck
deceased with the spade, but not otherwise than
that he was able to run away from me, and out of
the garden ; what became of him afterwards, or
how he came to be buried in my garden, I know
not. As for the evidence of Larsen and the dairymaid, who say that they saw me in the garden in the
night, it is either a foul lie or it is a hellish delusion. Miserable man that I am ! I have no one
on earth to speak in my defense—that I see clearly ;
if He in heaven likewise remains silent, I have only
to submit to His inscrutable will."

When, some weeks later, the trial came on,
two more fresh witnesses were produced. They declared that on the oft-mentioned night they were pro-

ceeding along the road which runs from the pastor's garden to the wood, when they met a man carrying a sack on his back, who passed them and walked on in the direction of the garden. His face they could not see, inasmuch as it was concealed by the overhanging sack ; but as the moon was shining on his back, they could plainly descry that he was clad in a pale green coat and a white night-cap. He disappeared near the pastor's garden hedge. No sooner did the pastor hear the evidence of the witness to this effect than his face turned an ashy hue, and he cried out in a faltering voice, "1 am fainting!" and was so prostrated in body that he had to be taken back to prison. There, after a period of severe suffering, to the intense astonishment of every one, he made, to his friend, the district magistrate who had first arrested him, the following strange confession :—"From my childhood, as far back as I can remember, I have ever been passionate, quarrelsome, and proud—impatient of contradiction, and ever ready with a blow. Yet have I seldom let the sun go down on my wrath, nor have I borne ill-will to any one. When but a lad I slew in anger a dog which one day ate my dinner, which I had left in his way. When, as a student, 1 went on foreign travel, I entered, on slight provocation, into a broil with a German youth in Leipsic, challenged him, and gave him a wound that endangered his life. For that deed, I feel it, I merited that which has now come upon me after long years; but the punishment falls upon my sinful head with tenfold weight now that I am broken down with age, a clergyman, and a father. Oh, Father in heaven! it is here that the wound is sorest."

After a pause of anguish, he continued: "I will now confess the crime which no doubt I have committed, but of which I am, nevertheless, not fully conscious. That I struck the unhappy man with the spade I know full well, and have already confessed; whether it were with the flat side or with the sharp edge I could not in my passion discern; that he then fell down, and afterwards again rose up and ran away—that is all that I know to a surety. What follows—heaven help me!—four witnesses have seen; namely, that I fetched the corpse from the wood and buried it; and that this must be substantially true I am obliged to believe, and I will tell you wherefore. Three or four times in my life, that I know of, it has happened to me to walk in my sleep. The last time (about nine years ago), I was next day to preach a funeral sermon over the remains of a man who had unexpectedly met with a dreadful death. I was at a loss for a text, when the words of a wise man among the ancient Greeks suddenly occurred to me, 'Call no man happy until he be in his grave.' To use the words of a heathen for the text of a Christian discourse, was not, methought, seemly; but I then remembered that the same thought, expressed in well-nigh the same terms, was to be met with somewhere in the Apocrypha. I sought, and sought, but could not find the passage. It was late, I was wearied by much previous labor; I therefore went to bed, and soon fell asleep. Greatly did I marvel the next morning when, on arising and seating myself at my writing desk, I saw before me, written in large letters in a piece of paper, 'Let no man be deemed happy before his end cometh (Syrach xi. 34).' But not this alone; I found likewise a funeral discourse—short, but as well written as any I had ever composed—and all in my own handwriting. In the chamber none other than I could have been. I knew, therefore, who it was that had written the discourse; and that it was no other than myself. Not more than half a year previous, I had, in the same marvelous state, gone in the night time into the church, and fetched away a handkerchief which I had left in the chair behind the altar. Mark now—

when the two witnesses this morning delivered their evidence before the court, then my previous sleep-walkings suddenly flashed across me; and I likewise called to mind that in the morning after the night during which the corpse must have been buried, I had been surprised to see my dressing-gown lying on the floor just inside the·door, whereas it was always my custom to hang it on a chair by my bedside. The unhappy victim of my un bridled passion must, in all likelihood, have fallen down dead in the wood ; and I must in my sleep-walking have followed him thither. Yes—the Lord have mercy !—so it was, so it must have been."

On the following day sentence of death was passed upon the prisoner—a sentence which many felt to be too severe, and which led to a friendly con-spiracy on his behalf ; and had it not been for his own refusal to be a party to anything unlawful, he might have escaped. The jailer was gained over, and a fisherman had his boat in readiness for a flight to the Swedish coast, where he would have been beyond the reach of danger. But Sören Qvist refused to flee. He longed, he said. for death ; and he would not add a new stain to his reputation by a furtive flight. He maintained his strength of mind to the last, and from the scaffold he addressed to the bystanders a discourse of much power, which he had composed in prison during his last days. It treated of anger and its direful consequences, with touching allusions to himself and the dreadful crime to which his anger misled him. Thereafter, he doffed his coat, bound with his own hands the napkin before his eyes, and submitted his neck to the execu- tioner's sword.

One-and-twenty years after the pastor, Sören Qvist of Veilby, had been accused, tried, condemned, and executed for the murder of his serving-man, an old beggarman applied for alms to the people of Aalsöe, the parish adjoining to Veilby. Suspi- cions were aroused by the exact likeness the beggar- man bore to Morten Bruns, of Ingvorstrup, who had lately died, and also by the curious and anxious in- quiries the man made concerning events long past. The pastor of Aalsöe, who had buried Morten Bruns, took the vagabond to his parsonage, and there the fellow, all unconscious of the portentous nature of the admission, acknowledged that he was Niels Bruns, the very man for whose supposed murder the pastor had suffered the shameful death of a crimi- nal. Had his brother Morten survived him, it is pretty certain the truth, concealed so long, had never been known, as Niels had only returned to the district in the hope of profiting by Morten's death, the news of which had accidentally reached him. He professed—and, indeed, plainly experienced—the utmost horror on hearing the dreadful history of the pastor's cruel fate. It was all Morten's doing, he said; but he was so overcome by the terrible narrative that he could scarcely gather strength to reply to the questions put to him. The result of his examination and confession may be summed up very briefly. Morten had conceived a mortal hatred of Sóren Qvist from the time that he refused him his daughter, and had determined on revenge. It was he who compelled Niels to take service with the pastor; he had spurred him on to the repeated offenses, in the expectation that violence would result, owing to the pastor's hasty temper; and had carefully nursed the feud which soon arose between master and man. Niels told him daily all that took place. On leaving the garden on that fatal day, he had run over to Ingvorstrup to acquaint his brother with what had happened. Morten shut him up in a private room that no one might see him. Shortly after midnight, when the whole village was asleep, the two brothers went to a place where the roads cross each other and where two days previously a suicide had been buried—a young man of about

Niels' age and stature. In spite of Niels' reluctance and remonstrance they dug up the corpse and took it into Morten's house. Niels was made to strip and don a suit of Morten's, and the corpse was clad, piece by piece, in Niels' cast-off clothes, even to the very ear-ring. Then Morten battered the dead face with a spade, and hid it in a sack until the next night, when they carried it into the wood by Veilby parsonage. Niels asked what all these preparations meant. Morten told him to mind his own business, and to go and fetch the parson's green dressing-gown and cap. This Niels refused to do, whereupon Morten went and fetched them himself.* "And now," he said to his brother, "you go your way. Here is a purse with a hundred dollars—make for the frontier, where no one knows thee; pass thyself under another name, and never set thy foot on Danish soil again as thou wouldst answer it with thy life!" Niels did as he was commanded, and parted from Morten forever. He had enlisted for a soldier, had suffered great hardships, had lost a limb, and had returned to his native place a mere wreck.

* It was not the custom in Jutland, in those days—it is hardly the custom now—to lock up the house at night.

V.

Case of Thomas Geddely.

THOMAS GEDDELY was a waiter in a public house
kept by a Mrs. Williams at York, and much frequented. The landlady was a bustling woman, a
favorite with her customers, and had the reputation
of being well-to-do. One morning it was found that
her scrutoire had been broken open and rifled of a
considerable sum; and as on that same morning
Thomas Geddely did not make his appearance, everybody concluded that he was the robber. A year
afterwards, or thereabouts, a man came to York who,
under the name of James Crow, plied for employ-
ment as a porter, and thus picked up a scanty living
for a few days. Meanwhile, from his unlucky likeness to Geddely he began to be mistaken for the thief.
Many people addressed him as Tom Geddely, and
when he declared that he did not know them, that
his name was James Crow, and that he had never
lived in York before, they would not believe him,
and attributed his denial to his natural desire to
escape the consequences of the robbery he had committed at the public house.

When subsequently his mistress was sent for, she singled him out from a number of people, and calling him Geddely, upbraided him with his ingratitude, and charged him with robbing her. When dragged before the justice of the peace, and examined in his presence, the man affirmed, as stoutly as any man could, that his name was not Geddely, that he had never known any person of that name, that he had never in his life lived in York before, and that his name was James Crow. He could not, however, get any one else to substantiate his affirmations; he could give but a poor account of himself, but was forced to admit that he led a vagabond life—and as the landlady and others swore positively to his person, he was committed to jail at York Castle to await his trial at the next assizes. When, in due time, the trial came on, he pleaded "not guilty," and denied as before that he was the person he was taken for; but the landlady of the inn and several other witnesses swore positively that he was the identical Thomas Geddely who was waiter when she was robbed; while a servant girl deposed that she had seen him on the very morning of the robbery in the room where the scrutoire was broken open, with a poker in his hand. As the prisoner had nothing to urge against the evidence but a simple denial, and as he could not prove an *alibi*, he was found guilty of the robbery, was condemned to death, and executed. He persisted to his latest breath in affirming that he was not Thomas Geddely, and that his name was Crow.

The truth of the poor fellow's declaration was established all too late. Not long after Crow's unjust punishment, the real Thomas Geddely, who, after the robbery, had fled from York to Ireland, was taken up in Dublin for a crime of the same stamp, and there condemned and executed. Between his conviction and execution, and again at the fatal tree, he confessed himself to be the very Thomas Geddely who had committed the robbery at York for which the unfortunate James Crow had suffered. A gentleman, a native of York, who happened to be at Dublin at the time of Geddely's trial and execution, and who knew him when he lived with Mrs. Williams, declared that the resemblance between the two men was so remarkable that it was next to impossible to distinguish their persons assunder.

VI.

Case of Joseph Lesurques.

ONE of the most lamentable cases of mistaken identity was that of Lesurques, the history of which may be summed up as follows :

In the month of April, 1796, a young man named Joseph Lesurques arrived in Paris from Douai, his native town. He was thirty-three years of age, and possessed a fortune equal to six hundred pounds a year. He hired apartments, and made preparations for residing permanently in Paris. One of his first cares was to repay one Guesno, of Douai, two thousand francs he had borrowed of him. On the following day Guesno invited Lesurques to breakfast. They accordingly went to a refreshment room, in company with two other persons, one of whom, named Couriol, happened to call just as they were sitting down to table. After breakfast they proceeded to the Palais Royal, and having taken coffee, separated. Four days afterwards, four horsemen, mounted on hired horses, were seen to drive out of Paris. They all wore long cloaks and sabres hanging from the waist. One of the party was Couriol.

Between twelve and one o'clock the four horsemen arrived at the village of Mongeron, on the road to Melun. There they dined, and then proceeded at a foot pace towards Lieursaint. They reached Lieursaint about three in the afternoon, and made a long halt at the inn, amusing themselves with billiards, and one of them having his horse shod. At half-past seven they remounted and rode off towards Melun. About an hour later the mail courier from Paris to Lyons arrived to change horses. It was then half-past eight, and the night had been for some time dark. The courier, having changed horses, set out to pass the long forest of Lenart. The mail at this period was a sort of post-chaise, with a large trunk behind containing the dispatches. There was one place only open to the public, at the side of the courier; and the place was occupied on that day by a man about thirty years of age, who had that morning taken it in the name of Laborde.

The next morning the mail was found rifled, the courier dead in his seat, and the postilion lying dead in the road—both being evidently slain with sabres. One horse only was found near the carriage. The mail had been robbed of seventy-five thousand livres in silver and bank bills. The officers of justice soon discovered that five persons had passed through the barrier on their way to Paris between four and five in the morning after the murders. The horse of the postilion was found wandering about the Place Royale ; and they ascertained that four horses, covered with foam and quite exhausted, had been brought, about five in the morning, to a man named Muiron, Rue des Fosses, Saint Germain l'Auxerrois, by two persons who had hired them the day before. These two persons were named Bernard and Couriol. Bernard was immediately arrested ; Couriol escaped. A description was obtained of the four who had ridden from Paris and stopped at Mongeron and Lieursaint, and also of the man who had taken his place with the courier under the name of Laborde. Couriol was traced to Chateau Thierry, where he was arrested, together with Guesno, the Douai carrier, and one Bruer, who happened to be in the same house. Guesno and Bruer proved *alibis* so clearly that they were discharged on arriving at Paris.

The magistrate, after discharging Guesno, told him to apply at his office the next morning for the return of his papers, which had been seized at Chateau Thierry ; at the same time he had sent a police officer to Mongeron and Lieursaint to fetch the witnesses, of whom he gave a list. Guesno, being desirous to obtain his papers as soon as possible, left

home the next day earlier than usual.   On his way to
the office he met Lesurques, who consented to accompany him.   They went to the office, and as Daubenton, the Juge-de-Paix, had not yet arrived, they
sat down in the antechamber to await his arrival.
About two o'clock the Juge-de-Paix, who had entered
his room by a back door, was thunderstruck on being
told by the police officer who had come back with the
witnesses, that two of them declared that two of the
actual murderers were in the house.   "Impossible!"
he exclaimed, "guilty men would not voluntarily
venture here."   Not believing the statement he
ordered the two women to be introduced separately ;
and examined each of them, when they repeated
their statement and declared they could not be
mistaken.   Warning them solemnly that life and
death depended on their truth, he had the accused
brought into the room one by one, and after conversing with them sent them again to the antechamber
where they waited as before.   When they had left
the room the magistrate again asked the women if
they persisted in their previons declarations.   They
did persist ; their evidence was taken down in writing ; and the two friends were immediately arrested.
No time was lost in pushing on the prosecution.
Seven persons were put upon their trial, amongst

whom were Couriol, Madeline Breban (his mistress), Lesurques, and Guesno. Lesurques was sworn to most positively by several, as being one of the party, at different places on the road, on the day of the robbery and murder. It should be born in mind that the case was quite conclusive against Couriol. "I attended them (said one witness) at dinner at Mongeron ; this one (Lesurques) wanted to pay the bill in assignats, but the tall dark one (Couriol) paid it in silver." A stable boy at Mongeron also identified him. A woman named Alfroy, of Lieursaint, and the innkeeper and his wife of the same place, all recognized him as of the party there—Lesurques declaring that he had never been present at either place. But the witnesses were positive, were unimpeached, were believed, and—were all mistaken. Lesurques and Couriol were convicted, Guesno, though as positively sworn to, proved his perfect innocence, and was acquitted. Lesurques called fifteen persons of known probity to prove an *alibi,* which was disbelieved in consequence of the folly of one of them, who falsified an entry in his book with the design of adding weight to the evidence in Lesurques's favor, but did it so clumsily that the falsification was discovered. Eighty persons of all classes declared the character of Lesurques to be irre-

proachable; but all was of no avail—he was condemned.

When the sentence was pronounced, rising from
his place, he calmly said—"I am innocent of the
crime imputed to me. Ah, citizens! if murder on
the highway be atrocious, it is not less a crime to
execute an innocent man."

Madeline Breban, though compromising herself,
wildly exclaimed—"Lesurques is innocent—he is
the victim of his fatal likeness to Dubosq."

Couriol then, addressing the judges, said—"I am
guilty; I acknowledge my crime; my accomplices
were Vidal, Rossi, Durochat, and Dubosq; but
Lesurques is innocent."

After the sentence had been pronounced, the
horror-stricken Madeline again presented herself before the judges to reiterate her declaration, and two
other witnesses attested to her having told them so
before the trial. The judges applied to the Directory
for a reprieve; and the Directory applied to the
Council of Five Hundred, requesting instructions for
their guidance, and concluding with the emphatic
question—"Ought Lesurques to die on the scaffold
because he resembles a criminal?" The answer was
prompt: "The jury had legally sentenced the accused, and the right of pardon had been abolished."

Left to his fate, poor Lesurques on the morning of his execution thus wrote to his wife:—"My deai friend, we cannot avoid our fate. I shall, at any rate, endure mine with the courage which becomes a man. I send some locks of my hair. When my children are older, divide it with them. It is the only thing that I can leave them."

Couriol had disclosed to Lesurques the history of Dubosq, and the fatal mistake which had been made, and accordingly, on the eve of his death, he had the following mournful letter inserted in the journals: "Man, in whose place I am to die, be satisfied with the sacrifice of my life; if you be ever brought to justice, think of my three children covered with shame, and of their mother's despair, and do not prolong the misfortunes of so fatal a resemblance."

On the 10th of March, 1797, Lesurques went to the place of execution dressed completely in white, as a symbol of his innocence. On the way from the prison to the place of execution, Couriol, who was seated in the car beside him, cried in a loud voice, addressing the people, "I am guilty; but Lesurques is innocent." On reaching the scaffold, Lesurques gave himself up to the executioners, and died protesting his innocence.

In consequence of his own misgivings, and of murmurs on the part of the public, Daubenton, the Juge-de-Paix, who had arrested Lesurques, and conducted the first proceedings, resolved to investigate the truth, which could only be satisfactorily done through the arrest and trial of the four persons denounced by Couriol as his accomplices. Two years elapsed in vain inquiries. At the end of that time, he discovered that Durochat—the man who, under the name of Laborde, had taken the place by the side of the courier—had been arrested for a robbery, and lodged in St. Pelagie.

When the trial of the villain came on, he was, through the exertions of Daubenton, recognized by the inspector of the mails as the man who traveled with the courier on the day of the assassination. When charged with the fact, he made at first some faint denials, and subsequently he confessed, relating the particulars of the crime, all which tallied with the statements made by Couriol. He stated that Vidal had projected the affair, and had communicated it to him as a *restaurant* in the Champs Elysees. The criminals were Couriol, Rossi, (*alias* Beroldy), Vidal, himself, and Dubosq. Dubosq had forged for him the passport in the name of Laborde, by means of which he easily procured another for

Lyons, to enable him to take his place in the mail. Bernard had supplied the four horses. They had attacked the carriage as the postilion was slackening his pace to ascend the hill. It was he (Durochat) who had stabbed the courier, at the instant that Rossi cut down the postilion with a sabre; Rossi had then given up his horse to him (Durochat), and had returned to Paris on that of the postilion. As soon as they arrived there, they all met at Dubosq's lodgings, where they proceeded to divide the booty. Bernard, who had only procured the horses, was there, and claimed his share, and got it. "I have heard," he added, "that there was a fellow named Lesurques condemned for this business; but, to tell the truth, I never knew the fellow, either at the planning of the affair, or at its execution, or at the division of the spoil."

Such was Durochat's confession as taken down in writing; he added a description of Dubosq, stating that on the day of the murder he wore a blonde wig.

Shortly after the arrest of Durochat, Vidal was also arrested. He was recognized by the witnesses and positively sworn to, but he denied everything, and was sent to the prison of La Seine. Towards the end of the year 1799, Dubosq, having been arrested for a robbery in the department of Allier, was recognized in the prison and brought to Versailles to be tried at the same time as Vidal before the criminal tribunal. It was seen by the registers that Dubosq was a thorough desperado; he had been sentenced to the galleys for life, but had escaped, and on four several occasions had broken prison. Like Vidal, he denied everything. Confined in the same cell with his old companion in guilt, Dubosq planned an escape; but this time he broke his leg in the attempt—Vidal alone getting clear away—to be retaken, however, after a brief interval, to be brought back to trial—and to execution.

Strange as it may seem, Dubosq had no sooner recovered from his fracture, than he found another opportunity of attempting an escape, and for the sixth time succeeded in breaking his bonds. As he could not live without rapine, however, he fell again into the hands of the police before the expiration of a year, and was brought before the tribunal at Versailles. The president ordered a blonde wig to be put on his head, and thus attired, he was recognized by the same witnesses who had sworn away the life of Lesurques, who now recanted their former testimony, and declared too late that they had been mistaken.

After the execution of Dubosq, in Febuary, 1802, there still remained one of the accomplices to be brought to justice. This man, Rossi, whose real name was Beroldy, was at length discovered near Madrid, and was given up to the French government. Unlike Vidal and Dubosq, he confessed his crimes, testifying the utmost remorse. In the declaration, which he confided to his confessor, he affirmed the entire innocence of Lesurques; but, for a reason which does not appear, made it a condition that the declaration should not be published until six months after his death.

According to law, the property of Lesurques had been confiscated on his conviction, and his widow and children reduced to indigence. One would have thought that a government which had erred so egregiously as to execute a man for a crime of which he was not guilty, would have been eager to make what atonement was possible to the family of the victim. Nothing of the sort. The widow and her advisers, relying on the confessions of the real criminals, and the retractions of the witnesses, applied for a revision of the sentence, so far as concerned Lesurques, in order to obtain a judicial declaration of his innocence and the restoration of his property. All their endeavors were vain.

The right of revision no longer existed in the French code. Under the Directory, the Consulate, and the Restoration, the applications of the widow and family were equally unsuccessful. All that they could obtain was the restoration, in the last two years of the elder Bourbons, of a part of the property sequestrated at the condemnation of the un- offending husband and father.

VII.

Case of Thomas Williams.

On the 7th of February, 1851, in the dead of night, the house of David Williams, situated at Truasth, in the county of Brecknock, was broken open by forcing the shutters and window of an outhouse. Williams, an old man, who with his wife alone occupied the cottage, was alarmed by the noise, and going to the head of the stairs, saw by the light of a candle the person of a man whom he recognized as one Tom Williams, a blacksmith living in the neighborhood, and who had formerly done some work in the house. This was only for a moment, as the light was struck out, and the burglar attacked old Williams and his wife in the dark. However, they proved too strong for him, and compelled him to take to flight. Nothing was stolen, but the drawer of a dresser in the kitchen had been ransacked, and some papers of no value turned out of it. Tom Williams, the blacksmith, was tried at the following spring assizes at Brecon for the burglary, and as the old man, who had known him from his boyhood, swore to him posi

tively, he was convicted, and sentenced to transportation. Happily for him, however, a person
named Morris was present at the trial, who, on
hearing the verdict, at once exculpated the convicted man, and directed the attention of the police
to one Powell, as the real criminal. Strict inquiry
was immediately instituted, the result of which was
that Powell was committed. He was tried before
the late Mr. Justice TALFOURD, and convicted on
evidence perfectly conclusive. It seems old Williams had lent Powell six hundred pounds on
mortgage, taking as security certain title deeds.
Williams commenced proceedings to recover principal and interest, and Powell committed the burglary
to possess himself of the documents; hence the
ransacking of the dresser drawer in which he believed they had been deposited. The blacksmith
was of course pardoned on the report of Mr. Justice
TALFOURD, and was discharged in September. But
the real criminal was also discharged, although his
guilt was clear as the sun at noonday. The jury
convicted him of breaking open the house "with
intent to steal the title deeds;" the indictment
charged his intent to be to "steal the goods and
chattels." The Appeal Court held the conviction
bad.

VIII.

Case of Professor Webster.

A CURIOUS case of identification occurred about twenty years ago. This was an instance in which the guilt of a crime was brought home to the perpetrator through the identifying of a body after it had been separated limb from limb, submitted to chemical processes, and to the inordinate heat of a furnace, and mingled with the countless bones of anatomical subjects in their common burying-place. One Professor Webster was brought to trial for the murder of Dr. Parkman. It was shown that the professor had urgent pecuniary motives at the time when the crime was committed, to get Dr. Parkman out of the way. The prisoner had a residence at the Medical College, Boston. He made an appointment to meet the deceased at this place at two o'clock on Friday, the 23rd of November, 1849, in order to discuss certain money matters. Dr. Parkman was seen about a quarter before two o'clock apparently about to enter the Medical College, and after that was never again seen alive. The prisoner affirmed that Dr. Parkman did not keep his appoint ment, and did not enter the college at all on that day. For a whole week nothing was discovered, and when search was made the prisoner interfered with it, and threw hindrances in the way.

On the Friday week and the day following there were found in a furnace connected with the prisoner's laboratory in the college, fused together indiscriminately with the slag, the cinders, and the refuse of the fuel, a large number of bones and certain blocks of mineral teeth. A quantity of gold, which had been melted, was also found. Other bones were found in a vault under the college. There was also discovered in a tea-chest, and embedded in a quantity of tan, the entire trunk of a human body and other bones. The parts thus collected together from different places, made the entire body of a person of Dr. Parkman's age, about sixty years, and the form of the body when reconstructed had just the peculiarities shown to be possessed by Dr. Parkman. In no single particular were the parts dissimilar to these of the deceased, nor in the tea-chest or the furnace were any duplicate parts found over and above what was necessary to compose one body.

The remains were further shown to have been separated by a person possessed of anatomical skill.

though not for anatomical purposes. Finally, three witnesses, dentists, testified to the mineral teeth found being those made for Dr. Parkman three years before. A mould of the doctor's jaw had been made at the time, and it was produced, and shown to be so peculiar that no accidental conformity of the teeth to the jaw could possibly account for the adaptation. This last piece of evidence was conclusive against the prisoner, and he was convicted. Without this closing proof the evidence would certainly have been unsatisfactory. The character of the prisoner, the possible confusion throughout the college of the remains of anatomical subjects, the undistinguished features, and the illusiveness of evidence derived from the likeness of a reconstructed body, were all facts of a nature to substantiate assumptions in favor of the prisoner's innocence. It is singular that the block of mineral teeth was only accidentally preserved, having been found so near the bottom of the furnace as to take the current of cold air, whose impact had prevented the thorough combustion that would otherwise have taken place.

IX.

Case of William Harrison.

ON the 6th of August, 1660, William Harrison, who was steward to Lady Campden, a person of good estate in Gloucestershire, left his home in order to collect her rents. There happened to reside in the neighborhood a humble family of the name of Perry, a mother and two sons, Joan, John, and Richard, of whom Joan, the mother, bore but an indifferent character, and John, one of the sons, was known to be half-witted. It so happened that days and weeks elapsed, and yet Harrison did not return nor were any tidings heard of him. Of course, the population of the place became excited, and rumors soon became rife that he had been robbed and murdered. From the mission on which he was known to have left his home, and his prolonged absence, the suspicion was not unnatural. The alarm which ensued, and the numberless inventions which were circulated, are supposed to have bewildered what little intellect the poor idiot had, for he actually went before a justice of the peace, and solemnly deposed to the murder of Harrison by his brother Richard, while his mother and himself looked on, and afterwards joined in robbing the deceased of a hundred and forty pounds. On this the whole three were sent to prison, and at the following assizes were doubly indicted for the robbery and the murder. The presiding judge, Sir CHARLES TURNER, refused to try them on the murder indictment, as the body had not been found; they were, however, arraigned on the charge of robbery, and pleaded guilty on some vague superstition that their lives would be spared. While in confinement John persisted in the charge, adding that his mother and brother had attempted to poison him in the jail for peaching. When the next assizes came, Sir ROBERT HYDE, considering the length of time which had elapsed, and the non-appearance of Harrison, tried them for the murder. The depositions of John, and the plea on the indictment for robbery, were given in evidence, and the whole three were forthwith convicted. On the trial John retracted his accusation, declaring that he was mad when he made it, and knew not what he said. They all suffered death. The mother was executed first, it being alleged that she influenced her sons, and that they would never confess while she was living; they died, however,

loudly protesting their innocence. But the disappearance of Harrison, the confession of John,
and the plea of "guilty" to the indictment for
robbery, seemed to invest the case with every
human certainty.

After this poor, ignorant, and deluded family
had lain in the grave for three years, the people of
Gloucester were startled by the reappearance in
their streets of the murdered Harrison! He accounted for his long absence thus, in a letter to Sir
Thomas Overbury. On returning homewards after
the receipt of Lady Campden's rents, he was set
upon by a gang of crimps, who forced him to the
seashore, where they hurried him on shipboard and
carried him off to Turkey. They there sold him
as a slave to a physician, with whom he lived for
nearly two years, when, his master dying, he made
his escape in a Hamburg vessel to Lisbon, and
was thence conveyed to England.

X.

Case of Thomas Wood.

On the 6th of October, 1806, Thomas Wood, a young seaman, was tried at Plymouth by naval court-martial. The offense charged was an active participation in a mutiny and murder on board the "Hermione," in 1797. At the time of his trial, he was only twenty-five years old, and therefore somewhere about sixteen when the mutiny took place. There was but one witness against him; one, however, whose testimony had considerable weight—the master of the "Hermione." This person most positively identified him as one of those chiefly implicated, and as having gone, when on board his ship, by the name of James Hayes. The identification undoubtedly was strong; but still, considering the personal changes which generally take place between the age of sixteen and twenty-five, and after an interruption of nine years in the intercourse, scarcely strong enough to warrant a conviction. But all doubt of the prisoner's guilt vanished at once before the voluntary statement which he put in, 'in the form of a written document. "At the time,' said the written statement, "when the mutiny took place, I was a boy in my fourteenth year. Compelled by the torrent of mutiny, I took the oath administered to me on the occasion. The examples of death which were before my eyes drove me for shelter among the mutineers, dreading a similar fate with those that fell if I sided with or showed the smallest inclination for mercy." To this frank and sweeping confession of his guilt he added a declaration of profound remorse for his crime, and wound up by throwing himself despairingly on the compassion of the court. The court found him guilty, passed upon him the sentence of death, and eleven days afterwards he was executed. In vain were all his supplications for compassion. In vain did his brother and sister interfere, proving, by a certificate from the Navy Office, that his written statement must have been a mere hallucination, seeing that the boy was at another place and in another ship when the crime was committed on board the "Hermione."

The subsequent establishment of this poor victim's innocence was most complete and satisfactory. The editor of a weekly journal, called the "Independent Whig," took up the matter very sternly, and denounced all the proceedings so indignantly from time to time that the members of the court-martial appealed to the Lords of the Admiralty for protection against the journalist. The Lords of the Admiralty responded to the appeal, and a prosecution was at once instituted. It was fortunate that the then law officers of the crown were Sir Arthur Pigott and Sir Samuel Romilly. These discreet men deemed it prudent to set on foot a strict inquiry into the facts before committing themselves to a public prosecution, "not, however," as Sir Samuel afterwards stated, "that either of us entertained any doubt as to the man's guilt." An inquiry was accordingly instituted by the solicitor of the Admiralty, the result of which was that Thomas Wood, who had been hanged for mutiny and murder, was proved to have been perfectly innocent, and was actually shown to have been doing his duty on board the "Marlborough" at Portsmouth at the very time that the crime was committed by the mutineers in the "Hermione." The reader naturally asks, How came Thomas Wood, if he was an innocent man, to confess himself guilty? The answer is not far to seek. Wood was a simple-minded Jack tar; he had no friends of any influence; he knew, or thought he knew, that no assertions of his would be of any avail against the positive evidence of the master of the "Hermione;" he therefore applied to another man to write a defense for him. Wood read the production of his comrade, and thinking it likely to excite the compassion of his judges, and that it would serve him better that a mere denial of the charges brought against him, adopted it. That the means chosen by his ignorant comrade for his defense proved his destruction, there can be no doubt. The confession acted as a bar to further inquiry, otherwise it is impossible to conceive that the certificate sent in by the brother and sister previous to the execution, and which showed the poor man's innocence, should not have been attended to. The truth was, that to all concerned in the condemnation of Thomas Wood, the facts were so clear, owing to the confession, that no regard whatever was paid to the exertions of his friends, and the official certificate was not merely slighted, it was probably never read.

XI.

Case of Connt Montgomery.

On the first floor of a large hotel in the Rue
Royale, at Paris, resided the Count and Countess de
Montgomery. The Count was a personage of rank,
and the possessor of considerable property, maintaining a numerous retinue of attendants, and an
almoner, who formed part of the establishment. On
the second and third floors of the same hotel the
Sieur d'Anglade resided with his lady in a style of
considerable respectability. The two families lived
on the most amicable terms. It so happened that on
one occasion the count and countess invited these
neighbors to accompany them on a visit to one of
their country seats. The invitation, at first accepted,
was, for some unexplained reason, subsequently declined when the count and countess were just on the
eve of their departure. Many of their numerous
suite accompanied the family, and amongst these was
the priest-almoner, Francis Gagnard. From some
presentiment, it was said, pressing on the mind of the
count, they returned to Paris the day before they
were expected, and in the evening they received a

visit from the d'Anglades. On the following day the
unwelcome discovery was made that the count's
strong box had been opened by a false key, and
completely plundered. It contents were thirteen
small sacks with a thousand silver livres in each. In
addition to these were near twelve thousand livres
in gold, some double pistoles, a hundred louis d'or,
of a new coinage called *au cordon*, and a pearl
necklace worth four thousand livres. The whole
had vanished.

The lieutenant of police having been consulted,
at once pronounced the crime to have been perpetrated by some one within the house, and seems
to have conceived and manifested a violent prejudice
against the d'Anglade family. On observing this
they immediately demanded that their apartments
should be examined, and a strict search was made,
their very beds having been ripped up, but nothing
whatever was found to implicate any one in the
floors which they inhabited. In an attic, however,
which had been used as a kind of lumber-room,
there were discovered, in an old trunk filled with
parchments and rubbish, seventy louis d'or *au
cordon*, wrapped up in a paper on which a genea-
logical table was printed, both of which Montgomery claimed, although the coin had no peculiar

mark, and was in general circulation. From this moment the suspicions entertained by the lieutenant were adopted by the count. He loudly avouched the honesty of all his servants, and invidiously adverted to the theft of a piece of plate from the Sieur Grimandet, a former tenant, the d'Anglades at the same time living in the hotel. These sus-picions were strengthened by the fact that it was known that d'Anglade had expensive habits, and that on their desiring him to count the coin he was observed to tremble. His trembling was the agita-tion of innocence under an accusation false but plausible. After this the small room in which the almoner, a page, and a *valet de chambre* slept, was subjected to a close search, and here, in a recess in the wall, were found five sacks containing a thou-sand livres each, and a sixth from which two hun-dred had been extracted. The d'Anglades were committed to prison, and it seems, by the law of France, the prejudiced police lieutenant who com-mitted was the judge by whom they were to be tried. D'Anglade appealed to the parliament against this foul prejudgment, but he appealed in vain. It would appear that Count Montgomery had his misgivings, for he ordered his almoner, the priest Gagnard, to say a solemn mass at the church

of Saint Esprit for the detection of the culprits;
and accordingly the "holy man" so fervently implored the aid of the Divine Being that the prosecutor's conscience was at rest. The almoner was
examined as a witness at the trial, though what was
the nature of his evidence does not appear; whatever it may have been, satisfactory proofs were
wanting to inculpate the accused. The public eye
was upon the judge, and, without plausible proof,
even a prejudiced judge shrank from pronouncing
judgment. But he had an alternative, which at
that time unhappily was legal. What the witnesses
failed in proving, the torture might goad the accused to confess; they therefore put d'Anglade to
the question, ordinary and extraordinary — they
tormented him even to the verge of death, and
then, covered over with wounds, his back dislocated, his whole frame shattered, all in ruins
save a noble nature, they bore him back to
prison beseeching God to manifest his innocence,
and to pardon his inhuman persecutors and his in-
exorable judge. Although they failed to prove his
guilt, they sentenced him to restore the amount
which had been stolen, and to serve for nine years
chained as a galley-slave. From this last degrada-
tion he was saved by death, for he sank in his

dungeon at Marseilles, having received the sacraments. His poor widow and orphan, stripped of everything, even of the bed on which they lay, were banished from Paris and its precincts, and cast upon the world, forsaken and heartbroken.

After the death of d'Anglade and the utter desolation of his family, their innocence was clearly demonstrated. Inquiry was instituted in consequence of some letters which, at first anonymous, appear to have been written by an Abbé de Fontpierre, and the truth was brought to light. This son of the church and expounder of doctrine was a member of a thieves' society, and, as such, an associate of one Belestré, who was the principal in the crime. What motive impelled Fontpierre to write the letters—whether it was some quarrel with Belestré, or remorse at the fate of d'Anglade—does not appear. Belestre could not have accomplished the crime without assistance, and such was afforded him by Francis Gagnard, the inmate of Montgomery's house, and his trusted almoner, the reverend divine who actually celebrated the sacred ceremony at Saint Esprit for the discovery of the criminals. Gagnard and Belestré, both natives of the town of Mons, had been associated from infancy. The former was the son of a jailer; he had

journeyed to Paris as an adventurer, and was
eking out a mere subsistence by saying masses at
Saint Esprit, when Montgomery admitted him on
his establishment. The return he made was the
furnishing his friend Belestré with wax impressions
of all the keys he found there. It turned out that
Belestré was a still greater villain than himself,
having been in the army, from which he deserted
after murdering his sergeant, and was afterwards
prowling about the dens of Paris, alternately a
gambler, a beggar, and a bully. Gagnard left
the service of Montgomery after the conviction of
d'Anglade, and following his criminal bent, soon
found himself in prison, and, strangely enough,
in the same cell with Belestré, arrested about the
same time on a different charge. In the mean
time the contents of the anonymous letters having much impressed the authorities, it occurred to
them to interrogate the count's late almoner and
his fellow prisoner as to the robbery in the Rue
Royale. They were first examined apart, and an
immediate prosecution was the result. The Abbé
de Fontpierre gave most important evidence.
Amongst other things he deposed, that being in
a room adjoining one in which the accused was
holding a revel, he heard Belestré say, "Come,

my friend, let us drink and be merry, while d'Anglade is at the galleys." "Poor man," answered the almoner, "I can't help being sorry for him; he is a good sort of man, and was always obliging to me." "Sorry!" said the other, with a laugh, "sorry for the man who has saved us from suspicion and made our fortune!" A woman named De la Comble deposed that Belestré frequently showed her a beautiful pearl necklace, which he said he had won at play. Upon Belestré there was a gazette of Holland, in which, after reference to the d'Anglade case, there was a positive statement that the men who were really guilty of that robbery had been since executed at Orleans for another crime. Of this it was supposed he had himself procured the insertion in order to lull inquiry. Unfortunately, however, for him and his confederate, there was also found on him a document, in Gagnard's writing, alluding to the anonymous letters, and advising him by some means or other to quiet or to rid himself of the Abbé de Fontpierre. In addition to this it was shown that Gagnard, who on entering the count's service was almost destitute, and who could have saved but little from his salary, had on leaving it a profusion of money, which he lavished in feasting and debauchery. Belestré, also, was proved at the same period to have pur-chased an estate at Mons, where his father was a humble tanner. Madame d'Anglade completely cleared up the paltry suspicions by which her husband had been sacrificed; but it is needless to detail the particulars of the exculpation, as the criminals made a full confession of their guilt. Indeed, Gagnard went farther, and declared that. had he been closely interrogated during the first inquiry, such was his confusion, he must have ad-mitted everything. But the mind of the judge was all intent on vindicating the prejudices in which he never should have indulged.

XII.

Case of Le Brun.

THERE lived in Paris a woman of fashion, known as Lady Mazel. Her house was roomy and lofty; on the ground floor was a large hall in which was a grand staircase; in a room opening into the hall slept the valet, whose name was Le Brun; the rest of this floor consisting of apartments in which the lady saw company. In the floor up one pair of stairs was the lady's own chamber, which was in front of the house, and was the innermost of three rooms from the grand staircase. The key of this chamber was usually taken out of the door and laid on a chair by the servant who was last with the lady, and who, pulling the door after her, shut it with a spring, so that it could not be opened from without. In this chamber, also were two doors — one communicating with a back staircase, the other with a wardrobe which also opened on the back stairs. On the second floor slept the Abbé Poulard; and on the third story were the chambers allotted to the servants; the fourth story consisted of lofts and granaries, whose doors were always open.

On the last Sunday in November, the two
daughters of Le Brun, the valet, who were fashionable milliners, waited on the lady, and were kindly
received; but, as she was going to church to the
afternoon service, she pressed them to come again
when she could have more of their company. Le
Brun attended his lady to church, and then went
to another himself, after which he went to several
places, and having supped with a friend, he went
home. Lady Mazel supped with the Abbé Poulard,
as usual, and about eleven o'clock retired to her
chamber, attended by her maids. Before they left
her Le Brun came to the door to receive his orders
for the next day; then one of the maids laid the
key of the room door on the chair next it—they
went out, and Le Brun following shut the door after
him.

In the morning he went to market, made his
purchases, and returning home transacted his
business as usual. At eight o'clock he expressed
surprise that his lady did not get up, as she
generally rose early. He went to his wife's lodging, which was close by, told her he was uneasy
that his lady's bell had not rung, and gave her
some money which he desired her to lock up; he
then went home again, and found the servants dis-

mayed at hearing nothing of their lady. When
one of them observed that he feared she had been
seized with an illness, Le Brun said, "It must be
something worse; my mind misgives me, for I
found the street door open last night after all the
family were in bed." They then sent for the lady's
son, M. de Savoniere, who hinted to Le Brun his
fear of an apoplexy. Le Brun replied that he
feared something worse, and again mentioned his
having found the street door open. A smith was
sent for, the door was broken open, and Le Brun,
running to the bed, after calling several times, threw
back the curtains and cried out, "Oh, my lady is
murdered!" He then ran to the wardrobe and
took up the strong box, and finding it heavy, said,
"She has not been robbed, how is this?" The
body, on examination, showed no less than fifty
wounds; they found in the bed a scrap of a cravat
of coarse lace, and a napkin made into a nightcap,
which was blood-stained, and had the family mark
on it. From the wounds on the lady's hand, it appeared she had struggled bravely with the assassin;
she could not ring for aid, the bell-strings being
twisted round the tester, and thus out of her reach.
A knife was found in the ashes almost consumed
by the fire; the key of the chamber had been

taken from the chair; but there were no marks of violence on any of the doors, nor were there any indications of a robbery, as a large sum of money and all the lady's jewels were found in the strong box and other places.

On being examined, Le Brun stated that after he left the maids on the stairs, he went down into the kitchen, and, sitting down by the fire, he fell asleep; that he slept, as he thought, about an hour, and going to lock the street door, he found it open; that he locked it, and took the key with him to his chamber. When searched, there was found in his pocket a key, the wards of which had been enlarged by filing, and which was found to open the street door, the antechamber, and both the doors in Lady Mazel's chamber. On trying the bloody nightcap on Le Brun's head, it was found to fit him exactly, whereupon he was committed to prison.

At the trial, it appeared that the lady had been murdered by some persons who had been admitted by Le Brun for the purpose. He could not himself have done it, because there was no blood upon his clothes, nor any scratch on his person, as there must have been on the murderer from the victim's struggling. But that Le Brun had let him in seemed clear. None of the locks were forced, and his story of finding the street door open, the circum-stances of the key and the nightcap, also of a ladder of ropes being found in the house, which might be supposed to be laid there by Le Brun to take off the attention from himself, were all interpreted as proofs of his guilt. It was inferred that he had an accomplice, because part of the cravat found in the bed was discovered not to be his, *but the maids deposed that they had washed such a cravat for one Berry, who had been a footman to the lady, and who was turned away about four months before for robbing her.* There was also found in the loft at the top of the house, under some straw, a shirt very bloody, but which evidently had never belonged to Le Brun. The accused had nothing to oppose to these strong circumstances but his long and faithful service, and his uniformly good character. It was resolved to put him to the torture in order to dis-cover his accomplices. This was done with such severity that he died in a few days of the injuries he received, declaring his innocence with his dying breath.

Poor Le Brun had scarcely been dead a month, when there came information from the provost of Sens, that a dealer in horses had lately set up there by the name of John Garlet, but whose real name was found to be Berry, and that he had been a footman in Paris. In consequence of this, he was taken up, and the suspicion of his guilt was increased by his attempting to bribe the officers. On searching him, a gold watch was found, which proved to be Lady Mazel's. A person in Paris swore to seeing him go out of Lady Mazel's, the night she was murdered; and a barber swore to shaving him next morning, when, on his remarking to his customer that his hands were very much scratched, Berry said he had been killing a cat. His guilt being evident, he was condemned to the torture, and afterwards to be broken alive on the wheel. Under the torture, he made, as many others have done, a false confession, declaring that at the instigation of Madame de Savoniere, Lady Mazel's daughter, he and Le Brun had undertaken to rob and murder the lady, and that Le Brun murdered her while he guarded the door to prevent surprise. But when brought to the place of execution, he recanted what he had said against Le Brun and Madame de Savoniere, and confessed "that he came to Paris on the Wednesday before the murder was committed. On the Friday evening he went into the house, and unperceived, got into one of the lofts, where he lay till Sunday morning, subsisting on apples and bread, which he had in his pockets ; that about eleven o'clock on Sunday morning, when he knew the lady had gone to church, he stole down to her chamber, and the door being open, he tried to get under the bed ; but it being too low, he returned to the loft, pulled off his coat and waistcoat, and returned to the chamber a second time, in his shirt. He then got under the bed, where he continued till the afternoon, when Lady Mazel went to church ; that knowing she would not come back soon, he left his hiding-place, and being incommoded with his hat, he threw it under the bed, and made a cap of a napkin which lay on a chair, secured the bell-strings, and then sat down by the fire, where he continued till he heard her coach drive into the courtyard, when he again got under the bed and remained there ; that Lady Mazel having been in bed about an hour, he got from under it, and demanded her money ; she began to cry out, and attempted to ring, upon which he stabbed her, and she resisting with all her strength, he repeated the stabs till she was dead ; that he then took the key of the wardrobe cupboard from the bed's head, opened the cupboard, found the key of the strong box, opened it and took out all the gold he could find, to the amount of about six hundred livres ;

that he then locked the cupboard, and replaced the key at the bed's head, threw his knife into the fire, took his hat from under the bed, left the napkin in it, took the key of the chamber from the chair, and let himself out; went to the loft, where he pulled off his shirt and cravat, and leaving them there, put on his coat and waistcoat, and stole softly down stairs; and finding the street door only on the single lock, he opened it, went out, and left it open; that he had brought a rope ladder to let himself down from a widow if he had found the street door double locked, but finding it otherwise, he left the rope ladder at the bottom of the stairs, where it was found."

Thus was this foul mystery cleared up—and thus were all the circumstances which appeared against Le Brun accounted for, consistently with his innocence. Le Brun perished, as d'Anglade had perished, through the headlong precipitancy of the criminal court and the judge.

XIII.

Case of Eliza Fenning.

A MOST melancholy case of circumstantial evidence happened in London, in the year 1815, the particulars of which must yet dwell in the memories of many still living. Eliza Penning was a servant girl, very young, and said to be very beautiful, living in Chancery Lane. She was but twenty-one years of age, the dutiful and only child of respectable parents, then alive. She was tried at the Old Bailey, in the month of April, 1815, before the recorder of London, for the crime of administering poison to her master and mistress, and her master's father—a capital felony under Lord EL-LENBOROUGH's Act. The only evidence to affect the prisoner was entirely circumstantial. The poison was contained in dumplings made by her, but it was proved by the surgeon, who gave evidence at the trial, that she had eaten of them herself, and had been quite as ill as any of the persons whom she was supposed to have intended to poison. Further, her eating of them could not be ascribed to art, or to any attempt to conceal her crime, for

she had made no effort whatever to remove the
strongest evidence of guilt, if guilt there was. She
had left the dish unwashed ; and the proof that
arsenic was mixed it it, was furnished by its being
found in the kitchen on the following day, exactly
in the state in which it had been brought from the
table.

It is hardly conceivable that, such being the circumstances, a conviction could have been possible.
"But," says Sir SAMUEL ROMILLY, from whose
manuscript this account is condensed, "the recorder
appeared to have conceived a strong prejudice
against the prisoner; in summing up the evidence,
he made some very unjust and unfounded observations to her disadvantage, and she was convicted."
Petitions signed, not by hundreds, but by thousands,
besought the throne for mercy. The master of the
girl was requested to add his name to the petitioners
on her behalf, but the recorder dissuaded him, and
at his instance he refused. All intercession was
fruitless, and Eliza Penning was ordered for execution. She mildly, but earnestly, asserted her innocence to the last, and prayed to God some day to
make it manifest. When the religious ceremonies
were over, the sad procession moved towards the
scaffold. As the last door was opening which still

concealed her from the public gaze, Mr. Cotton, the ordinary, made a final effort: "Eliza, have you nothing more to say to me?" It was an awful moment, but her last words in this world were, "Before the just and Almighty God, and by the faith of the Holy Sacrament I have received, I am innocent of the offense of which I am charged." The door then opened, and she stood robed in white, before the people. Two old offenders were executed with her, "and," says a bystander, "as all three stood under the beam, beneath the sun, she looked serene as angel." The stormy multitude was hushed at once, and while all eyes wept, and every tongue prayed for her, she passed into eternity.

When the curtain had fallen upon this tragedy, the fury of the people knew no bounds, and the house of the prosecutor was protected only by the presence of a considerable force. The temper of the times was such that nothing could prevent a popular demonstration at the funeral, and a mournful and striking one it must have been. The broken-hearted parents led the way, followed by six young females clad in white, and then by eight chief mourners. At least ten thousand persons accompanied the hearse, and thus, every window filled, and every housetop crowded, they reached the cemetery of St. George the Martyr, where the remains of the innocent girl was interred.

Sir SAMUEL ROMILLY further states, that after Eliza Fenning's conviction, and while the error was reparable, "an offer was made to prove that there was in the house of Eliza's master, when the poisoning took place, a person who had labored, a short time before, under mental derangèment, and who, in that state, had declared his fears that he should destroy himself and his family." This statement was made to the recorder himself, and evidence of its truth was offered, but that functionary affirmed that the production of any evidence of the kind would be wholly useless. That the crime was committed by a maniac, there can be but small doubt. The testimony of Mr. Gibson, who was then connected with the firm of Corbyn & Co., Holborn, is all but conclusive on the point. This gentleman stated that "about September or October, in the preceding year, a Mr. —— (the name, for obvious reasons, was not made public), called on me in Holborn. He seemed in such a wild and deranged state, that I took him into a back room, where he used the most violent and incoherent expressions— 'My dear Gibson, do, for Heaven's sake, get me secured or confined, for if I am left at liberty I shall do some mischief; I shall destroy myself and my wife. I must and shall do it unless all means of destruction are removed out of my way; therefore do, my good friend, have me put under some restraint; *something from above* tells me I must do it, and, unless I am prevented, I shall cer· tainly do it." Mr. Gibson felt it his duty to communicate this to the poor maniac's family, but they were heedless of the warning, and he was left at liberty.

XIV.

Case of Richard Coleman.

ABOUT the middle of the last century, Richard Coleman was indicted at the Kingston assizes, in Surrey, for the murder of Sarah Green. Coleman was a man of some education, was married and had several children, and was clerk to a brewer when the affair happened which cost him his life. One Sarah Green, a woman of a humble class, was attacked by three men, who maltreated her so cruelly that she afterwards died. These men had the appearance of brewers' servants,' and while she was under treatment in the hospital, she declared that a clerk in Berry's brewhouse was one of them, though it was not clear to whom she alluded. Two days after the transaction, Coleman went into an alehouse for refreshment, where he met with one Daniel Trotman, whom he knew. Having called for some spirits and water, Coleman was stirring it with a spoon, when a stranger who was present, asked him what he had done with the pig—alluding to a pig which had been lately stolen in the neighborhood. The retort led to a violent quarrel, in the course of which, the stranger insinuated that Coleman had been concerned in the murder of Sarah Green. Coleman answered the insinuation only by further aggravating his opponent. There was no breach of the peace, and the parties separated at length, with mutual ill-temper and personal abuse.

A day or two after this quarrel, Daniel Trotman and another man went before a magistrate in the Borough, and charged Coleman with the crime. The magistrate, not supposing that Coleman was guilty, sent a man with him to the hospital where the wounded woman lay, and a person pointing out Coleman, asked her if he was one of the per sons who assailed her. She said she believed he was, but as she declined to swear positively to his having any concern in the affair, the magistrate, Justice CLARKE, admitted him to bail. A short time afterwards Coleman was again taken before the magistrate, when nothing positive being sworn against him, the justice would have absolutely discharged him; but Mr. Wynne, the master of the injured girl, requesting that he might be once more taken to see her, a time was fixed for that purpose, and the justice took Coleman's word for his appearance. He came punctually to his time

bringing with him the landlord of an alehouse where
Sarah Green had been drinking on the night of
the crime with the three men who were really guilty ;
and this publican, and other people, declared on
oath that Coleman was not one of the party. On
the following day, Justice CLARKE went to the
hospital to take the examination of the woman on
oath. Having asked her if Coleman was one of the
men who had attacked her, she said she could not
tell, as it was dark at the time, but Coleman being
called in, an oath was administered to her, when
she swore that he was one of the three assailants.
Spite of her oath, the justice, who thought the poor
girl not in her right senses, and was convinced in his
own mind of the innocence of Coleman, permitted
him to depart, on his promise of bringing bail the
following day, to answer the complaint at the next
assizes for Surrey ; and he brought his bail and gave
security accordingly.

Sarah Green dying in the hospital, the coroner's
jury sat to inquire the cause of her death ; and having found a verdict of willful murder against Richard
Coleman and two persons then unknown, a warrant
was issued to take Coleman into custody. Though
conscious of his innocence, yet such was the agitation of his mind at the idea of being sent to prison

on such a charge, that Coleman absconded, and secreted himself at Pinner, near Harrow-on-the-Hill. The king being then at Hanover, a proclamation was issued by the lords of the regency, offering a reward of fifty pounds for the apprehension of the supposed offender ; and to this the parish of Saint Saviour, Southwark, added a further sum of twenty pounds. Coleman read in the "Gazette" an advertisement for his apprehension, but was still so thoughtless as to conceal himself, though perhaps an immediate and voluntary surrender would have been his wisest course. However, to assert his innocence, he caused the following advertisement to be printed in the newspapers :

"I, Richard Coleman, seeing myself advertised in the 'Gazette' as absconding on account of the murder of Sarah Green, knowing myself not any way culpable, do assert that I have not absconded from justice, but will willingly and readily appear at the next assizes, knowing that my innocence will acquit me."

The authorities, not choosing to wait for his promised appearance, however, made strict search after him, and he was apprehended at Pinner on the 22nd of November, and lodged in Southwark jail till the time of the assizes at Kingston, Surrey

At the trial several persons swore positively that Coleman was at another place at the time the crime was committed ; but their evidence was not believed, and he was convicted principally upon the evidence of Daniel Trotman, and the declaration of the dying woman. After conviction, Coleman behaved like a man possessed of conscious innocence, and betrayed no fear in dying for a crime which he had not com mitted. At the place of execution, he delivered to the chaplain who had attended him a paper, in which he declared, in the most solemn and explicit manner, that he was altogether innocent of the crime alleged against him. He was executed at Kennington Common, on the 12th of April, 1749— and died with perfect resignation, lamenting only the distress in which he should leave a wife and two children.

About two years after Coleman's death, it was discovered that three working brewers named James Welch, Thomas Jones, and John Nichols, were the persons who had actually occasioned the death of Sarah Green. These wretches had been intimately acquainted from their childhood, and had kept the murder a secret, till it was discovered in the following manner. Welch, and a young fellow named James Bush, were walking together in the neighborhood of Newington, when their conversation happened to turn on the subject of persons who had been executed for offenses of which they had not been guilty—"Among whom," said Welch, as if by a sudden impulse, "was Richard Coleman Nichols, Jones, and I, were the persons who committed the murder for which he was hanged." Welch then went on to relate the circumstances of the crime—his companion listening to the disclosure with feelings that may be imagined. Bush scarcely credited the story thus abruptly communicated, and for a time said nothing about it to any one; at length, however, he told his father what he had heard, and his father meeting shortly afterwards with Thomas Jones, and willing to test the truth of so strange a tale, abruptly charged him with being one of the murderers of Sarah Green. Jones trembled and turned pale at the charge, but soon assuming a degree of courage, said: "What does it signify? The man is hanged, and the woman is dead, and nobody can hurt us." In consequence of this acknowledgment, Nichols, Jones, and Welch were apprehended, when all of them steadily denied their guilt. Nichols, however, subsequently turned against his companions, and was admitted as evidence for the crown.

The prisoners being brought to trial at the next
Surrey assizes, were both of them convicted on the
testimony of Nichols, and sentence of death was
passed upon them. After conviction, they behaved with the utmost contrition, and made a
full confession of their crime. They likewise
signed a declaration which they begged might be
published, containing the fullest assertions of Cole
man's *innocence.*

XV.

Case of William Shaw.

ANOTHER case, in which an innocent man was convicted on the evidence of a dying person, was that of William Shaw, of Leith. Shaw was an artisan, and lived in that town respectably for his station in life, his family consisting but of an only daughter, who resided with him; she had formed an unfortunate attachment to a young man whom the father knew to be of bad character, and therefore sternly discountenanced his addresses. This gave rise to continual dissension, until, at length, it one day rose to such a height, that James Morrison, the tenant of an adjoining room, could not avoid overhearing the conversation. The voices of father and daughter were recognized, and the words, "cruelty," "barbarity," and "death," were over and over again angrily enunciated. The father at last left the room abruptly, locking the door behind him, and leaving the daughter a prisoner. After some little time, deep noises were heard from within, which gradually becoming fainter, the alarmed neighbors procured the assistance of a bailiff, and

burst open the door. Ghastly, indeed, was the
spectacle which presented itself. There lay the
young woman on the floor, weltering in her blood —
a knife, the instrument of her death, beside her.
To the question whether her father had been the
cause of her sad condition, she was just able to
make a faint affirmative gesture, and expired. At
this moment the father reappeared. His horror
may be imagined; every eye was fixed on him,
and some specks of blood upon his shirt-sleeves
seemed to confirm strongly the dreadful accusation
which his daughter's dying gesture had too clearly
intimated. Vainly attempting to account for the
stained sleeve by the rupture of some swathe with
which he had bound his wrist, he was hurried
before a magistrate, and, upon the depositions of
all the parties, committed to prison upon suspicion.
He was shortly after brought to trial, when, in his
defense, he acknowledged his having confined his
daughter to prevent her intercourse with Lawson,
the young man to whom he objected; and that he
had quarreled with her on the subject the evening
she was found murdered, as the witness Morrison
had deposed; but he averred that he left his
daughter unharmed and untouched, and that the
blood found upon his shirt was there in conse-

quence of his having bled himself some days before, and the bandage becoming untied. These assertions did not weigh a feather with the jury when opposed to the strong circumstantial evidence of the daughter's expressions of "barbarity, cruelty, death," together with that apparently affirmative motion of her head, and of the blood so, as it seemed, providentially discovered on the father's shirt. On these severally concurring circumstances was William Shaw found guilty and executed.

After this unfortunate man had swung for weeks upon his gibbet—for he was gibbeted in chains, exposed to the four winds of heaven and the gaze of every passer-by—it was shown, beyond the possibility of doubt, that he was not merely guiltless, but that he had fallen a sacrifice to his regard for her whom he was accused of having murdered. The incoming tenant who succeeded Shaw, while rummaging in the chamber where Catherine Shaw died, discovered in a cavity on one side of the chimney, where it appeared to have fallen, a paper written by the wayward girl, announcing her intention of committing suicide, and ending with the words, "My inhuman father is the cause of my death;" thus explaining her expiring gesture. This document being shown, the handwriting was

recognized and avowed to be Catherine's by many
of her relatives and friends. It became the public
talk, and the magistracy of Edinburgh, on a
scrutiny, being convinced of its authenticity,
ordered the body of William Shaw to be given
to his relatives for interment. Willing to make
some reparation to his memory, and to show some
sympathy with the feelings of his relatives, they
caused a pair of colors to be waved over his grave.
It was all the compensation they could award.

XVI.

Case of De Moulin.

JAQUES DU MOULIN, a French refugee, having brought over his family and a small sum of money, employed it in purchasing lots of goods that had been condemned at the custom-house, which he again disposed of by retail. As these goods were such as, having a high duty, were frequently smuggled, those who dealt in this way were generally suspected of increasing their stock by illicit means, and smuggling, or purchasing smuggled goods, under color of dealing only in goods that had been legally seized by the king's officers, and taken from smugglers. This trade, however, did not, in the general estimation, impeach his honesty, though it gave no sanction to his character; but he was often detected in uttering false gold. He came frequently to persons of whom he had received money, with several of these pieces of counterfeit coin, and pretended that they were among the pieces which had been paid him; this was generally denied with great eagerness, but, if particular circumstances did not confirm the contrary, he was always peremptory and obstinate in his charge. This soon brought him into disrepute, and he gradually lost not only his business, but his credit. It happened that, having sold a parcel of goods, which amounted to seventy-eight pounds, to one Harris, a person with whom he had before had no dealings, he received the money in guineas and Portugal gold, several pieces of which he scrupled ; but the man having assured him that he himself had carefully examined and weighed those very pieces, and found them good, Du Moulin took them, and gave his receipt.

In a few days he returned with six pieces, which he averred were of base metal, and part of the sum which he had a few days before received of him for the lot of goods. Harris examined the pieces, and told Du Moulin that he was sure there were none of them among those which he had paid him, and refused to exchange them for others. Du Moulin as peremptorily insisted on the contrary, alleging that he had put the money in a drawer by itself, and locked it up till he offered it in payment of a bill of exchange, and then the pieces were found to be bad, insisting that they were the same to which he had objected. The man now became angry, and charged Du Moulin with intending a fraud. Du Moulin appeared to be rather piqued than intimidated at this charge; and having sworn that these were the pieces he received of Harris, Harris was at length obliged to make them good; but as he was confident Du Moulin had injured him by a fraud, supported by perjury, he told his story wherever he went, exclaiming against him with great bitterness, and met with many persons who made nearly the same complaints, and told him that it had been a practice of Du Moulin's for a considerable time. Du Moulin now found himself universally shunned; and hearing what Harris had reported from all parts, he brought his action for defamatory words, and Harris, irritated to the highest degree, stood upon his defense; and, in the mean time, having procured a meeting of several persons who had suffered the same way in their dealings with Du Moulin, they procured a warrant against him, and he was apprehended upon suspicion of counterfeiting the coin. Upon searching his drawers, a great number of pieces of counterfeit gold were found in a drawer by themselves, and several others were picked from other money, that was found in different parcels in his scrutoire; upon further search, a flask, several files, a pair of moulds, some powdered chalk, a small quantity of aqua regia, and several other implements, were discovered. No

doubt could now be made of his guilt, which was
extremely aggravated by the methods he had taken
to dispose of the money he made, the insolence
with which he had insisted upon its being paid him
by others, and the perjury by which he had supported his claim. His action against Harris for defamation was also considered as greatly increasing
his guilt, and everybody was impatient to see him
punished. In these circumstances he was brought
to his trial, and his many attempts to put off bad
money, the quantity found by itself in his scrutoire,
and, above all, the instruments of coining, which,
upon a comparison, exactly answered the money
in his possession, being proved, he was upon this
evidence convicted, and received sentence of death.

It happened that a few days before he was to have
been executed, one Williams, who had been bred a
seal engraver, but had left his business, was killed
by a fall from his horse ; his wife who was then
big with child, and near her time, immediately
fell into fits, and miscarried. She was soon sensible
that she could not live, and therefore sending for
the wife of Du Moulin, she desired to be left alone,
and gave her the following account:

That her husband was one of four, whom she
named, that had for many years subsisted by coun-

terfeiting gold coin, which she had been frequently
employed to put off, and was therefore intrusted
with the whole secret; that another of these persons
had hired himself to Du Moulin as a kind of footman and porter, and being provided by the gang
with false keys, had disposed of a very considerable
sum of bad money, by opening his master's scrutoire, and leaving it there in the stead of an equal
number of good pieces, which he took out; that by
this iniquitous practice, Du Moulin had been de-
frauded of his business, his credit, and his liberty,
to which in a short time his life would be added,
if application was not immediately made to save
him. By this account, which she gave in great
agonies of mind, she was much exhausted, and having given directions where to find the persons whom
she impeached, she fell into convulsions, and soon
after expired. The woman immediately applied to
a·magistrate, and having related the story she had
heard, procured a warrant against the three men,
who were taken the same day, and separately
examined. Du Moulin's servant steadily denied
the whole charge, and so did one of the other two;
but while the last was examining, a messenger who
had been sent to search their lodgings, arrived with
a great quantity of bad money, and many instru-

ments for coining. This threw him into confusion, and the magistrate, improving the opportunity by offering him his life if he would become an evidence for the king, he confessed that he had been long associated with the other prisoners and the man that was dead, and he directed where other tools and money might be found, but he could say nothing as to the manner in which Du Moulin's servant was employed to put it off. Upon this discovery, Du Moulin's execution was suspended; and the king's witness swearing positively that his servant and the other prisoner had frequently coined in his presence, and giving a particular account of the process, and the part which each ot them usually performed, they were convicted, and condemned to die. Both of them, however, still denied the fact, and the public were still in doubt about Du Moulin. In his defense, he had declared that the bad money which was found together was such as he could not trace to the persons of whom he had received it; that the parcels with which bad money was found mixed, he kept separate, that he might know to whom to apply if it should appear to be bad; but the finding of the moulds and other instruments in his custody was a particular not yet accounted for, as he only alleged in general terms that he knew not how they came there, and it was doubted whether the impeachment of others had not been managed with a view to save him who was equally guilty, there being no evidence of his servant's treachery but that of a woman who was dead, reported at second hand by the wife of Du Moulin, who was manifestly an interested party. He was not, however, charged by either of the convicts as an accomplice, a particular which was strongly urged by his friends in his behalf; but it happened that while the public opinion was thus held in suspense, a private drawer was discovered in a chest that belonged to his servant, and in it a bunch of keys, and the impression of one in wax; the impression was compared with the keys, and that which it corresponded with was found to open Du Moulin's scrutoire, in which the bad money and implements had been found. When this particular, so strong and unexpected, was urged, and the key produced, he burst into tears, and confessed all that had been alleged against him. He was then asked how the tools came into his master's scrutoire; and he answered, that when the officers of justice came to seize his master, he was terrified for himself, knowing that he had in his chest these instru-

ments, which the private drawer would not con
tain, and fearing that he might be included in the
warrant, his consciousness of guilt kept him in
continual dread and suspicion; that for this reason,
before the officers went up stairs, he opened the
scrutoire with his false key, and having fetched
his tools from his box in the garret, he deposited
them there, and had just locked it when he heard
them at the door.

In this case, even the positive evidence of Du
Moulin, that the money he brought back to Harris
was the same he had received of him, was not true,
though Du Moulin was not guilty of perjury, either
willfully or by neglect, inattention or forgetfulness.
And the circumstantial evidence against him, however strong, would only have heaped one injury
upon another, and have taken away the life of an
unhappy wretch, from whom a perfidious servant
had taken everything else.

XVII.

Case of the Schmidts.

IN the town of M——, in Germany, resided a goldsmith, named Christopher Ruprecht, aged upwards of sixty; rich, illiterate, quarrelsome, covetous; rude in speech, vulgar in his habits; whose chief indulgence consisted in frequenting low alehouses, and mingling in such haunts with the most disreputable among the lower classes of his fellow citizens. His selfishness and repulsive manners had alienated from him all his relations, with the exception of a sister, who resided with him, and a married daughter, who still continued, notwithstanding his peculiarities of temper, to visit him regularly, though as much from interest perhaps as affection.

The favorite resort of Ruprecht was a small alehouse of the meanest order, situated at the end of a dark winding lane, and receiving as a title, from its gloomy situation, and the orgies of which it was the scene, the emphatic monosyllable usually applied to the place of darkness. About half-past eight o'clock, on the evening of the 7th of February, 1817, the goldsmith repaired to this place according to his custom, took his seat among the circle which generally assembled round the inn fire on the first floor, and in his usual overbearing style, joined in the current conversation. In this manner the time was spent till past ten o'clock, when Ruprecht despatched the landlord to the ground floor for a further supply of beer. As the master of the house was reascending the stairs to the company with the liquor wanted, a voice from the passage or outer door below, was heard inquiring if Ruprecht was above; and on the landlord replying—without turning his head—in the affirmative, he was desired by the person below to tell the goldsmith to come down. On receiving the message, Ruprecht rose immediately, and left the room. A minute had scarcely elapsed afterwards, when the company heard distinctly a loud groaning from below stairs, followed by a sound as of a heavy body falling in the passage. All present, to the number of eleven, hurried down stairs, where they found the goldsmith lying near the house door, still alive, but covered with blood flowing from a large wound on his head. At a little distance lay his leather cap, which had been cut through by the blow. The only words which the wounded man uttered, when lifted up, were: "The villain—the villain with the axe!" and once afterwards, "My daughter, my daughter!" She was immediately sent for, but his mind apparently wandered, and he did not recognize her.

No trace of the author of the deed, or of any weapon, was visible in the neighborhood. On examination, the wound was found to be about four inches long, extending along the left side of the head from front to back, and deeper in the center than at the ends. From the force required to inflict such a blow, it was obvious that it must have been done outside the door, as the passage within was so low, that no weapon could have been raised sufficiently high to produce such an injury. After receiving it, the goldsmith, must have been able to stagger into the passage before falling. On the left side of the door without, was a stone seat, two feet high, on which, it was supposed, the murderer must have taken his stand, awaiting his victim, and directed, from this position, the deadly stroke. Though Ruprecht's words implied that the weapon had been an axe, the medical inspector was of opinion that a saber, wielded by an experienced hand, was more likely to have been the instrument. The main hope of explaining this point. and of discovering the author of the deed, rested on the revelations which the goldsmith himself might be able to make. It was not, however, till the evening of the following day, that he appeared sufficiently in his senses to warrant the judge in commencing his examination. The wounded man's answers were given in monosyllables. He was asked :

"Who struck you ?"

" Schmidt."

" What is this Schmidt—where does he reside ?'"

" In the Most." (The Most is a street of the town.)

" With what did he strike you?"

" A hatchet."

" How did you know him ?"

"By his voice."

" Was he indebted to you ?"   Ruprecht shook his head.

"What was his motive ?"

"A quarrel."

The wounded man was so much exhausted by these responses, that scarcely any other questions could be put to him, excepting the request, that he would again name the individual who had struck him.   His repeated answer was, " Schmidt—woodcutter."

Who, then, was this Schmidt?—a name, it is to be observed, not less common in Germany than Smith is in England. It turned out that there were three Schmidts, woodcutters, in the town, two of whom were brothers, and lived in the Most, the street indicated by the goldsmith; while the third, Christopher Schmidt, lived in the street called the Hohen Pflaster. The brothers were usually named from their different heights, the Great Schmidt and the Little Schmidt, and they proved to be old acquaintances of Ruprecht, but to have recently ceased to be on familiar terms with him, chiefly because the Great Schmidt had given evidence against him in an action of damages. Regarding Christopher Schmidt, it was ascertained that, at a former period of his life, he had been imprisoned under a charge of accession to a robbery. Before proceeding to the arrest of any of these individuals, Ruprecht, whose skull had in the interval been trepanned, in order to raise the depressed bone, was again asked, at a favorable moment, a string of questions similar to the former, and gave the same responses, excepting in one important point. On being asked whether the Great or the Little Schmidt was the guilty person, he tried to speak, but failed. He was then asked if the Most was the street, but was silent. To the next question, "If the Hohen Pflaster was the man's residence?" he answered with difficulty, but distinctly, "Yes," and then relapsed into the state of insensibility which was common to him.

All three Schmidts being thus implicated in suspicion, they were taken into custody, for the purpose, in the first place, of being confronted with the wounded man, and to have the guilty individual, if possible, identified by him. But Ruprecht, though sensible, was unable to open his eyes, and the main object of the interview was thus defeated. The behavior of the suspected persons was, however, so very different, as to excite the strongest hopes that the matter would be cleared up. The brothers Schmidt were calm and composed on being brought into the goldsmith's presence; they spoke to him, called him by name, and expressed the greatest sympathy for his situation. Christopher Schmidt, on the contrary, was agitated and restless; when asked if he knew the person in bed, he first said he did not know him, and then that he did know him; first, that he remained in his mother-in-law's house on the night of the murder till eleven, and afterwards, that he was in his own house in bed at nine. He at the same time protested his entire innocence, and appealed to the testimony of his wife, his mother-in-law, and his neighbors. His agitation and contradictions drew the suspicion of all from the other Schmidts upon him, and he was committed by the judge to prison. All hope of further information from the victim himself, was put an end to by his death on the following day, the second from the accident.

Subsequent investigations tended to increase the suspicions against Christopher Schmidt, which his behavior on the first occasion had awakened. On inspecting his house, the handle of his axe, near the blade, was found to be streaked with blood ! The truth of the report as to his former imprisonment he did not attempt to deny, but alleged that he had been merely made the innocent instrument of conveying stolen property from one place to another. On undergoing another examination, his contradictions were even more glaring than before. To the question, "How he came to know Ruprecht in bed, when he stated that he had never seen him before," he said that he knew him from having heard of his accident, and from being aware of the object of his own visit to the goldsmith's house. He stated that he had been with his wife and child

to his mother-in-law's house, where they wrought
at some in-door work, to save candles at home.
It was impossible to ascertain from his answers
the time at which he had come from his mother-in-
law's house to his own. He first averred that he
had come home with his child at nine, and that his
wife had come an hour after him; then, that his
wife had returned with him at ten o'clock; then
that he was asleep, and did not know when she
came; and made fresh contradictions, in short, with
regard to time, at every query put to him. All
these things—his variations, his agitation, his downcast and suspicious look, his previous imprisonment, the spots upon his axe, the expression of
the dying man, which pointed most strongly to
him—when taken together, formed a strong combination of circumstances against Christopher
Schmidt. Indeed, his guilt was scarcely doubted of
by any one.

On the other hand, after men's minds became
capable of calmer reflection on the subject, the very
grossness of these contradictions seemed to lead to
the inference, that they arose from a deficiency of
intellect, or from a mind disordered by temporary
anxiety and fear, or from both causes, rather than
from a desire to conceal the truth. The report of

the neighbors, when their evidence was collected, corroborated this conjecture; his stolidity and dull- ness of intellect was such as to have acquired for him the common nickname of "The Sheep." He never was capable, it was found, of expressing him- self clearly, and it followed that, under such cir- cumstances as a charge of murder, this deficiency must evidently have been greatly aggravated. From such a character as this, the statement, illogical as it was, that he knew Ruprecht in bed from having heard of his accident, was natural enough. With regard to the contradictory repre- sentations regarding the hour of his return, the inconsistency might be in part explained away by supposing his wife to have first gone home with him, seen him to bed with the child, and after- wards to have returned to her mother's for a short period before she finally came to sleep in her own house. This was, in fact, substantially proved by subsequent investigations of Schmidt's mother-in- law and wife. They, with other witnesses, proved that the wife, having seen her husband home, went back to her mother's to finish some work, and after an hour or an hour and a half's stay, returned to her own domicile. It was remarkable, however, that these two witnesses differed considerably with respect to the hours at which these events took place. These discrepancies were held to arise from the fact, that the night in question was a long and dark one in February, and that no clocks were within reach of the parties. This gave a favorable color also to Schmidt's own inconsistencies as to time, particularly when taken in connection with the man's unquestionable stupidity.

But—admitting the wife's statement to be correct—Christopher Schmidt was left alone for an hour and a half at the very time the deed was com-committed. The ale-house where it took place, however, was a mile and a quarter from Schmidt's dwelling ; and to have been the actor in the deed, he must have sprung from bed at the moment of his wife's departure, hurried to the spot, committed the murder, and then been in bed a quarter of an hour afterwards. Was this energetic villainy likely to have been exhibited by one so slow and sluggish in intellect and behavior as Schmidt was proved to be? The thing was felt by all, on reflection, to be barely possible.

But, again, the blood on the handle of the axe? The accused, on being questioned respecting this, said, that if such stains existed, of which he knew nothing, they must have proceeded from a swelling in the hand—which he showed—that had burst some days before. The swelling, it was replied, is in the *right* hand, while the stains are upon the upper of the handle, which is always held in the *left* hand. "I am *left-handed*," said the accused; and on inquiry among his associates, it was found to be the case. Further examination, also, showed that the axe of Schmidt could not have been the instrument of death, the wound in the head being four inches long, while the axe's blade was barely three inches. A strong additional testimony in Schmidt's favor, was the discovery that he had actually been free of all guilt, as he had represented, on the occasion of his former imprisonment, and that his general character everywhere was that of a sober, industrious, peaceable man.

Thus, one by one, the grounds of suspicion which had at first appeared to be assuming so firm and compact a form, crumbled away, and, though not yet finally liberated, it was apparent to all that Christopher Schmidt would be acquitted. But, as the clouds of suspicion passed from Christopher, they gathered for a time round the heads of his namesakes, the Great and Little Schmidts of the Most. These men, it was recollected, knew

Ruprecht, which Christopher did not; they had, moreover, been actually placed in an inimical position with respect to the deceased. They had borne evidence against him, in an action instituted by two respectable surveyors, whose names the goldsmith had publicly vilified. Ruprecht had lost the cause, and had been sentenced to a short confinement on bread and water. At his liberation, he had set on foot an action of retaliation against the surveyors, which was still undecided at the time of the murder. Could the surveyors have made use of their former witnesses, the Schmidts, to rid themselves of their pertinacious opponent? The high character of the men rendered this supposition improbable; and after it had lived for but a short time on the public breath, it was completely extinguished by the coming forward of several witnesses, who spoke to the fact of the brothers Schmidt having come home early on the night of the goldsmith's death, and not having left the house till next morning.

While all grounds for suspicion to rest upon were thus disappearing as far as the parties first implicated were concerned, some new discoveries, or rather conjectures, were made, which drew the eyes of justice to an entirely different quarter

Two other Schmidts, woodcutters also, were found out, not living in the town indeed, but in the suburbs. One of these men was woodman to Berenger, Ruprecht's son-in-law, and this circumstance seems to have originated a new train of thinking in the minds of the official persons of the town, though no ground of suspicion could be found against the newly discovered Schmidts. One of Ruprecht's first expressions, it will be remembered, after receiving the blow, was, "My daughter! my daughter!" These words had been naturally in-terpreted at the time into an expression of anxiety to see her, but circumstances subsequently emerg-ing, seemed to render it doubtful whether his ex-clamation did not bear a less favorable meaning. The matrimonial life of Berenger and his wife had long been, it appeared, an unhappy one; Berenger had often made complaints against his wife to her father. Recently, some steps taken by the husband had ended in making the wedded pair's life a little more harmonious, but they had, at the same time, exasperated Ruprecht's mind in the highest de-gree against Berenger. A short time before his death, the goldsmith had been heard to call his son-in law a villain; and he had also for some time past entertained the resolution of making a will,

leaving all to his daughter, and beyond her husband's control. This resolve he had announced to
his daughter, about two months before his death,
and also to his apprentice, Hogner. Nay, within a
few hours of his accident, he had sent for Hogner
to assist in arranging his papers, preparatory to
the execution of the will on the following Sunday.
This intention he had expressed in the hearing of
of the maid servant. These remarkable circumstances directed the attention of justice to Berenger,
who might have heard of the old man's determination ; and a sufficient motive for a desire on his
part to get rid quickly of the goldsmith would
thus have been established.

Berenger, according to account, showed no emotion or sympathy on hearing of the accident, and
his wife, it was said, showed also a want of feeling.
One of her first concerns was to see whether her
father had his keys about him ; and having ascer
tained that he had, she took possession of and
walked away with them. She had, besides, shown
a strong anxiety to criminate one of the Schmidts.
reporting several speeches against him, from her
father's lips, which no one else had heard. Several
other minor incidents seemed to bear against the
Berengers. In interpreting her father's dying words

with this view, it was thought that the old man, feeling himself struck with what he conceived to be an axe, would immediately revert in his mind to the woodcutters, the Schmidts, who had borne a part against him in the suit then pending, and which occupied at the time much of his attention. This was the sense now put upon the goldsmith's mention of the name of Schmidt.

Here also, however, as in the former cases, the grounds of suspicion vanished, one by one, into thin air. That the words "my daughter" bore no meaning unfavorable to the Berengers, was proved by the statement of Ruprecht's sister, that such was her brother's common expression when anything troubled him; it was also proved, on better inquiry, that Berenger's wife had shown deep feeling for her father, and had only taken away his keys on the surgeon suggesting that the murder might be a prelimary to robbery; it was, however, sworn by the wife, the apprentice, and the maid servant, that they had never spoken of the will—a thing, indeed, most unlikely for the wife to do, when she alone was to to be benefited by it; and, finally, there was distinct evidence that Berenger himself, at least, had not been the murderer, as, at the time of it, he was quietly seated in the parlor of the Golden Fish. By this and other evidence, the suspicion against the Berengers fell to peices.

Even after all these failures, the investigation was not abandoned. A soldier, who was indebted to Ruprecht, and who had been threatened by him, on the day of the accident, with hard measures, was the person next brought under examination. After the fabric of evidence in this case also had gathered strength, it was at once overturned by a clear proof of an alibi.

Here, at last, justice was obliged to give up the pursuit; nor has any light since been thrown on this strange story.

XVIII.

Case of Mistaken Medical Testimony.

THE following narrative, while it strikingly exhibits the fallible and uncertain nature of circumstantial evidence, affords also a convincing proof of the indispensable necessity of procuring medical testimony of the highest order, in all criminal cases relating to injuries of the person. The narrator, Mr. Perfect, a surgeon at Hammersmith, sent the statement to the editor of the *Lancet* (Mr. Wakley) in January, 1839 :—

"It is now thirty years ago, that accidentally passing the Packhorse, Turnham Green, my attention was attracted by a mob of persons of the lowest order assembled around the door of that inn, who were very loud in their execrations against some person who was suspected of having murdered his brother; in corroboration of which, I was told that his bones were found near the premises where he formerly resided, upon view of which a jury was then sitting, after an adjournment from the day preceding. I found that two surgeons had been supœnaed to inspect the remains, and I had no doubt but that every information as to their character had been obtained; curiosity alone, therefore, induced me to make way into the room, where I found that the coroner, and, I believe, a *double jury*, were sitting for the second day, and were engaged in an investigation which tended to show that a farmer and market gardner at Suttoncourt Farm, had, a few years before, a brother living with him, who was engaged in the farm, but whose conduct was dissolute and irregular to a degree that often provoked the anger of his elder brother, and sometimes begat strife and violence between them; that the temper of the elder brother was as little under control as the conduct of the younger; and, in fine, that they lived very uncomfortably together.

" One winter night, when the ground was covered with snow, the younger brother absconded from the house (for they both lived together), by letting himself down from his chamber window; and when he was missed the ensuing morning, his footsteps were clearly tracked in the snow to a considerable distance, nor were there any other footsteps *but his own*. Time passed on, and after a lapse of some few years no tidings were heard of his retreat, nor per-

haps have there ever been since. Some alterations
in the grounds surrounding the house having been
undertaken by a subsequent tenant (for the elder
brother had then left the farm), a skeleton was
dug up, and the circumstance appeared so conclusive that one brother had murdered the other,
that the popular clamor was raised to the utmost,
and a jury impanneled to investigate the case.

"After listening attentively to these details, I
ventured to request of the coroner to be allowed
to examine the bones, which I found were contained in a hamper basket at the further end of
the room, and I felt much flattered by his immediate compliance, for he desired the parish beadle,
who was in attendance, to place them upon the
table; and having himself disposed them in their
natural order, I found that they represented a
person of short statute, and from the obliteration
of the sutures of the skull, and the worn-down
state of the teeth, must have belonged to an aged
person. But what was my surprise when I reconstructed the bones of the skeleton, and found the
lower bones of the trunk to be those of a female.
I immediately communicated the fact to the jury,
and requested that the two medical men who had
before given their opinions might be sent for, one

of whom attended, and without a moment's hesitation corroborated my report.

"I need not add that the proceedings were instantly at an end, and an innocent man received the *amende honorable*, in the shape of an apology, from all present, in which the coroner heartily joined. It has since been proved beyond all doubt that the spot where the bones were found was formerly the site of a large gravel pit, in which hordes of gipsies not only assembled, but occasionally buried their dead, and perhaps more skeletons are yet to be found in that vicinity."

XIX.

Case of James Baxwell.

IN the year 1841, at Gibraltar, there occurred one of those extraordinary cases, which show us how ineffectively the romancist, even when his imagination is strained to the uttermost, can portray the extremes of passion of which human nature is susceptible. A communication, bearing date Feberuary 20th, from the rock-built fortress which England keeps as a key to the Mediterranean, relates the following particulars :

A respectable merchant, named James Baxwell, born at London, had removed in early life to Gibraltar, induced partly by the circumstance of his being of the same religious persuasion to which the people of his adopted country belonged. For many years he occupied a small dwelling near the base of Mount St. Michael, so renowned for its caves and crystallizations. He carried on a successful traffic in all the articles of British manufacture introduced into Spain. He acquired, in truth, a very considereble fortune in this way. All the country knew that he had a large amount of treasure lying by him, not to speak of the capital belonging to him, which was embarked in commerce. His name was one of credit in all the principal houses of exchange in Europe.

James Baxwell had a daughter, an only daughter, aged seventeen, and of remarkable beauty. Her countenance and figure combined in a most agreeable manner the peculiar charms of the Englishman with the soft and languishing characteristics of the Spaniard. Young as she was, she had been for some two or three years an object of devoted admiration to all the youths around Gibraltar. At church they devoured her with their eyes; and many, many a one thought to himself that happy above all men would be he who could win the smiles of Elezia Baxwell. But Elezia bestowed her smiles upon no one. She seemed, to those whose involuntary sighs she excited, to carry maidenly modesty to freezing coldness. At mass, *her* eyes were ever bent upon her book, regardless of all the glances cast upon her by others.

Such was, at least, the case, till shortly before the events to be narrated. At length, however, Elezia did see one who awakened in herself some of the emotions which she had caused in others. At mass, one day, she observed the eyes of a young stranger fixed upon her with an expression of admiration and respect. To her he seemed a being superior to all the young men she had ever yet beheld. From that moment, her calm and self-possessed demeanor left her for ever. Abroad and at home, she was restless and uneasy. But, ere long, the stranger found an opportunity of being introduced to her, and mutual avowals of love followed at no great distance of time.

Assured of the affections of Elezia, the young stranger then presented himself to Mr. Baxwell. "I am named William Katt," said he to the merchant; "I am, like yourself, an Englishman; I am of respectable family and character, young, and wealthy. Give me your daughter — we love one another."

"Never!" said James Baxwell, to whom the position and circumstances of the young man were not unknown; "never! You belong to the denominant religion of England, by which my fathers suffered so much and so long. You are a Lutheran and my daughter is a Catholic. Such a union could not be happy; nor will I ever give my consent to it. Elezia shall never be yours!" The daughter, informed of this declaration, threw herself at the feet of her father, and endeavored to move him from his purpose. Her lover did the same. But the father remained obstinate, and a violent scene took place between Elezia and her parent. The blood of the fiery South coursed in the daughter's veins, and she declared that she *would* marry the object of her choice, despite of all opposition. James Baxwell, on the other hand, declared that he would sooner kill her with his own hands, than see her carry such a resolution into effect. As to William Katt, who stood by at this scene, he kept silence. What thoughts were revolving in his mind, it would be difficult to say.

Two days afterwards, an alarming noise was heard by the neighbors to issue from a cave immediately adjoining the merchant's house, and used by him for some domestic purposes. The noise consisted at first of loud cries, which gradually became fainter, and at length died altogether away. The auditors looked at each other with amazement, and many were the conjectures as to the cause of the sounds alluded to. A solution of the mystery was not long in suggesting itself. Elezia had disappeared; she was no longer to be seen about her father's house. After many low murmurs had circulated, the father was interrogated respecting his daughter. He said that she was missing, certainly; but whither she had gone, he knew not. He had nothing whatever to do, he said, with her disappearance.

This explanation was not satisfactory. · The whisper went abroad that James Baxwell had assassinated his daughter, to prevent her marriage with William Katt, and, ultimately, this conjecture was so forcibly pressed on the attention of the public authorities, that they were compelled to arrest James Baxwell, and inquire into the matter. The dwelling of the merchant was examined, but nothing criminatory was found. "The cave! the cave is the place!" cried some of the crowd. The magistrates then descended into the cave, and there, on lifting some loose stones, they found a portion of Elezia's dress, sprinkled all over with blood. They also discovered a small quantity of hair, clotted with gore, and that hair was recognized by many as having been taken from the head of Elezia.

Baxwell protested his innocence. But the proof seemed strong against him, and he was regularly brought to trial. The result was his conviction for the murder of his daughter, and his condemnation to death.

On receiving sentence, the unhappy merchant trembled to excess, and afterwards seemed utterly overpowered by the dreadful nature of his situation. He continued in a state almost of total insensibility during the interval between his trial and the day

appointed for his execution. On the morning of the
latter day, the jailer came to announce to him, for
the final time, that the moment was at hand. The
merchant was seized again with a fearful trembling,
and he cried, what he had reiterated to all who saw
him in his confinement: "Before my Maker, I swear
that I am guiltless of my child's death!"

They led him out to the scaffold. There he found,
among others, William Katt, who, it should have
been said, was the most important witness against
him at his trial, having repeated to the court the
threat of assassination which had been uttered by
James Baxwell in his presence against Elezia. No
sooner did the doomed merchant behold Katt, than
he exclaimed. at the very foot of the scaffold: "My
friend, in one minute I shall be in eternity. I wish
to die in peace with all men. Give me your hand—
I pardon you freely for the injury your evidence has
done to me." Baxwell said this with some composure, but the effect of his words upon Katt were
very striking. He became pale as death, and could
not conceal the depth of his agitation

Baxwell mounted the steps of the gallows slowly,
and gave himself up to the hands of the executioner,
to undergo death by the rope. According to the
ancient custom of Gibraltar, the executioner com-

menced his last duties by crying in a loud voice : "Justice is doing! Justice is done!" He then placed the black bonnet on the head of the condemned merchant, and pulled it down in front, so as to cover the eyes. He had just done this, when he was stopped in his proceedings by a loud cry .from the side of the scaffold : "*It is I who am guilty—I alone!*"

This cry came from William Katt. The magistrates in attendance instantly called him forward, and demanded an explanation. The young man avowed that he had carried off Elezia, with her consent, to be his wife, and that she was now residing not far off, in concealment. But to her he did not communicate other measures which he had taken, chiefly to revenge himself for the scorn of her father. He had contrived to cut off a portion of her hair while she slept. He had clotted it with the blood of a lamb, and had also sprinkled in the same way a part of Elezia's dress, which he had purloined. These articles he had placed in the cave, and there, also, had he emitted personally those cries which had borne so heavily against the merchant. The generous pardon which the merchant had bestowed on him at the scaffold, had awakened (the young man said) instantaneous remorse in his breast, and compelled him to avow the truth.

This confession was partly made at the scaffold, and partly afterwards. As soon as Katt had spoken out decisively, the executioner had turned to James Baxwell, to take from him the insignia of death. The merchant, almost unobserved, had sunk down into a sitting posture. The black bonnet was drawn by the executioner from off his eyes and head. It was found that he was a corpse! No exertions had the slightest effect in awakening in him the spark of life. The physicians, saying all they could on such a subject, declared that he had died from the effects of strong imagination.

William Katt was conducted to prison amid the clamors of the populace, there to await judgment for his misdeeds.

Elezia, the unhappy daughter of an unhappy father, retired to a convent for life immediately on learning all that had passed.

XX.

Case of John Miles.

WILLIAM RIDLEY kept the Red Cow, a public house at Exeter. John Miles was an old acquaintance of Ridley's, but they had not seen each other for some time (Miles living some distance off), when they met one morning, as the latter was going a little way to receive some money. They adjourned to the next public house, and, after drinking together, Ridley told Miles that he must go about the business which brought him from home, which was to receive a sum of money, but made him promise to wait for his coming back. Ridley returned, and they drank together again. Ridley now insisted upon Miles' accompanying him home to dinner. They dined, they drank, they shook hands, repeated old stories, drank and shook hands again and again, as old acquaintances in the lower class, after long absences, usually do; in fine, they both got, at last, pretty much in liquor.

The room they sat in was backwards, detached as it were from the house, with a door that went immediately into a yard, and had communication with the street, without passing through the house.

As it grew late, Mrs. Ridley came into the room, and not seeing her husband there, made inquiry after him of Miles. Miles being much intoxicated, all that could be got out of him was, that Ridley went out into the yard some time before, and had not returned. Ridley was called, Ridley was searched after, by all the family; but neither answering, nor being to be met with, Miles, as well as he was able for intoxication, went his way.

Ridley not coming home that night, and some days passing without his returning, or being heard of, suspicions arose, in the mind of Mrs. Ridley, of some foul play against her husband on the part of Miles; and these were not a little increased on the recollection that her husband had received a sum of money that day, and that Miles had replied to her inquiries after him in a very incoherent, unintelligible manner, which, at the time, she had attributed to his being in liquor.

These suspicions went abroad, and at length a full belief took place in many, that Miles was actually the murderer of Ridley; had gone out with him, robbed and murdered him, disposed of the body, and slid back again to the room where they were drinking, unseen by any one.

The officers of justice were sent to take up Miles.

and he giving, before the magistrate, a very unsatis-factory relation of his parting with Ridley, which he affirmed was owing to his having been intoxicated when Ridley went out of the room from him, but which the magistrate ascribed to guiltiness, he was committed to Exeter jail for trial.

Whilst Miles was in confinement, a thousand reports were spread, tending to warp the minds of the people against him. Supernatural as well as natural reasons were alleged as proof of his guilt. Ridley's house was declared to be haunted; frequent knockings were heard in the dead of the night; two of the lodgers avowed they had seen the ghost. And to crown the whole, an old man, another lodger, positively affirmed, that once, at midnight, his curtains flew open, the ghost of Ridley appeared, all bloody, and, with a piteous look and hollow voice, declared he had been murdered, and that Miles was the murderer.

Under these prepossessions amongst the weak and superstitious, and a general prejudice even in the stronger minds, was John Miles brought to trial for the willful murder of William Ridley. Circum-stances upon circumstances were deposed against him; and as it appeared that Miles was with Ridley the whole day, both before and after his receiving the money, and that they spent the afternoon and evening together alone, the jury, who were neighbors of Ridley, found Miles guilty, notwithstanding his protestations, on his defense, of innocence, and he was shortly after executed at Exeter.

It happened, that, some time after, Mrs. Ridley left the Red Cow to keep another ale house, and the person who succeeded her, making several repairs in and about the house, in emptying the necessary, which was at the end of a long dark passage, the body of William Ridley was discovered. In his pockets were found twenty guineas, from whence it was evident he had not been murdered, as the robbing of him was the sole circumstance that could be and was ascribed to Miles for murdering of Ridley. The truth of Miles' assertions and defense now became doubly evident; for it was recollected that the floor of the necessary had been taken up the morning before the death of Ridley, and that, on one side of the seat, a couple of boards had been left up; so that, being much in liquor, he must have fallen into the vault, which was uncommonly deep; but which, unhappily, was not adverted to at the time of his disappearance !

XXI.

The Obstinate Juryman.

Two men were seen fighting together in a field. One of them was found, soon after, lying dead in that field. Near him lay a pitchfork which had apparently been the instrument of his death. This pitchfork was known to have belonged to the person who had been seen fighting with the deceased; and he was known to have taken it out with him that morning. Being apprehended and brought to trial, and these circumstances appearing in evidence, and also that there had been, for some time, an enmity between the parties, there was little doubt of the prisoner's being convicted, although he strongly persisted in his innocence; but, to the great surprise of the court, the jury, instead of bringing in an immediate verdict of guilty, withdrew, and, after staying out a considerable time, returned and informed the court, that eleven, out of the twelve, had been, from the first, for finding the prisoner guilty; but that one man would not concur in the verdict. Upon this, the judge observed to the dissentient person, the great strength of the circumstances, and asked him how it was possible, all circumstances *sidered*, for him to have any doubts of the guilt of the accused?" But no arguments that could be urged, either by the court or the rest of the jury, could persuade him to find the prisoner guilty; so that the rest of the jury were at last obliged to agree to the verdict of acquittal.

This affair remained, for some time, mysterious; but it at length came out, either by the private acknowledgment of the obstinate juryman to the judge who tried the cause (who is said to have had the curiosity to inquire into the motives of his extraordinary pertinacity), or by his confession at the point of death (for the case is related both ways), that he himself had been the murderer! The accused had, indeed, had a scuffle with the deceased, as sworn on the trial, in which he had dropped his pitchfork, which had been, soon after, found by the juryman, between whom and the deceased an accidental quarrel had arisen in the same field; the deceased having continued there at work after the departure of the person with whom he had been seen to have the affray; in the heat of which quarrel, the juryman had unfortunately stabbed him with that very pitchfork, and had then got away totally unsuspected; but finding, soon after, that the other person had been apprehended, on suspicion of being the murderer, and fearing, as the circumstances appeared so strong against him, that he should be convicted, although not guilty, he had contrived to get upon the jury, as the only way of saving the innocent without endangering himself.

XXII.

Case of John Harkins and George Simpson

JOHN HAWKINS and George Simpson were indicted for robbing the mail, on the 16th of April, 1722. Hawkins, in his defense, set up an *alibi*, to prove which, he called one William Fuller, who deposed, that Hawkins came to his house on Sunday, the 15th of April, and lay there that night, and did not go out until the next morning. Being asked by the court, "By what token do you remember that it was the 15th* of April?" he replied, "By a very good token, for he owed me a sum of money for horse hire, and on Tuesday, the 10th of April, he called upon me and paid me in full, and I gave him a receipt; and I very well remember, that he lay at my house the Sunday night following." The receipt was now produced. "April the 10th, 1722. Received of Mr. John Hawkins, the sum of one pound ten shillings, in full of all accounts, per me, William Fuller." Upon inspecting the receipt, the court asked Fuller who wrote it. He replied, "Hawkins wrote the body of it, and I signed it."

---

* The robbery was committed about two o'clock on the morning of the 16th.

Court. "Did you see him write it?"

Fuller. "Yes."

Court. "And how long was it after he wrote it, before you signed?"

Fuller. "I signed it immediately, without going from the table."

Court. "How many standishes do you keep in the house?"

Fuller. "Standishes?"

Court. "Aye, standishes· it is a plain question."

Fuller. "My Lord, but one; and that is enough for the little handwriting we have to do."

Court. "Then you signed the receipt with the same ink that Hawkins wrote the body of it with?"

Fuller. "For certain."

Court. "Officer, hand the receipt to the jury. Gentlemen, you will see that the body of the note is written with one kind of ink, and the name at the bottom with another very different; and yet this witness has sworn, that they were both written with the same ink, and one immediately after the other. You will judge what credit is to be given to his evidence!"

Thus, the authenticity of the receipt, and the credit of the witness, were overthrown by the sagacity of the court! But while the judge, Lord Chief Baron MONTAGUE was summing up the evidence, he was interrupted by the following occurrence: The person who reports the trial was then taking notes of the proceedings; his ink, as it happened, was very bad, being thick at the bottom, and thin and waterish at the top, so that, accordingly as he dipped the pen, the writing appeared very pale or pretty black. This circumstance being remarked by some gentlemen present, they handed the book to the jury; the judge perceiving them very attentively inspecting it, called to them: "Gentlemen, what are you doing? What book is that?" They told him that it was the writer's book, and that they were observing how the same ink appeared pale in one place, and black in another. The judge then told them—"You ought not, gentlemen to take notice of any thing but what is produced in evidence"; and, turning to the writer, demanded—"what he meant by showing that book to the jury?" And being informed by the writer that it was taken from him, he inquired "who took it, and who handed it to the jury?" But this the writer could not say, as the gentlemen near him were all strangers to him, and he had not taken any particular notice of the person who took his book.

That a jury ought not to take notice of any thing but what is produced in evidence, has been said to be law; but, on the contrary, it has been held, and surely very properly, that a juryman may find from his own knowledge; ·indeed, what evidence can convince a person that *is* which he knows *not* to be?

Hawkins and Simpson were convicted and executed; indeed, the evidence against them was very strong; but, had the fate of Hawkins depended upon the single testimony of Fuller, he would, but for this occurrence, have fallen a sacrifice to the acuteness of the judge! who appears to have been much displeased at the accidental confutation of his remarks on the receipt, although it was an accident in favor of life; and, had it not been in a case where other evidence was so strong against the accused, it must have been looked upon as the special interposition of Providence.

XXIII.

A Man Wrongly Convicted of Parricide.

A MAN was tried for, and convicted of, the murder of his own father. The evidence against him was merely circumstantial, and the principal witness was his sister. She proved that her father possessed a small income, which, with his industry, enabled him to live with comfort; that her brother, the prisoner, who was his heir at law, had long expressed a great desire to come into the possession of his father's effects; and that he had long behaved in a very undutiful manner to him, wishing, as the witness believed, to put a period to his existence by uneasiness and vexation; that, on the evening the murder was committed, the deceased went a small distance from the house, to milk a cow he had for some time kept, and that the witness also went out to spend the evening and to sleep, leaving only her brother in the house; that, returning home early in the morning, and finding that her father and brother were absent, she was much alarmed, and sent for some neighbors to consult with them, and to receive advice what should be done; that, in company with these neighbors, she went to the hovel in which her father was accustomed to milk the cow, where they found him murdered in an inhuman manner, his head being almost beat to pieces; that a suspicion immediately falling on her brother, and there being then some snow upon the ground, in which the footsteps of a human being, to and from the hovel, were observed, it was agreed to take one of the brother's shoes, and to measure therewith the impressions in the snow; this was done, and there did not remain a doubt but that the impressions were made with his shoes. Thus confirmed in their suspicions, they then immediately went to the prisoner's room, and after a diligent search, they found a hammer, in the corner of a private drawer, with several spots of blood upon it, and with a small splinter of bone, and some brains in a crack which they discovered in the handle. The circumstances of finding the deceased and the hammer, as described by the former witness, were fully proved by the neighbors whom she had called; and upon this evidence the prisoner was convicted and suffered death, but denied the fact to the last. About four years after, the witness was extremely ill, and understanding that there were no possible hopes of her recovery, she confessed that her father and brother having offended her, she was determined they should both die ; and, accordingly, when the former went to milk the cow, she followed him with her brother's hammer, and in his shoes; that she beat out her father's brains with the hammer, and laid it where it was afterwards found ; that she then went from home to give a better color to this wicked business, and that her brother was perfectly innocent of the crime for which he had suffered. She was immediately taken into custody, but died before she could be brought to trial.

XXIV.

Case of Mistaken Medical Testimony.

JOHN STRINGER was tried at the Lent assizes, held at Kingston, in the county of Surry, in the year 1765, before the late Lord Chief Baron SMYTHE, for the murder of his wife, and found guilty. The trial being on the Saturday, he was ordered for execution on the Monday following. The case was thus: Stringer, a man in low circumstances, had brought his wife, who had long been in an ill state of health, from London to Lambeth, for the benefit of the air; here they lived for some time; generally in great harmony; but not without those little quarrels and scuffles, so common with persons in their rank of life. Upon the woman's death, some of the neighboring females, who had been occasionally witnesses to these litttle accidental bickerings between the husband and wife, took it in their heads that he had murdered her, notwithstanding she had never been heard to make the least complaint of her husband during the course of her illness; and the man was brought to trial in consequence.

Some trifling evidence being given of the little

differences that had arisen between them ; and the opinion of a young surgeon, that some appearances on the corpse were somewhat the appearances of a mortification, occasioned by bruises ; Stringer, on these slight circumstances, was convicted, and left for execution !

Mr. Carsan, a surgeon of great experience in the neighborhood, had, on the report of the murder, from mere curiosity, examined the body, and was so clear that there were no marks of violence thereon, that he had not the least apprehension of the possibility of Stringer's being convicted : but hearing of the conviction, and confident of the innocence of the unhappy man, and actuated by the love of justice and humanity, he instantly, on the Sunday, waited on, and represented the case to the Archbishop of Canterbury ; his grace gave Mr. Carsan a letter to Baron SMYTHE, who, convinced by his statement of the matter, that himself and the jury had been too precipitate in forming an opinion of the guilt of Stringer, granted an immediate respite ; which gave Mr. Carsan an opportunity of laying the whole case before his majesty, and he had the satisfaction of saving an innocent man from an undeserved and ignominious death.

XXV.

The Evidence of Torture.

IN the year 1764, a citizen of Liege was found dead in his chamber, shot in the head. Close to him lay a discharged pistol, with which he had apparently been his own executioner. Firearms are the chief manufacture of that city; and so common is the use of pistols at that place, that every peasant, who brings his goods to the markets there, is seen armed with them; so that the circumstance of the pistol did not, at first, meet with so much attention as it might have done in places where those weapons are not in such common use. But, upon the researches of the proper officer of that city, whose duty, like that of our coroner, it is to inquire into all the circumstances of accidental deaths, it appeared that the ball which was found lodged in the head of the deceased could never, from its size, have been fired out of the pistol which lay by him; thus it was clear that he had been murdered; nor were they long in deciding who was the murderer. A girl, of about sixteen, the niece of the deceased, had been brought up by him, and he had been always supposed to have intended to leave her his effects, which were something considerable; but the girl had then lately listened to the addresses of a young man whom the uncle did not approve of, and he had, upon that occasion, several times threatened to alter his will, and leave his fortune to some other of his relations. Upon these, and some other concurrent circumstances, such as having been heard to wish her uncle's death, &c., the girl was committed to prison.

The torturing a supposed criminal, in order to force confession, is certainly the most cruel and absurd idea that ever entered into the head of a legislator. This being observed by the writer of this narrative, who was then at Liege, to a magistrate of that place, on this very occasion, his defense was,— "We never condemn to the torture but upon circumstances on which you in England would convict; so that the innocent has really a better chance to escape here than with you." But, until it is proved that pain has a greater tendency to make a person speak truth than falsehood, this reasoning seems to have little weight.

This unhappy girl was, therefore, horridly and repeatedly tortured; but still persevering in asserting her innocence, she at last escaped with life;—if it could be called an escape, when it was supposed she would never again enjoy health or limbs, from the effects of the torture.

The writer has since learned, that, some years afterwards, her innocence became manifest, by the confession of the real assassins, who, being sentenced to the wheel for other crimes, confessed themselves the authors of this of which the girl was suspected ; and that, several pistols having been discharged at the deceased, they had, intending that it should appear a suicide, laid a pistol near him, without adverting that it was not the same by which he fell.

XXVI.

Case of Jonathan Bradford.

JONATHAN BRADFORD kept an inn, in Oxford-
shire, on the London road to Oxford. He bore a
very unexceptionable character. Mr. Hayes, a gentleman of fortune, being on his way to Oxford, on a
visit to a relation, put up at Bradford's. He there
joined company with two gentlemen, with whom he
supped, and, in conversation, unguardedly mentioned that he had then about him a sum of money.
In due time they retired to their respective chambers ;
the gentlemen to a two-bedded room, leaving, as is
customary with many, a candle burning in the
chimney corner. Some hours after they were in bed,
one of the gentlemen, being awake, thought he heard
a deep groan in an adjoining chamber ; and this
being repeated, he softly awaked his friend. They
listened together, and the groans increasing, as of
one dying and in pain, they both instantly arose, and
proceeded silently to the door of the next chamber,
whence they had heard the groans, and, the door
being ajar, saw a light in the room. They entered,
but it is impossible to paint their consternation, on

perceiving a person weltering in his blood in the bed, and a man standing over him with a dark lantern in one hand, and a knife in the other! The man seemed as petrified as themselves, but his terror carried with it all the terror of guilt. The gentlemen soon discovered that the murdered person was the stranger with whom they had that night supped, and that the man who was standing over him was their host. They seized Bradford directly, disarmed him of his knife, and charged him with being the murderer. He assumed, by this time, the air of innocence, positively denied the crime, and asserted that he came there with the same humane intentions as themselves; for that, hearing a noise, which was succeeded by a groaning, he got out of bed, struck a light, armed himself with a knife for his defense, and was but that minute entered the room before them. These assertions were of little avail; he was kept in close custody till the morning, and then taken before a neighboring justice of the peace. Bradford still denied the murder, but, nevertheless, with such apparent indications of guilt, that the justice hesitated not to make use of this most extraordinary expression, on writing out his mittimus: "Mr. Bradford, either you or myself committed this murder."

This extraordinary affair was the conversation of the whole country. Bradford was tried and condemned, over and over again, in every company. In the midst of all this predetermination, came on the assizes at Oxford. Bradford was brought to trial; he pleaded—not guilty. Nothing could be stronger than the evidence of the two gentlemen. They testified to the finding Mr. Hayes murdered in his bed; Bradford at the side of the body with a light and a knife; that knife, and the hand which held it, bloody; that, on their entering the room, he betrayed all the signs of a guilty man; and that, but a few moments preceding, they had heard the groans of the deceased.

Bradford's defense on his trial was the same as before the gentlemen: he had heard a noise; he suspected some villany was transacting; he struck a light; he snatched the knife, the only weapon near him, to defend himself; and the terrors he discovered were merely the terrors of humanity, the natural effects of innocence as well as guilt, on beholding such a horrid scene.

This defense, however, could not be considered but as weak, contrasted with the several powerful circumstances against him. Never was circumstantial evidence more strong! There was little need of the prejudice of the county against the murderer to strengthen it; there was little need left of comment from the judge, in summing up the evidence; no room appeared for extenuation; and the jury brought in the prisoner guilty, even without going out of their box.

Bradford was executed shortly after, still declaring that he was not the murderer, nor privy to the murder of Mr. Hayes; but he died disbelieved by all.

Yet were these assertions not untrue! The murder was actually committed by Mr. Hayes' footman; who, immediately on stabbing his master, rifled his breeches of his money, gold watch, and snuff-box, and escaped back to his own room; which could have been, from the after circumstances, scarcely two seconds before Bradford's entering the unfortunate gentleman's chamber. The world owes this knowledge to a remorse of conscience in the footman (eighteen months after the execution of Bradford), on a bed of sickness. It was a death-bed repentance, and by that death the law lost its victim.

It is much to be wished that this account could close here, but it cannot! Bradford, though innocent, and not privy to the murder, was, nevertheless, the murderer in design: he had heard, as well as the footman, what Mr. Hayes declared at supper, as to the having a sum of money about him; and he went to the chamber of the deceased with the same diabolical intentions as the servant. He was struck with amazement; he could not believe his senses; and, in turning back the bed-clothes, to assure himself of the fact, he, in his agitation, dropped his knife on the bleeding body, by which both his hands and the knife became bloody. These circumstances Bradford acknowledged to the clergyman who attended him after his sentence.

XXVII.

Case of Leavitt Alley.

THE most remarkable murder trial which Boston has seen since the famous Webster-Parkman case, was that which resulted in a verdict that Leavitt Alley was not guilty of the murder of Abijah Ellis. There is at many points a wonderful parallelism in the two trials. The victims were both men of wealth, and of strikingly similar habits ; both were hard creditors, and the incentive alleged in each case was the inability of the murderer to meet a certain payment. The horrible circumstances attending·the finding of Ellis's body—just after the mysterious shooting of Charles Lane, a wealthy merchant, in his own doorway—and the consequent excitement, equaled in intensity only by the discovery of the charred remains of Dr. Parkman, a score of years before, will serve to recall the salient features of the case.

Some workmen near the Cambridge gas works, discovered two barrels, containing the mutilated body, floating in the Charles river. They were packed with horse manure and shavings, and in one of the barrels was discovered a piece of brown paper

with the name of M. Schouler, a billiard manufacturer. Investigation proved that a teamster, Leavitt
Alley, was in the habit of removing these shavings
to his stable. Following the clew to the stable, it
was found that a dry manure heap had been recently
disturbed ; blood was also found upon some boards
near by.

It was proved that on the previous morning Alley
had started from his stable with four barrels, and a
teamster, in jumping from the wagon, had ascertained
that two of them were heavy. Two of the barrels
were not satisfactorily accounted for, while a man
testified to seeing the team and barrels with a man
strongly resembling Alley upon the mill-dam, where
they were supposed to have been thrown into the
river. Alley was owing Ellis some two hundred dollars, was in great need of money, and Ellis was known
to have been searching for the suspected man on the
night when the murder was probably committed. A
new axe which Alley had purchased a short time
before was missing, and its very existence was denied.
In addition, blood stains were found upon the clothing worn by Alley, which were identified by experts
as human gore ; and a woman had heard strange
noises, like the rolling of barrels, in the stable on the
fatal night. Lastly, it was shown that Alley had

been abundantly provided with money after the death of Ellis.

The testimony for the government was entirely circumstantial. It was not claimed that any human eye saw, or human ear heard, the doing of the atrocious deed. The case had been carefully worked up and prepared by the best detective skill and professional ability that could be brought to bear upon it, and, as the facts already given were clearly brought out, the outlook for the prisoner was certainly a dark one as compared with the Webster trial, when the whole case turned upon the identification by a dentist of a gold plate. The stains of blood found in the prisoner's stable and on his clothing were submitted to chemical tests, by skillful experts, and then examined through a microscope, and pronounced by them to be not only human blood, but that of the murdered man. A physician testified, from an examination of the deceased's stomach, that he must have met his death between six and nine o'clock on the fatal evening; and altogether the case against Alley was about as strong a one as circumstantial evidence ever presents.

The prisoner's counsel, however, appeared to fully appreciate the situation, and developed an unexpected strength. To controvert the theory that Alley had committed the murder in a quarrel, they introduced evidence from prominent citizens of New Hampshire that he had always been a quiet and peaceable man, with a reputation for honesty and integrity above reproach, in the face of which the commission of so horrible a crime seemed most unlikely. The prosecution had claimed that Alley was in debt to Ellis, and without money to meet an engagement which fell due at the time of the murder; but the defense clearly proved that the prisoner possessed considerable property in New Hampshire and had money in a bank.

A strong point against the accused had been the fact that, though he had not much ready money on hand just before the murder, immediately after it he had considerable in his possession. But the defense disposed of this by evidence that a loan of one hundred and twenty-five dollars was repaid by his son the evening before the murder. There remained the evidence of the blood, which the prosecution had professed to prove was not only human blood, but that of the victim himself. But the defense introduced experts, who not only denied that the blood in question was that of a human being, but showed that the best scientific authorities agree that the difference between human and animal blood cannot be determined after it has dried, as was the fact in this case.

On the whole, therefore, the scientific testimony not only served to confuse the jury, but positively helped the prisoner's case. The defense then proceeded to still further dissipate the web of circumstantial evidence which had been woven around Alley by satisfactorily accounting for every hour of his time from the moment Ellis disappeared till the time his body was discovered.

When the defense rested their case, public opinion and expectation had naturally, and justly, very much changed, and the probability of his conviction had practically disappeared. No one had seen the murder, and the natural indisposition to condemu a man on circumstantial evidence alone was strengthened by the fact that much of what appeared strongest in this evidence had been overthrown by the defense. These considerations, joined with the traditional principle of holding every man innocent till his guilt is proved beyond the shadow of a doubt, resulted in a verdict of not guilty— a decision of the case with which the public will not be inclined to find fault.

XXVIII.

The Blue Dragoon.*

In the town of M——, in Holland, there lived, towards the close of the last century, an elderly widow, Madame Andrecht. She inhabited a house of her own, in company with her maid-servant, who was nearly of the same age. She was in prosperous circumstances; but, being in delicate health and paralyzed on one side, she had few visitors, and seldom went abroad except to church or to visit the poor. Her chief recreation consisted in paying a visit in spring to her son, who was settled as a surgeon in a village a few miles off. On these occasions, fearing a return of a paralytic attack, she was invariably accompanied by her maid, and, during these visits, her own house was left locked up, but uninhabited and unwatched.

---

* The following singular story of circumstantial evidence is from a collection of criminal trials, published at Amsterdam, under the title " Oorkonen uit de Gedenkschriften van het Strafregt, en uit die der menschlyke Mishappen ; te Amsterdam. By J. C. Van Kersleren, 1820 " Notwithstanding the somewhat romantic complexion of the incidents, it has been included as genuine in the recent German collection, *Der Neue Pitaval*, 7 Band.

On the 30th June, 17—, the widow, returning to M——, ·from one of these little excursions, found her house had been broken open in· her absence, and that several valuable articles with all her jewels and trinkets, had disappeared. Information was immediately given to the authorities, and a strict investigation of the circumstances took place without delay.

The old lady had been three weeks absent, and the thieves of course had had ample leisure for their attempt. They had evidently gained access through a window in the back part of the house communicating with the garden, one of the panes of which had been removed, and the bolts of the window forced back, so as to admit of its being pulled up. The bolts of the back door leading into the garden had also been withdrawn, as if the robbers had withdrawn their plunder in that direction. The other doors and windows were uninjured ; and several of the rooms appeared to have been unopened. The furniture, generally, was untouched ; but the kitchen utensils were left in confusion, as if the robbers had intended removing them, but had been interrupted or pursued.

At the same time it was evident they had gone very deliberately about their work. The ceilings and aoors of a heavy old press, the drawers of which had

been secured by strong and well constructed locks
had been removed with so much neatness that no
part of the wood-work had been injured. The ceil-
ing and doors were left standing by the side of the
press. The contents, consisting of jewels, articles of
value, and fine linens, were gone. Two strong boxes
were found broken open, from which gold and silver
coin, with some articles of clothing, had been abstracted. The value of the missing articles amounted
to about two thousand Dutch guldens. The house,
however, contained many other articles of value,
which, singular enough, had escaped the notice of
the thieves. In particular, the greater part of the
widow's property consisted of property in the funds,
the obligations for which were deposited, not in the
press above mentioned, but in an iron chest in her
sleeping room. This chest she had accidentally removed, shortly before her departure ; placing it in a
more retired apartment, where it had fortunately
attracted no attention.

The robbery had, apparently, been committed by
more than one person ; and, it was naturally suspected, by persons well acquainted with the house,
and with the circumstances of its inhabitants. The
house itself, which was almost the only respectable
one in the neghborhood, was situated in a retired

street. The neighboring dwellings were inhabited by the poorer classes, and not a few of the less reputable members of society. The inner fosse of the town, which was navigable, flowed along the end of the garden through which the thieves had, apparently, gained admittance, being separated from the garden only by a thin thorn hedge. It was conjectured that the thieves had made their way close to the hedge by means of a boat, and from thence had clambered over into the garden, along the walks and flower-beds of which foot-marks were traceable.

The discovery of the robbery had created a general sensation, and the house was surrounded by a crowd of curious idlers, whom it required some effort on the part of the police to prevent from intruding into the premises. One of them only, a baker, and the inhabitant of the house opposite to that of the widow, succeeded in making his way in along with the officers of justice. On his exit, he assumed an air of mystery, answered equivocally, and observed that people might suspect many things of which it might not be safe to speak.

In proportion, however, to his taciturnity, was the loquaciousness of a woolspinner, Leendert Van N——, the inhabitant of the corner house next to that of the widow. He mingled with the groups who were discussing the subject; dropped hints that he had his own notions as to the culprits, and could, if necessary, give a clue to their discovery. Among the crowd who were observed to listen to these effusions, was a Jew dealer in porcelain, a suspected spy of the police. Before evening, the woolspinner received a summons to the town-house, and was called upon by the Burgomaster for an explanation of the suspicious expressions he had used. He stammered, hesitated, pretended he knew of nothing but general grounds of suspicion, like his neighbors; but being threatened with stronger measures of compulsion, he at last agreed to speak out, protesting at the same time, that he could willingly have spared persons against whom he had no grudge whatever, and would have been silent for ever, if he had foreseen the consequence of his indiscretion.

The substance of his disclosure was to this effect: —Opposite the German post-house, at the head of the street, in which the woolspinner lived, there was a little alehouse. Nicholas D—— was the landlord. He was generally known among his acquaintances, not by his baptismal or family name, but by the appellation of the Blue Dragoon, from having formerly served in the horse regiment of Colonel Van Wackerbarth, which was popularly known by the name of the Blues. About two years before, he had become acquainted with and married Hannah, the former servant of Madame Andrecht, who had been six years in that situation, and possessed her entire confidence. Unwilling to part with her attendant, and probably entertaining no favorable notion of the intended husband, Madame Andrecht had long thrown impediments in the way of the match, so that the parties were obliged to meet chiefly at night, and by stealth. Nicholas found his way into the house at night through the garden of his acquaintance the woolspinner, and across the hedge which divided it from Madame Andrecht's. Of these nocturnal visits the woolspinner was at first cognizant, but, fearful of getting into a scrape with his respectable neighbor, he was under the necessity of intimating to the dragoon, that if he intended to continue his escalades, he must do so from some other quarter than his garden. Nicholas obeyed apparently, and desisted ; but, to the surprise of the woolspinner, he found the lovers continued to meet not the less regularly in Madame Andrecht's garden. One evening, however, the mystery was explained. The woolspinner, returning home after dark, saw tied to a post in the canal, close by Madame Andrecht's garden, one of those small boats which were generally used by the dragoons for bringing forage from the magazine; and he at once conjectured that this was the means by which the dragoon was enabled to continue his nocturnal assignations. With the recollection of this passage in the landlord's history was combined a circumstance of recent occurrence, trifling in itself, but which appeared curiously to link in with the mode in which the robbery appeared to have been effected. Ten days before the discovery of the house-breaking, and while the widow was in the country, the woolspinner stated that he found, one morning, a dirty colored handkerchief lying on the grass bank of the fosse, and exactly opposite his neighbor's garden. He took it up and put it in his pocket, without thinking about it at the time. At dinner he happened to remember it, mentioned the circumstance to his wife, showed her the handkerchief, and observed jestingly, " If Madame Andrecht were in town, and Hannah were still in her service, we should say our old friend the Blue Dragoon had been making his rounds and had dropped his handkerchief." His wife took the handkerchief, examined it, and exclaimed, " In the name of wonder, what is that you say? Is not Hannah's husband's name Nicholas D——?" pointing out to him at the same time the initials N. D. in the corner.

Both, however, had forgotten the circumstance till the occurrence of the robbery naturally recalled it to the husband's mind.

The woolspinner told his story simply; his conclusions appeared unstrained; suspicion became strongly directed against the Blue Dragoon, and these suspicions were corroborated by another circumstance which emerged at the same time.

During the first search of the house, a half burnt paper, which seemed to have been used for lighting a pipe, was found on the floor, near the press which had been broken open. Neither Madame Andrecht nor her maid smoked; the police officers had no pipes when they entered the house; so the match had in all probability been dropped on the ground by the house-breakers.

On the examination of the remains of the paper, it appeared to have been a receipt, such as was usually granted by the excise to innkeepers for payment of the duties on spirits received into the town from a distance, and which served as a permit entitling the holder to put the article into his cellars. The upper part of the receipt, containing the name of the party to whom it was granted, was burnt, but the lower part was preserved, containing the signature of the excise officer, and the date of the permit; it

11

was the 16th March of the same year. From these materials it was easy to ascertain what innkeeper in the town had, on that day, received such a permit for spirits. From an examination of the excise register, it appeared that on that day Nicholas D—— had received and paid the duties on several ankers of Geneva. Taken by itself, this would have afforded but slender evidence that he had been the person who had used the paper for a match, and had dropped it within Madame Andrecht's room ; but, taken in connection with the finding of the hand-kerchief, and the suspicious history of his nocturnal rambles which preceded it, it strengthened in a high degree the suspicions against the ex-dragoon.

After a short consultation, orders were issued for his apprehension. Surprise, it was thought, would probably extort from him an immediate confession. His wife, his father—a man advanced in years—and his brother, a shoemaker's apprentice, were appre-hended at the same time.

A minute search of the house of the innkeeper followed ; but none of the stolen articles were at first discovered, and indeed nothing that could excite suspicion, except a larger amount of money than might perhaps have been expected. At last, as the search was on the point of being given up, there was found in one of the drawers a memorandum book. This was one of the articles mentioned in the list of Madame Andrecht's effects; and, on inspection, there could be no doubt that this was the one referred to—for several pages bore private markings in her own handwriting, and in a side pocket were found two letters bearing her address. Beyond this, none of the missing articles could be traced in the house.

The persons apprehended were severally examined. Nicholas D—— answered every question with the utmost frankness and unconcern. He admitted the truth of the woolspinner's story of his courtship, his nightly scrambles over the hedge, and his subsequent visits to his intended by means of the forage boat. The handkerchief he admitted to be his property. When and where he had lost it he could not say. It had disappeared about six months before, and he had thought no more about it. When the pocket-book which had been found was laid before him, he gave it back without embarrassment, declared he knew nothing of it, had never had it in his possession, and shook his head with a look of surprise and incredulity when told where it had been found.

The other members of his household appeared

equally unembarrassed ; they expressed even greater astonishment than he had done, that the pocket-book, with which they declared themselves entirely unacquainted, should have been found in the place where it was. The young wife burst out into passionate exclamations ; she protested it was impossible ; or if the book was really found on the spot, that it was inexplicable to her how it came there. The Saturday before (her apprehension having taken place on a Thursday), she had brushed out the press from top to bottom—and nothing of the kind was then to be found there.

In this stage of the inquiry, a new witness entered upon the scene. A respectable citizen, a dealer in wood, voluntarily appeared before the authorities, and stated that his conscience would no longer allow him to conceal certain circumstancs which appeared to bear upon the question, though, from an unwillingness to come forward or to appear as an informer against parties who might be innocent, he had hitherto suppressed any mention of them.

Among his customers was the well-known carpenter, Isaac Van C——, who was generally considerably in arrears with his payments. These arrears increased ; the wood merchant became pressing ; at last he threatened judicial proceedings. This brought matters to a point. A few days before the discovery of the robbery at Madame Andrecht's the carpenter made his appearance in his house, and entreated him to delay proceedings, which he said would be his ruin, by bringing all his creditors on his back. "See," said he, "in what manner I am paid myself," putting a basket on the table, which contained a pair of silver candlesticks and a silver coffee-pot. "One of my debtors owes me upwards of sixty guldens; I have tried in vain to get payment, and have been glad to accept of these as the only chance of making anything of the debt. From the silversmiths here I could not get the half the value for them; I must keep them by me till I go to Amsterdam, where such things are understood; but I shall leave them with you in pledge for my debt." The wood merchant at first declined receiving them, but at length, thinking that it was his only prospect of obtaining ultimate payment, he yielded, and the articles remained on his hands.

A few days afterwards, the robbery became public; the list of the silver articles contained a coffee-pot and candlesticks; and the wood merchant, not doubting that the articles pledged had formed part of the abstracted effects, placed them in the hands of the police.

The court ordered the basket with the plate to
be placed, covered, upon the table, and sent forthwith for the carpenter. He arrived in haste, but
seemed prepared for what followed, and without
waiting for the interrogatories of the judge, he proceeded with his explanation.

Pressed by his creditor the wood merchant, the
carpenter, in his turn, proceeded to press his own
debtors. Among these was the Blue Dragoon,
Nicholas D——, who was indebted to him in an
account of sixty guldens for work done on his
premises. Nicholas entreated for delay, but the
carpenter being peremptory, he inquired whether
he would not take some articles of old silver plate in
payment, which, he said had belonged to his father,
and had been left him as a legacy by an old lady
in whose family he had been coachman. It was at
last agreed that the carpenter should take the plate
at a certain value as a partial payment, and it was
accordingly brought to his house the same evening
by the dragoon. The latter advised him, in the event
of his wishing to dispose of the plate, to take it to
Amsterdam, as the silversmiths of the place would
not give him half the value for the articles. The
carpenter asked him why he had not carried it to
Amsterdam himself. "So I would," he answered,

"if you had given me time. As it is, give me your promise not to dispose of it here—I have my own reasons for it."

If this statement was correct—and there seemed no reason to doubt the fairness of the carpenter's story—it pressed most heavily against the accused. He was thus found in possession of part of the stolen property, and disposing of it, under the most suspicious circumstances, to a third party

He was examined anew, and the beginning of his declaration corresponded exactly with the deposition of the carpenter. The latter had worked for him; he was sixty guldens in his debt. He was asked if he had paid the account: he answered he had not been in a condition to do so. He was shown the silver plate, and was told what had been stated by the carpenter. He stammered, became pale, and protested he knew nothing of the plate; and in this statement he persisted in the presence of witnesses. He was then shown the gold which had been found in his house. It belonged, he said, not to himself, but to his father-in-law.

This part of the statement, indeed, was confirmed by the other inmates of his family; but, in other respects, their statements were calculated to increase the suspicions against him. Nicholas, for instance,

had stated that no part of his debt to Isaac had been
paid—that in fact he had not been in a condition to
do so—while the other three members of the household, on the contrary, maintained that a few months
before he *had* made a payment of twenty guldens to
Isaac, expressly to account of this claim. Nicholas
became vastly embarrassed when this contradiction
between his own statement and the evidence of the
witnesses was pointed out to him. For the first time
his composure forsook him—he begged pardon for
the falsehood he had uttered. It was true, he said,
that he had counted out twenty guldens, in the
presence of the members of his family, and told
them it was intended as a payment to account of
Isaac's claim ; but the money had not been paid to
his creditor. He had been obliged to appropriate
it to the payment of some old gambling debts, of
which he could not venture to inform his wife.

This departure from truth on the part of the
accused had apparently but slender bearing on the
question of the robbery ; but it excited a general
doubt as to his statements, which further inquiry
tended to confirm. The carpenter, anxious to remove any suspicion as to the truth of his own story,
produced a sort of account-book kept by himself,
in which, under the date of 23d June, there was

the following entry, — "The innkeeper, Nicholas D——, has this day paid me the value of thirty guldens in old silver." The houskeeper and apprentice of the carpenter also deposed that they had been present on one occasion when the dragoon had proposed that their master should take the silver in payment.

The dragoon was removed from his provisional custody to the prison of the town ; the others were subjected to a close surveillance, that all communication between them might be prevented. As all of them, however, persisted in the story, exactly as it had at first been told, stronger measures were at length resorted to. On the motion of the burgomaster, as public prosecutor, "that the principal party accused, Nicholas D——, should be delivered over to undergo the usual preparatory process for compelling confession," namely the torture, the court, after consideration of the state of the evidence, unanimously issued the usual warrant against him to that effect.

The torture was to take place the next day, when the following letter, bearing the post-mark of Rotterdam, was received by the court :

"Before I leave the country, and betake myself where I shall be beyond the reach either of the court of M—— or the military tribunal of the garrison, I would save the poor unfortunate persons who are now prisoners at M——. Beware of punishing the innkeeper, his wife, his father, and brother, for a crime of which they are not guilty. How the story of the carpenter is connected with theirs, I cannot conjecture. I have heard of it with the greatest surprise. The latter may not himself be entirely innocent. Let the judge pay attention to this remark. You may spare yourselves the trouble of inquiring after me. If the wind is favorable, by the time you read this letter I shall be on my passage to England.

"Joseph Christian Ruhler,
"Former Corporal in the Company of Le Lery."

The court gladly availed themselves of the apportunity afforded by this letter to put off the torture. At first sight it did not appear a mere device to obtain delay. A company under Captain Le Lery was in garrison in the town ; in that company there was a corporal of the name of Ruhler, who some weeks before had deserted and disappeared from his quarters. All inquiries after him since had proved in vain. The court subsequently learned from the report of the officer in command, that he had disappeared the evening before the day when the news of the robbery became public. He had been last seen by the guard in the course of the afternoon before his disappearance. Some connection between the events appeared extremely probable.

But a new discovery seemed suddenly to demolish the conclusions founded on the letter. It had been laid before the commanding officer, who at once declared the handwriting was counterfeited; it was not that of Ruhler, which was well known, nor had it the least resemblance to it. The evidence of several of his comrades, and a comparison of the handwriting with some regimental lists, undoubtedly in the handwriting of Ruhler, proved this beyond a doubt.

The strongest efforts were now made to discover the true writer of the letter; and meantime the torture was put off, when two other important witnesses made their appearance upon the stage. Neither had the least connection with the other; nay, the circumstances which they narrated appeared in some respects contradictory, and while they threw light on the subject in one quarter, they only served to darken it in another.

A merchant in the town, who dealt in different wares, and lived in the neighborhood of Madame Andrecht's house, had been absent on a journey of business during the discovery of the robbery, and the course of the subsequent judicial proceedings. Scarcely had he returned and heard the story of the robbery, when he voluntarily presented himself next

morning before the authorities, for the purpose, as
he said, of making important revelations, which
might have the effect of averting destruction from
the innocent.

At the time when the robbery must have taken
place, he had been in the town. The carpenter,
Isaac Van C——, called upon him one day, begging
the loan of the boat, which he was in the custom
of using for the transport of bales and heavy pack-
ages to different quarters of the town. The boat
generally lay behind the merchant's house, close to
his warehouse, which was situated on the bank of
the town fosse already alluded to. Isaac assured
him he would require the boat only for a night or
two, and would take care that it was returned in
the morning in good condition. To the question
why he wanted the boat at night, he, after some
hesitation, returned for answer, that he had engaged to transport the furniture of some people who
were removing, and who had their own reasons for
not doing so in daylight, implying that they were
taking French leave of their creditors. "And you
propose to lend yourself to such a transaction?"
said the merchant, peremptorily refusing the loan of
the boat. The carpenter interrupted him; assured
him he had only jested; that his real object was

only to amuse himself in fishing with some of his comrades ; and that he had only not stated that at first, as the merchant might be apprehensive that the operation would dirty his boat. The merchant at last yielded to the continued requests of the carpenter, and agreed to lend him the boat, but upon the express condition that it should be returned to its place in the morning. In this respect the carpenter kept his word ; when the merchant went to his warehouse in the morning, he saw the carpenter and his apprentice engaged in fastening the boat. They went away without observing him. It struck him, however, as singular, that they appeared to have with them neither nets nor fishing tackle of any kind. He examined the boat, and was surprised to find it perfectly clean and dry, whereas, if used for fishing, it would probably have been found half filled with water, and dirty enough. In this particular, then, the carpenter had been detected in an untruth. The boat had not been fastened to its usual place ; the merchant jumped into it for that purpose, and from a crevice in the side he saw something protruding ; he took it out ; it was a couple of silver forks wrapped in paper. Thus the carpenter's first version of the story—as to the purpose for which he wanted the boat—was the true one after all. He *had* been assisting some bankrupt to carry off his effects. Angry at having been thus deceived, the merchant put the forks in his pocket, and set out forthwith on his way to Isaac's. The carpenter, his apprentice, and his housekeeper, were in the workshop. He produced the forks. "These," said he, "are what you have left in my boat. Did you use these to eat your fish with?"

The three were visibly embarrassed. They cast stolen glances upon one another; no one ventured to speak. The housekeeper first recovered her composure. She stammered out,—"that he must not think ill of them; that her master had only been assisting some people who were leaving the town quietly, to remove their furniture and effects." As the transaction was unquestionably not of the most creditable character, this might account for the visible embarrassment they betrayed; when he demanded, however, the names of the parties whose effects they had been removing, no answer was forthcoming. The carpenter at last told him he was not at liberty to disclose them then, but that he should learn them afterwards. All three pressingly entreated him to be silent as to this matter. He was so; but in the mean time made inquiry quietly as to who had left the town, though without success.

Shortly after, his journey took place, and the transaction had worn out of mind, till recalled to his recollection on his return, when he was made aware of the whole history of the robbery ; and forthwith came to the conclusion, that there lay at the bottom of the matter some shameful plot to implicate the innocent, and shield those whom he believed to be the true criminals, namely, Isaac Van C——, his apprentice, and housekeeper, the leading witnesses, in fact, against the unfortunate dragoon.

The judge issued an immediate order for the arrest of the carpenter and his companions, before publicity should be given to the merchant's disclosures. No sooner were they apprehended, than a strict scrutiny was made in the carpenter's house.

This measure was attended with the most complete success. With the exception of a few trifles, the whole of the effects which had been abstracted from Madame Andrecht's were found in the house. The examination of the prisoners produced a very different result from those of Nicholas, and his comrades. True, they denied the charges, but they did so with palpable confusion, and their statements abounded in the grossest contradictions of each other and even of themselves. They came to re-

criminations and mutual accusations; and, being
threatened with the torture, they at last offered to
make a full confession. The substance of their
admissions was as follows .

Isaac Van C——, his apprentice, and his housekeeper, were the real perpetrators of the robbery
at Madame Andrecht's. Who had first suggested
to them the design does not appear from the evidence. But with the old lady's house and its
arrangements they were as fully acquainted as the
dragoon. The apprentice, when formerly in the
service of another master, had wrought in it, and
knew every corner of it thoroughly. They had
borrowed the boat for the purpose of getting access
across the canal into the garden, and used it for
carrying off the stolen property, as already mentioned. On the morning when the robbery became
public, the master and the apprentice had mingled
with the crowd to learn what reports were in circulation on the subject. Among other things the apprentice had heard that the woolspinner's wife had
unhesitatingly expressed her suspicions against the
Blue Dragoon. Of this he informed his comrades,
and they, delighted at finding so convenient a scape-
goat for averting danger from themselves, forthwith
formed the design of directing, by every means in

their power, the suspicions of justice against the innkeeper.

The apprentice entered the drinking room of the innkeeper, and called for some schnapps, at the same time asking for a coal to light his pipe. While the innkeeper went out to fetch the coal, the apprentice took the opportunity of slipping the widow's memorandum book, which he had brought in his pocket, betwixt the drawers.

If these confessions were to be trusted, the dragoon and his family seemed exculpated from any actual participation in the robbery. Still, there were circumstances which these confessions did not clear up. That the carpenter had himself pledged the silver plate with the wood merchant, without having received it from Nicholas, was now likely enough; he had accused him, probably, only to screen himself. But how came Nicholas's handkerchief to be found at the side of the hedge? How came the exc se receipt, which belonged to him, to be used as a match by the thieves? The carpenter and his comrades declared that as to these facts they knew nothing; and as they had now no inducement to conceal the truth, there could be no reasonable doubt that their statement might. in these particulars, be depended upon.

12

The suspicion again arose that other accomplices must be concerned in the affair; and the subject of the letter from the corporal who had deserted, became anew the subject of attention. If not written by himself, it might have been written at his suggestion, and in one way or other he might have a connection with the mysterious subject of the robbery.

In fact, while the proceedings against the carpenter and his associates were in progress, an incident had occurred, which could not fail to awaken curiosity and attention with regard to this letter. The schoolmaster of a village about a league from the town presented himself before the authorities, exhibited a scrap of paper on which nothing appeared but the name Joseph Christian Ruhler, and inquired whether, shortly before, a letter in this handwriting and subscribed with this name, had not been transmitted to the court? On comparing the handwriting of the letter with the paper exhibited by the schoolmaster, it was unquestionable that both were the production of the same hand.

The statement of the schoolmaster was this:

In the village where he resided, there was a deaf and dumb young man, named Henry Hechting,

who had been sent by the parish to the schoolmaster for board and education. He had succeeded
in imparting to the unfortunate youth the art of
writing; so perfectly, indeed, that he could communicate with any one by means of a slate and
slate-pencil which he always carried about with him.
He also wrote so fair a hand, that he was employed
by many persons, and even sometimes by the authorities, to transcribe or copy writings for them.
Some time before, an unknown person had appeared in the village, had inquired after the deaf
and dumb young man in the schoolmaster's absence,
and had taken him with him to the alehouse to write
out something for him. The unknown had called
for a private room, ordered a bottle of wine, and,
by means of the slate, gave him to understand that
he wanted him to make a clean copy of the draft
of a letter which he produced. Hechting did so at
once without suspicion. Still, the contents of the
letter appeared to him of a peculiar and questionable
kind, and the whole demeanor of the stranger
evinced restlessness and anxiety. When he came,
however, to add the address of the letter, "To Herr
Van der R——, Burgomaster of M——," he hesitated to do so, and yielded only to the pressing entreaties of the stranger, who paid him a gulden for

his trouble, requesting him to preserve strict silence as to the whole affair.

The deaf and dumb young man, when he began to reflect on the matter, felt more and more convinced that he had unconsciously been made a party to some illegal transaction. He at last confessed the whole to his instructor, who at once perceived that there existed a close connection between the incident which had occurred and the criminal procedure in the noted case of the robbery. The letter of the corporal had already got into circulation in the neighborhood, and was plainly the one which his pupil had been employed to copy. The schoolmaster set on foot a small preliminary inquiry. He hastened to the innkeeper of the village inn, and asked him if he could recollect the stranger who some days before had ordered a private room and a bottle of wine, and who had been for some time shut up with the deaf and dumb lad. The host remembered the circumstance, but did not know the man. His wife, however, recollected that she had seen him talking on terms of cordial familiarity with the corn miller, Overblink, as he was resting at the inn with his carts. The schoolmaster repaired on the spot to Overblink, inquired who was the man with whom he had conversation and shaken hands some days before at the inn ; and the miller without much hesitation, answered, that he remembered the day, the circumstance, and the man, very well ; and that the latter was his old acquaintance the baker, H——, from the town. The schoolmaster hastened to lay these particulars before the anthorities.

How, then, was the well-known baker, H——, implicated in this affair, which seemed gradually to be expanding itself so strangely ? The facts as to the robbery itself seemed exhausted by the confessions of the carpenter and his associates. They alone had broken into the house—they alone had carried off and appropriated the stolen articles. And yet, if the baker was entirely unconnected with the matter, what could be his motive for mixing himself up with the transaction, and writing letters, as if to avert suspicion from those who had been first accused ? Was his motive simply compassion ? Was he aware of the real circumstances of the crime, and its true perpetrators ? Did he know that the Blue Dragoon was innocent ? But if so, why employ this mysterious and circuitous mode of assisting him ? Why resort to this anxious precaution of employing a deaf and dumb lad as his amanuensis? why such signs of restlessness and apprehension,—such anxious injunctions of silence ? Plainly the baker was not

entirely innocent : this was the conviction left on the
minds of the judges ; for it was now recollected that
this baker was the same person who, on the morning
when the robbery was detected, had contrived to
make his way into the house along with the officers
of justice. It was he who had lifted from the
ground the match containing the half-burnt receipt,
and handed it to the officers present. His excessive
zeal had even attracted attention before. Had he,
then, broken into the house independently of the
carpenter? Had he, too, committed a robbery—and
was he agitated by the fear of its detection? But all
the stolen articles had been recovered, and all of
them had been found with the carpenter. The
mystery, for the moment, seemed only increased ;
but it was about to be cleared up in a way wonderful
enough, but entirely satisfactory.

While the schoolmaster and the miller Overblink
were detained at the council-chamber, the baker
H—— was taken into custody. A long and circumstantial confession was the result, to the particulars
of which we shall immediately advert. From his
disclosures, a warrant was also issued for the apprehension of the woolspinner, Leendert Van N——
and his wife—the same who had at first circulated
the reports and suspicions against the dragoon ; and

who had afterwards given such plausible, and, as it appeared, such frank and sincere information against him before the court. Both had taken the opportunity of making off; but the pursuit of justice was successful—before evening they were brought back and committed to prison.

The following disclosures were the result of the confessions of the guilty, and of the other witnesses who were examined.

On the evening of the 29th June, there were assembled in the low and dirty chamber of the wool-spinner, Leendert Van N——, a party of card-players. It has already been mentioned that this quarter of the town was in a great measure inhabited by the disreputable portion of the public—only a few houses, like those of Madame Andrecht, being occupied by the better classes. The gamblers were the Corporal Ruhler, of the company of Le Lery, then lying in garrison in the place, the master baker H——, and the host himself, Leendert Van N——. The party were old acquaintances; they hated and despised each other, but a community of interests and pursuits drew them together.

The baker and corporal had been long acquainted; the former baked the bread for the garrison company, the latter had the charge of receiving it from him. The corporal had soon detected various frauds committed by the baker, and gave the baker the choice of denouncing them to the commanding officer, or sharing with him the profits of the fraud. The baker naturally chose the latter, but hated the corporal as much as he feared him ; while the latter made him continually feel how completely he considered him in his power.

A still deadlier enmity existed between the corporal and the woolspinner and his wife. The latter had formerly supplied the garrison with gaiters and other articles of clothing, and he had reason to believe that the corporal had been the means of depriving him of this commission, by which he had suffered materially. But the corporal had still a good deal in his power ; he might be the means of procuring other orders, and it was necessary, therefore, to suppress any appeaarance of irritation, and even to appear to court his favor.

These worthy associates were playing cards on the evening above-mentioned ; they quarreled ; and the quarrel became more and more embittered. The long suppressed hatred on the part of the baker and the woolspinner burst forth. The corporal retorted in terms equally offensive ; he applied to them the epithets which they deserved. From words they proceeded to blows, and deadly weapons were laid hold of on both sides. But two male foes and a female fury, arrayed on one side, were too much for even a soldier. The corporal, seized and pinioned from behind by the woman, fell under the blows of the woolspinner. As yet the baker had rather hounded on the others than actually interfered in the scuffle; but when the corporal, stretched on the ground, and his head bleeding from a blow on the corner of the table, which he had received in falling, began to utter loud curses against them, and to threaten them all with public exposure—particularly that deceitful scoundrel the baker—the latter, prompted either by fear or hatred, whispered to the woolspinner and his wife that now was the time to make an end of him at once; and that if they did not, they were ruined.

The deadly counsel was adopted; they fell upon the corporal; with a few blows life was extinct. The deed was irrevocable; all three had shared in it; all were alike guilty, and had the same reason to tremble at the terrors of the law. They entered into a solemn mutual engagement to be true to each other and to preserve inviolable secresy as to the crime.

On the night of the murder, they had devised

no plan for washing out the blood, and removing
the body, which of course required to be disposed of,
so that the disappearance of Ruhler might cause no
suspicion. The next morning, however, they met
again at the woolspinner's house to arrange their
plans. Suddenly a noise was heard in the street,—
it was the commotion caused by the news of the discovery of the robbery at Madame Andrecht's. The
culprits stood pale and confounded. What was
more probable than that an immediate search in
pursuit of the robbers, or of the stolen articles,
would take place into every house of this suspected
and disreputable quarter. The woolspinner's house
was the next to that which had been robbed; the
flooring was at that moment wet with blood; the
body of the murdered corporal lay in the cellar.

The object, then, was to give to the authorities
such hints as should induce them to pass over the
houses of the baker and the woolspinner. The
woolspinner's wife had the merit of devising the
project which occurred to them. The Blue Dragoon
was to be the victim. A robbery had taken place.
Why might he not have been the criminal? He had
often scaled the hedge—had often entered the house
at night during his courtship. But then a corroborating circumstance might be required to ground

the suspicion. It was supplied by the possession of a handkerchief which he had accidentally dropped in her house, and which she had not thought it necessary to restore to him.

The invention of the baker came to the aid of the woolspinner's wife. One token was not enough; a second proof of the presence of the dragoon in Madame Andrecht's house must be devised. The baker had, one day, been concluding a bargain with a peasant before the house of the dragoon. He required a bit of paper to make some calculation, and asked the host for some, who handed him an old excise permit, telling him to make his calculations on the back. This scrap of paper the baker still had in his pocket-book. This would undoubtedly compromise the dragoon. But then it bore the name and handwriting of the baker on the back. This portion of it was accordingly burnt; the date and the signature of the excise officer were enough for the diabolical purpose it was intended to effect. It was rolled up into a match, and deposited by the baker (who, as already said, had contrived to make his way along with the police into the house) upon the floor, where he pretended to find it, and delivered it to the authorities.

The machinations of these wretches were unconsciously assisted by those of the carpenter and his confederates. The suspicion which the handkerchief and the match had originated, the finding of the pocket-book within the house of the dragoon appeared to confirm and complete,—an accidental concurrence of two independent plots, both resorted to from the principle of self-preservation, and having in view the same object.

But this object, so far as concerns the baker and the woolspinner, had been too effectually attained. They had wished to excite suspicion against Nicholas, only with the view of gaining time to remove the corpse, and efface the traces of the murder. This had been effected—their intrigue had served its purpose; and they could not but feel some remorse at the idea that an innocent person should be thereby brought to ruin.

They met and consulted as to their plans. A scheme occurred to them which promised to serve a double purpose,—by which delay might be obtained for Nicholas, while at the same time it might be made the means of permanently ensuring their own safety. To resuscitate the murdered Corporal Ruhler in another quarter, and to charge him with the guilt of the robbery, might serve both ends. It gave a chance of escape to Nicholas; it accounted for the disappearance of the corporal. Hence the letter which represented him as alive, as the perpetrator of the robbery, and as a deserter flying to another country ; which they thought would very naturally put a stop to all further inquiry after him.

But their plan was too finely spun, and the very precautions to which they had resorted, led to discovery. If they had been satisfied to allow the proposed letter to be copied out by the woolspinner's wife, as she offered, to be taken by her to Rotterdam, and put into the post, suspicion could hardly have been awakened against them ; the handwriting of the woman, who had seldom occasion to use the pen, would have been unknown to the burgomaster or the court. The deaf and dumb youth, to whom they resorted as their copyist, betrayed them ; step by step they were traced out,—and, between fear and hope, a full confession was at last extorted from them.

Sentence of death was pronounced against the parties who had been concerned in the housebreaking as well as in the murder, and carried into effect against all of them, with the exception of the woolspinner's wife, who died during her imprisonment. The woolspinner alone exhibited any signs of penitence.

XXIX.

The Miller's Niece.

NEAR the town of C———, in Yorkshire, there lived, in the last century, an old bachelor, who had thriven well as a miller. His name was John Smith; but he was generally known in his neighborhood only by the title of "Old Johnny." He was a man of, at least, average honesty, not ill-disposed, very illiterate, and wholly devoted to worldly gain. Old Johnny was never seen at church; his mill was his place of worship. He was a sincere money-worshiper; and never attempted to disguise the fact by contributions to any charities or religious institutions. The house in which he lived was situated close behind his mill, on the bank of the river which flows at the foot of the hill on which the town is built. On that side of the stream there were no other houses; but, within a stone-throw of his mill, on the side of the river nearer the town, there was collection of cottages known by the name of Fording-place, and noted as a resort for vagabonds. About half a mile further up the river, there was a respectable house inhabited by Stephen Bracewell, an attorney, and his only son Richard, who belonged to the same profession. Old Johnny's house was one of those substantial stone-built farm houses, with a large porch, low windows, and stone floors, which are still to be seen in many of the rural districts of Yorkshire and Lancashire.

Margaret, the miller's niece, presided over his domestic economy. She was a sensible, shrewd, and well-domesticated young woman, the only relative of whom the old man took any notice, and had made herself seem indispensable to the miller's comfort by her good management of his household. There was only one point of disagreement between the miller and his neice, and this was in the encouragement which she gave to the addresses of Richard, the son of the attorney whom we have mentioned. Though Richard was a young man of good character, he had no great worldly prospects; besides, in some business which they had transacted together, Old Johnny had quarrelled with Stephen Bracewell. This, added to his dislike of losing a ood housekeeper, made the miller violently opposed to the proposed match, and he never failed to show a discontented aspect when Richard had visited the mill. Besides this opposition, Richard had to en-

counter a rival candidate for Margaret's hand in a
man of a very singular character. There lived a
few woolen weavers at Fording-place, and among
them was a man rather beyond the middle age, of
the name of Singleton. In some way he had acquired more knowledge than his neighbors; for he
could read, and even write. His hopeless passion
for Margaret, or some other cause, had impaired his
intellect, and he excited the curiosity of his neighbors by the accounts of his "visions," which he
committed to paper, and in which Margaret often,
much to her own dissatisfaction, played the most
prominent part. Though certainly crazy, he was
frequently consulted as a medical adviser by his
ignorant neighbors, and even by people who came
from a distance for the purpose; for he was deep
in all the mysteries of an old herbal, which told
wondrous tales of the "starry influences" of Mars,
Jupiter, Saturn, and all the other planets upon
medical plants.

In this collection of cottages there was one miserable old house, notorious throughout the neighborhood as the resort of a gang of very disorderly
characters. An old woman, of a most unfavorable
aspect, with her daughter Nell, were the tenants of
this old building, in which they sheltered a party

of vagabonds, of whom the two most notorious were known by the names of Will and Ned Crooks. A frequent visitor at this infamous abode was a young man of the most dissolute character, whose relatives kept a public house in the town. He had, it appears, some independent property, which he consumed among the basest of companions in the practice of the lowest debauchery.

Old John the miller had frequently had serious disputes with the inmates of Nell Crooks' establishment on account of their inroads upon his property ; and he had threatened a prosecution against the brothers, Will and Ned, for stealing his poultry.

One day young Nell made her appearance at the mill, to urge a petition, in behalf of her friends, that Margaret would persuade the "auld fellow" not to proceed with the prosecution.

Margaret only answered that she should not interfere in the business at all ; but that her uncle's patience was quite worn out by the numerous depredations made upon his property. Still the stout young advocate urged her petition.

But Margaret still persisted in her refusal, and, after trying in vain the force of a climax of entreaties, Nell had recourse to abusive and threatening speeches.

13

In the evening of the same day, both Margaret and her uncle went out to transact some little business with a man who rented a small piece of land belonging to the miller. The house of this little farmer was situated up in the fields, about half a mile distant from the mill. The path to it led along by the mill-stream, as far as a little copse, where the stream joined its parent river, from which it had been separated awhile that it might turn Old Johnny's wheel. At the farmer's house he drank, during his talk on business, rather more than his usual quantity of good ale; but, when he left the house, he flung aside the proffered assistance of Margaret's arm.

The night was misty, and Margaret frequently lost sight of her uncle's figure, as he walked a few yards in advance; but he now and then declared his presence by breaking forth in some half-tipsy ejaculation.

About half-past nine o'clock Margaret arrived at home, and immediately asked the servant-maid if her uncle had not just entered the house, when the housekeeper answered "No;" but added, that a young man had shortly before crossed the mill-stream, and gone over the ford. The niece expressed some surprise, but said that her uncle must be somewhere about the premises. and would soon be coming in. Half an hour passed away, and then a footstep was heard in the porch.

"That is not the master," said the servant-maid.

"No," said Margaret, "it is Richard Bracewell," as she rose and opened the door for her visitor.

Shortly afterwards the servant-maid left the house, professing to feel great anxiety on account of her master's non-appearance. She did not enter the house again until Richard Bracewell had departed. When she came in Margaret asked, "Have you seen my uncle?"

"No," replied Susan.

"Then have you seen Master Richard Bracewell?"

"No," said Susan.

"Strange!" exclaimed Margaret; "for he has just left the house to search for my uncle."

"Then he has not crossed the ford," said Susan, "for I have only just now come over."

"But what should you be doing on the other side of the river?" said Margaret.

"Why, looking for my master, to be sure," the girl replied.

"Why should you think he had crossed the ford?" said Margaret.

"Nay, gracious Heaven only knows where he is," said the girl, with a confused look.

For three days no tidings were heard either ot the disolute Will Naylor, or of the old miller ; and all the neighborhood was full of excitement about these mysterious disappearances. The excitement of the people rose higher, when it was observed that Will Crooks was also missing. But on the evening of the third day the whole neighborhood was amazed by a singular incident.

Jonas Singleton, the crazy weaver, was in the habit, when his work was done, of taking a walk in the fields, over the ford, either for the purpose of seeing "visions," (as he called his hallucinations,) or of collecting medicinal herbs. He frequently returned from one of these rambles with a long story of some "vision" he had seen in the fields, and in which realities and strange fancies were most curiously intermingled. Accounts of these "visions" he would write out in a fair, legible hand ; then throw them aside and soon forget them, or give them to the first person who asked him if he had any "new visions !" Sometimes he would put one of his papers into the hand of a child, telling him to give it to his father, and saying "there is something in it which concerns him." He also had frequently sent his papers through the hands of Susan to her mistress, until Margaret had forbidden the girl to receive any more of them. It was a curious circumstance, that he generally prefaced these visions with a statement of the exact spot on which he stood, and of the quarter of the heavens toward which his face was turned. Thus he would begin—"Standing in the west corner of the miller's field, near the copse, (where the cuckoo-pint flourishes,) moon in her first quarter—hazy weather— face south-south-west—I saw," &c. Though he wrote down these "visions" with all possible solemnity, he must have had some lurking sense of their reality, as he betrayed no emotion even when he had seen "burials of his neighbors," &c. He seldom communicated any of his visions in any other way than by writing, and, as the whole neighborhood was accustomed to his marvelous stories, if he had reported that he had discovered a chest of gold in the field, nobody would have run to look after it. But, on the evening of the third day after the miller's disappearance, this eccentric visionary returned from his usual ramble with an altered demeanor, excited and perturbed, so that he could hardly speak articulately. He seemed to have made some discovery which urged him to speak, and, when his strange conduct had excited the curiosity of some neighbors who gathered round him, he burst forth with a revelation which astonished all present. "In the corner of the miller's field," said he, "just where the mill-stream flows by the copse, there lies in the water the body of old John Smith. *Why* he lies there, Mistress Margaret must tell; or, perhaps, Master Richard Bracewell may be able to give some information upon it, as he is a lawyer."

This sounded like a reality, and several of the hearers ran immediately to the place specified, and found that Singleton had, for once, seen nothing more than the fact. There, in the mill-stream, darkly shaded by overhanging boughs, lay the swollen corpse of the miller. The face was livid, and there were marks of bruises upon the temples.

By this time, the magistrate had heard of the occurrence, and issued orders that the body should be conveyed to a room beneath the town-hall. The coroner's inquest sat upon it the next day, and a verdict was returned, "Found in the mill-stream at the foot of the miller's field; but how the deceased came there, the jury cannot say."

Meanwhile great excitement was felt throughout the neighborhood, on account of the continued absence of Richard Bracewell, Will Crooks and

Will Naylor. At Fording-place the "visions" of Singleton and the insinuations of Nell had worked up the people to such a fury against Richard Bracewell and Margaret, that the latter was hardly safe in the mill; and, accordingly, Mr. Bracewell, the elder, gave her shelter in his house.

On the 14th day of November, Richard Bracewell returned, wet and weary, late in the evening, to his father's house. When this became known, and it was also circulated by the zealous Susan, that Mr. Bracewell had ransacked all the chests and drawers at the mill, and that Margaret had taken with her several valuable articles, popular indignation knew no bounds. A new excitement was raised when Will Crooks, on the following day, reappeared at the house of old Nell. His first question was if Master Bracewell had returned, and this was soon answered by the entrance of the person in question, attended by his father.

"Now, Will Crooks," said the younger Bracewell, "I wish to ask you, for the last time, if you can tell me anything of Naylor?"

Will Crooks refused to utter a word respecting Naylor, and told Bracewell to look to his "own business," which was "ugly enough."

Further altercation was prevented by the entrance

of the officers of justice, who at once apprehended all the parties present, on suspicion of having been concerned in the death of John Smith, and the disappearance of William Naylor.

In the morning of the same day, young Nell had laid a statement before the magistrate, that, on the evening of the miller's disappearance, young Bracewell had been drinking with Will Crooks at the Black Dog, and that both left the house together, about half-past eight o'clock. She had also repeated all that Susan had told of the conduct of her mistress on that fatal evening. On these grounds a warrant had been issued for the apprehension of the two Bracewells, Margaret, and Will Crooks. On the next day an examination of the prisoners took place. Mr. Bracewell the elder was liberated on bail, on account of the statement of his housekeeper, which asserted an *alibi ;* but the others were sent to the prison, and fully committed to take their trial at the York assizes.

Shortly afterwards, Ned Crooks, and the old mistress of the infamous establishment at Fording-place, were apprehended on suspicion. The prisoners were removed to York Castle, and placed in separate cells.

The bills against Mr. Bracewell the elder, old

Nell Crooks, Ned Crooks, and young Nell, were ignored ; but true bills were found against Richard Bracewell, jun., Margaret Smith, and William Crooks, for having been concerned in the death of John Smith.

During the interval between the commitment and the assizes, Mr. Bracewell, senior, was actively engaged in collecting witnesses for his, son and Margaret Smith. Richard determined to conduct his own defense.

The first indictment was read, charging all the three prisoners at the bar with having been concerned in causing the death of John Smith, miller, &c., by drowning or other means.

To this all the prisoners pleaded "not guilty."

The first witness called was Susan Holmes, formerly a servant at the mill. The substance of her statement was as follows :

"I lived, for a year and a month, servant under Margaret Smith at the mill. I was generally on good terms with my mistress. I believe she has a hot temper, and does not like to be contradicted. I believe there was unpleasantness sometimes between master and mistress about Richard Bracewell. It had been getting worse, I think, a little before master disappeared. I was in the house all the time while master and mistress went to Robert Wilkinson's. Mistress came in about half-past nine. It was later than I expected. She looked rather warm as 1 should say. I don't think her face is easily colored by a little walking or any sort of work. She asked me if master had come in—did not seem much surprised when I told her 'No.' She opened the door for Richard Bracewell. She had not been in the house five minutes when he came in. He looked flushed—not very much in liquor, I should say. He could walk steadily. I had seen a man cross the plank over the mill-stream just before mistress came in. You can see the plank from the kitchen window. I am sure it was not master. It was a misty night, but I could see his figure, and by his walking quickly I judged it was a young man. I cannot say it was Richard Bracewell.''

Cross-examined.—'' I went out soon after Richard Bracewell came in. I called at Nell Crooks'; I had been there before. Edward Crooks never paid me particular attentions. Young Nell was at home, and I talked with her awhile. When I returned I did not see Bracewell. I have been to Nell Crooks' several times since then.''

The next witness called was Thomas Batters, the landlord of the Black Dog.

Examined by Mr. Bailey. — '' The prisoners, Richard Bracewell and William Crooks, were at my house on the evening of the 7th of November last. They drank two quarts of ale between them. Crooks had been at the house nearly all day. Bracewell came in about half-past seven o'clock. They left the house about half-past eight. They were not drunk. Crooks had been at my house the evening before with William Naylor the young man who is missing. I cannot say how much ale they drank that night, the 6th of November. They went away very late. It was past midnight. Naylor was very drunk. He could not have walked without Crooks' assistance. I have never seen Naylor since he left my house with Crooks that evening. He was generally drunk. He spent a great deal of money ; more than his own independent propeity would cover, I believe. Bracewell has never been at my house since the 7th of November."

Jane Hartley, Mr. Bracewell's housekeeper, was next examined.

"I have lived at Mr. Bracewell's, the attorney's, now for more than three years. Richard, the prisoner at the bar, I have always considered a steady young man. He took his dinner at home on the 7th of November. After dinner I did not see him again until late at night. He came in flushed and seeming tired ; did not take any supper, but drank a tankard of ale. He went out, soon after breakfast, on the morning of the 8th, and I did not see him again until the 14th day of November."

Robert Wilkinson, a small farmer, testified :

"I rented a few acres of land under the deceased, John Smith. He was at my house on the evening of the 7th of November last. I paid him a small account for meal and bran. He was in very good spirits and took some ale. I cannot say justly how much ; but it might be something moie than three half-pints. It was not small beer. My wife generally brews good ale. I don't often take more than a pint of it at a time. The deceased, John Smith, often

called at my house. I never knew him to be out late
at night. He was no ways given to drink. His
niece, Margaret, did not say much while she was in
my house with him. They seemed good friends
when they left. I saw nothing of John after that,
until I saw his body in the mill-stream just by the
copse."

Robert Walker, surgeon, stated as follows :

"I saw the body of the deceased, John Smith, on
the eleventh of November, but did not open it. I
cannot say there were marks from blows upon the
head or face. The skin was discolored ; but it
might be the effect of immersion in water. The body
had evidently been in the water a considerable time.
I should say as long as two or three days."

The witnesses for the defense were called

Sarah Stokes, an old nurse, testified as follows :

"I am a nurse, and attended the late John Smith
during an illness, about two years ago, and I can
testify that the conduct of Margaret Smith, the
prisoner, was always exceedingly kind towards her
uncle."

Mary Barnes, who had lived as servant-maid at
the mill, confirmed the statement of the first witness. Next, a woman, who had called at the mill
for milk on the morning after the miller was lost,
stated that the grief and trouble of Margaret were
evident.

John Green also, servant-man to Robert Wilkinson, stated that the path along by the mill-stream

was mossy, so that a footstep upon it would be inaudible at a little distance.

Edward Norris, a man who worked in the mill, stated that the mill-stream would, at certain times, be strong enough to to carry down a man's body as far as from the plank to the copse.

These were all the witnesses who came forward for the defense.

Richard Bracewell was then allowed to make his own defense.

. . . . "You have heard an individual of the name of William Naylor mentioned in the evidence given by the witness Thomas Batters, landlord of the Black Dog. Gentlemen, I must make some statements respecting that young man's character, to explain the interest which I felt, and the exertions I made on his behalf. He had been my school-fellow. He had good qualities, though they all seemed drowned in one vice — that of habitual, I might almost say constant, intemperance. His father left a sum of money for him, under the control of my father, to be paid quarterly. Unhappily, the young man was brought up to do no business or profession. He fell into the lowest company, and often, I have good reason to believe, lost sums of money, by unfair means, in such company. He had been miss-

ing from home since the 4th of November last ; but,
as his habits were so very reckless and irregular, this
excited little surprise. His mother-in-law, however,
was alarmed when she discovered, on the sixth of
the same month, that he had taken a considerable
sum of money from her till, and requested me to
make my best efforts to find him, and recover some
portion of the money. I knew, as all the neighbors
knew, that he was very often in company with the
brothers William and Edward Crooks. I went to
the Black Dog on the evening of the 7th, and found
William Crooks there. I gave him liquor, to conceal
from him the object of my visit. When I inquired
after Naylor, he seemed unwilling to give me any
information. We left the Black Dog together, and
I followed him to the house of Nell Crooks, in Fording-place, where he lodges. Here I was violently
abused by the woman of the house, and a young
woman generally known by the name of Young
Nell, with whom Naylor was intimate. I left this
house, and called at several public houses, inquiring
for Naylor ; at one of these houses I saw John
Green, the servant-man of Robert Wilkinson,
farmer, who informed me that he had seen William
Crooks and William Naylor together, on the evening of the 6th instant. He told me that Naylor

appeared to be very drunk, and that he watched
the two men until they approached a hovel in the
Bridge-field, near to which was a manure heap. He
would have followed them, but knew the character
of the men. I determined to prosecute my search
in the morning. After leaving John Green, I walked
to the mill. I can give no particular reason for going
there, beyond the motive which led me there as often
as opportunity allowed. With regard to the lateness
of the hour—half-past nine—I may observe, that the
deceased, John Smith, generally retired to bed at
nine o'clock, and I had frequently visited the house
after that time. I had not been in the house five
minutes before Margaret Smith told me, with some
anxiety, that her uncle was missing, and I did not
stay ten minutes longer in the house, after I heard
that. Yet I cannot say that I felt any great anxiety
on his account. Margaret Smith also told me that
she thought her uncle was somewhat affected by the
ale he had drank, and that he had threatened to
'cloot' me, if he found me in his house.

"As I left the mill, I said I would make some
inquiry after him ; but still I thought he must be
about the place, and, as I did not wish to meet him,
I neither looked for him nor called after him. I
·alled at the house of an acquaintance, where 1

stayed a few minutes, and then went home to my father's house, where I drank a tankard of ale, and immediately went to bed. The next morning I communicated my business to my father. put some money in my pocket, and went out, soon after breakfast, to renew my inquiries after the missing William Naylor. I went, first to John Green before mentioned, whom I found at work in the Bridgefield. We went to the manure-heap, mentioned before, and, turning over the straw, found marks as if the body of a man had recently lain there. I confess I had very dark suspicions of the treatment which the missing man had received from his com panion, the prisoner, William Crooks. I then went up into the town, and had some conversation, at the Fleece tavern, with Mrs. Naylor, the mother-in-law of the missing individual. She told me that he had talked of leaving her, and going to visit some relatives near Burnley. I communicated to her my worst fears, and she earnestly begged me to make all possible inquiries after him. I rode on the coach to Burnley, where I, also, had friends, whc pressed me to stay with them a few days. I did so ; and employed much of my time in searching for Naylor, but to no purpose. His friends denied all knowledge of his having been in the neighbor·

hood. I wrote from Burnley to my father on the business." . . .

The witnesses called to corroborate Bracewell's statement were, a relative from Burnley, Mrs. Naylor, and the landlords of the public houses mentioned in his story. John Green, the servant-man of Robert Wilkinson, also confirmed all the statements with which his name was connected; and his brother, James Green, asserted that he had observed, on the morning of the 8th of November, the mark of a slipping foot at the edge of the mill-stream, a little above the copse on the way to the mill.

No witnesses appeared in favor of the prisoner Crooks.

The court was then adjourned, and met again in half-an-hour. The judge then proceeded with his summary of the evidence; but before he had uttered many words, Sergeant Jackson entered the court, and stated that he had fresh evidence now to lay before the jury, in the shape of a confession just made and signed by the prisoner, William Crooks. Bracewell and Margaret seemed amazed at this announcement, and there was great astonishment throughout the court while the sergeant read the following document:

"I, William Crooks, do solemnly declare that,

on the evening of the 7th of November last, I met the prisoner, Richard Bracewell, by appointment, at the Black Dog. He brought a short bludgeon in his pocket, and, after he had drunk several pints of ale, we set out to waylay the deceased, John Smith, near the copse. As the deceased was coming down the field, Bracewell whispered to me, 'The old villain has his niece with him.' But the niece stayed behind as her uncle approached the copse. It was a little after nine o'clock. We let him go past the copse a little way and then Bracewell said to me, 'Now's your time, Crooks!' I then went after the miller; but Bracewell kept concealed in the copse. I struck the deceased twice on the head with the bludgeon, then drew the body to the mill-stream, and pushed it in. I then went into the copse. In a few minutes Bracewell and I came out of the copse, and drew the body down to the shady place where it was found. Bracewell promised me good pay; and, soon afterwards, we separated. This I solemnly declare, is the whole truth of the way in which the miller met his death.

"Signed, WILLIAM CROOKS, + *his mark.*
"In presence of,   WILLIAM BAILEY, *Barrister.*
"SAMUEL KNUBBS, *Jailer.*"

The judge then asked the prisoner, Crooks, if he

had anything to add to this statement? He refused
to say another word. Bracewell was then asked if
he would make any reply to the statement just read
over.

"My lord," said he, "I am utterly amazed at
the awful wickedness of the man who has brought
forward this false confession. It is throughout a
lie; but I still beg for time—time, my lord, that the
truth may become apparent."

The judge then addressed the jury, and they retired. After a long absence they returned with the
verdict—"We find the prisoners, Richard Bracewell
and William Crooks, GUILTY OF WILLFUL MURDER—
the prisoner, Margaret Smith, NOT GUILTY."

The prisoners were next asked if they had anything to say why sentence should not be pronounced. Crooks refused to speak. "For *time*,
my lord, is all my prayer," was the answer given
by Bracewell.

The judge then put on his black cap, and pronounced sentence of death upon the condemned
prisoners, warning them to prepare for a speedy
execution. They were then conducted to their cells.

Crooks was sitting in his cell on the eve of execution. Young Nell had visited him during the
day to inquire for Naylor; but he had repulsed her

with violence. Mr. Bracewell, the elder, with Margaret Smith, and the chaplain of the prison, now entered his cell. The chaplain earnestly entreated the prisoner, if he had anything more to confess, that he would not delay. Margaret fell upon her knees, and added the most touching prayers to the exhortations of the chaplain. The conscience of the prisoner seemed to be writhing in torture, until, late in the night, he bade them get pen and paper, and take down his last words in this world. The jailer and other witnesses were called in, and the prisoner make a second and last confession, as follows :

"Every word in my former confession is false, except that Richard Bracewell met me at the Black Dog on the 7th of November last. He came to inquire after Naylor. I was drinking with Naylor all day, on the 6th. He had plenty of money, and told me he meant to leave the country. He got very drunk towards evening, and said he would go to Nell Crooks, and bid good-bye to Young Nell. I took him into the cow-house in the Bridge-field, and there struck him one heavy blow on the head with a short bludgeon. He groaned and fell, as 1 thought, dead on the spot. 1 buried his body in the manure-heap. I have never seen him, nor heard of

him, from that day to this. I solemnly declare that
Richard Bracewell never plotted with me against any
man's life; but that all he ever had to do with me
was to ask me about William Naylor. I state this
for truth, as I hope God will have mercy on my
miserable soul."

In consequence of this confession, Richard Bracewell was reprieved. The next morning, William
Crooks was hanged in the presence of an unfeeling
crowd, among whom were many of the people of
Fording-place and the neighborhood; and Young
Nell conspicuously exhibited her assumed grief on
the occasion. The moment before the fatal bolt was
drawn, the miserable man turned in reply to a question put to him by the chaplain, and confirmed solemnly, with his last breath, the statement he had
made on the previous night.

Still Richard Bracewell was kept in confinement;
but wonders had not yet ceased. A few days only
after the execution of Crooks, a man arrived at
Fording-place who declared himself to be the missing, *the murdered man*—William Naylor! The
identity was proved by numerous witnesses, Young
Nell being in the number. He was examined before
the magistrates, and made the following statement:

"My name is William Naylor. You must all

recognize me. My mother-in-law is Mrs. Naylor of the Fleece. I need say nothing of my habits and character when I lived here; but I will tell you all I remember of the circumstances connected with my disappearance from this part of the country. I had been drinking for weeks. Richard Bracewell had refused to pay me money in advance. I had taken a considerable sum from the till of the Fleece. I had some notion of paying it back when I could. I was drinking with Will Crooks on the night I was seen there. He took me to a cow-house in the Brdge-field. I forget how we quarreled. I think we said something about hell. I remember a heavy blow on my head that made fire flash all around me, and then I remember nothing more until I found myself lying in a manure-heap in the morning. I lurked about in the copse of the miller's field all the day, and considered that this was a good opportunity for leaving the country. I determined to set out at night-fall. I was in the copse at night, I should say about nine o'clock. I was hardly in my right senses from the drink and the blow; but I remember well, I was frightened by hearing a gurgling noise in the stream, and I fancied I saw some great black body floating in the water; but I did not stay to examine it. I left the copse and went over the plank by the mill. I saw nobody. I then crosed the ford, and walked nearly to Burnley that night, but did not call on my friends there. I have plenty of witnesses to prove where I have been ever since that time."

The result of the examination proved the truth of this statement, and Richard Bracewell was liberated a few days afterwards.

XXX.

The Boorn Case.

IN 1812 there lived in Manchester a man named Barney Boorn, who had two sons Stephen and Jesse, and a son-in-law named Russel Colvin, all living with him. Colvin was an eccentric man, supposed to be insane at times, and frequently absented himself for days without notice and without giving any account of his adventures. At last he was missing so long that people began to make inquiries, and suspicions of foul play were aroused. Months and years passed, and yet there was no explanation of Colvin's absence. Some of the neighbors remembered that the Boorn brothers, very shortly after his disappearance, had declared that Colvin was dead, and that they had "put him where potatoes would not freeze." They had not been on good terms with him, and this added to the prejudice against them.

NOTE.—For a full report of this case see a pamphlet recently published by Hon. ⎍ₑₙᵤₐᵣ⎍ Sargeant, one of the counsel. *Journal Office, Manchester, Vt.*

Singularly enough, other circumstances began to accumulate against the brothers. Some children found a dilapidated hat, which was recognized as the one Colvin wore at the time of his disappearance. Search was then made for the bones of the supposed murdered man. Soon afterwards a dog uncovered some bones beneath an old stump, which at first were pronounced to be human bones, but subsequently were found not to be. An uncle of the boys had a dream in which Colvin came to his bedside and told him he had been murdered. A barn in the neigborhood was mysteriously burned, and it was at once conjectured that the murdered man had been buried under it, and that the fire was intended to destroy all traces of the crime. All these circumstances added to the excitement against the Boorns. Stephen was then out of the State, but Jesse was arrested. He confessed that his brother Stephen had told him a short time previously that he and Colvin had quarreled, and that he had killed Colvin by a blow on the head. The people of the neighborhood and for miles around spent the next few days in another search for Colvin's bones, but none were found.

Stephen Boorn was brought home. He denied the statement of Jesse and asserted his innocence.

The brothers were imprisoned to await the meeting of the Grand Jury. The principal witness before that body was a forger, who had been confined in jail with the Boorns. He reported in detail a confession of the murder by Jesse Boorn, and both the boys were indicted. This was in September, 1819, more than seven years after the disappearance of Colvin. In November the trial took place. Meanwhile Stephen was induced by the remarks upon the hopelessness of their case to confess the crime, in the expectation of mercy from the court. This confession was the chief evidence against them. Notwithstanding that it was drawn out by hope of obtaining a more favorable verdict, and that no body had been found as proof of the murder, or even that Colvin was dead, the brothers were convicted and sentenced to be hanged on the 28th of January, 1820. The character of the evidence upon which they were convicted will attract the attention of lawyers at this time as showing what remarkable changes have taken place in criminal jurisprudence. So decisive did the testimony against them appear to be that the mother of the convicts was expelled from the Baptist church, and the father was held as a prisoner for a time, upon the suspicion that they must have been accessory to the murder.

A few of the citizens who were disposed to be merciful, signed a petition for the commutation of the sentence against the Boorns. The legislature voted to change the sentence of Jesse to imprisonment for life, but refused to interfere with that of Stephen. It occurred to Stephen in an interview with his counsel that it would be a good plan to advertise for Colvin in the newspapers. Up to that point his counsel had believed him guilty, but he assured them that his confession was untrue and that he was innocent. The following notice was therefore printed in the Rutland *Herald:*

"MURDER.—Printers of newspapers throughout the United States are desired to publish that Stephen Boorn, of Manchester, in Vermont, is sentenced to be executed for the murder of Russel Colvin, who has been absent about seven years. Any person who can give information of said Colvin may save the life of the innocent by making immediate communication. Colvin is about five feet five inches high, light complection, light colored hair, blue eyes, about forty years of age.

"Manchester, Vt., Nov. 26, 1819."

Newspapers traveled slowly then, and Stephen's friends had but little hope that this would save him even if his story was true. Three days afterwards, says Mr. Sargeant's pamphlet, the *New York Evening Post* copied it, and "the next day it happened that the notice was read aloud in one of the hotels in New York. Another man standing near, named Whelpley, said he had formerly lived in Manchester, and was well acquainted with Colvin, and related many anecdotes and peculiarities concerning him. Mr Tabor Chadwick, of Shrewsbury, N. J., was also standing near, and listened to the conversation, which made a deep impression upon his mind. On thinking the matter over after his return home it occurred to him that a man then living with his brother-in-law, Mr. William Polhemus, of Dover, New Jersey, answered exactly the description of Colvin as given by Whelpley." Finally, he wrote a letter to *The Evening Post*, giving his conclusions. Whelpley saw it, went to Dover, identified Colvin, and, after great effort, induced him to visit Manchester. There was great rejoicing in the town, and Stephen Boorn was brought from the prison to fire the cannon that celebrated his deliverance.

XXXI.

Henry Ranthorpe.

HENRY RANTHORPE, a literary man, had made some slight success as provincial journalist and a political pampleteer. He had a tragedy in his truuk, a plot of a comedy in his head, and one five-pound note in his pocket; and he must needs come up, to win golden opinions and earn golden sovereigns in the great world of London. He had, moreover, made what is called an improvident marriage; that is, he had married a pretty girl without a farthing, who nevertheless was a very good wife. They took cheap lodgings in "the wilds of Pimlico." The tragedy had not been accepted; at least the manager had not vouchsafed a reply. Nevertheless, he worked at the comedy laboriously and hopefully. As he had, however, not been for years in a London theater, he thought, wisely enough, that it would considerably assist him if he saw a play acted at the house where *he* intended *his* five acts to be brought out. He had no special interest with actors or critics by which to secure an "order;" and his wife agreed with him that the expenditure of half a crown, low as their finances were, would nevertheless be a wise outlay. Meanwhile a pair of boots, the only shoe-leather which he had brought with him from the country, had become so heelless, dilapidated, and shabby, that he made an investment in a pair of cheap shoes, and discarded the ruined bluchers. How to dispose of them was now his difficulty. He was ashamed to give them away at his lodgings; and they were not, after a grave consultation on the subject between his wife and himself, deemed worth of repair. He proposed taking them out into the street at night, and willfully making away with them, when he descried a dusty-looking cupboard high up in the wall of the bed-room, into which he threw his once serviceable boots. The cupboard-door would not close; but the cupboard being high up and in a corner, the bluchers did not show.

He started on his trip to the theater, leaving his fond and self-denying little wife to her tea, her needlework, and anticipations of his report of the evening's entertainment. He entered the pit entrance of the ——— Theater just after the first rush of half-past-six punctual folk had gone in; deposited his solitary half-crown, the only money

which, with the exception of a few pence, he had
about him ; and received his check-ticket, and was
about to pass on, full of disappointment at not having been earlier, and of excitement at the prospect
of a little novel amusement. To his intense astonishment, he had scarcely proceeded a yard when the
money-taker called out to him and a policeman
who was standing by simultaneously. The man
in the little box had twisted the half-crown, which
was a bad one ; was gesticulating wildly, and de-
claiming incoherently ; and Henry Ranthorpe, in a
few moments, was in the custody of the officer.
It was in vain that he protested his innocence, produced his card, gave his address, mentioned the
names of two or three friends he knew in London.
The money-taker winked knowingly to the officer,
who smiled tranquilly ; and to the station-house
they went. The inspector took the charge, heard the
evidence, and he was placed in a wretched dark
cell, where a riotous drunkard was singing and crying in turns. Afraid to alarm his wife by sending
to her to state the the misfortune that had befallen
him, he secured, by the good offices of the inspector,
who was struck with his respectable appearance
and his manner, a messenger, whom he sent with
a note to his landlord, and to a friend in Piccadilly,

who was a respectable householder. They arrived, and gave so satisfactory an account of him, that the inspector, overstepping his duty, permitted him to go ; and he reached home rather earlier than his wife expected him, with very little to say about the comedy which he was to have enjoyed, but with a full and impassioned narrative of the calamity that had befallen him. They sat together over their crust of bread-and-cheese and glass of beer, vowing vengeance against the manager of the theater and his employees, and discussing the expediency of bringing an action for false imprisonment.

They little knew how really narrow the escape had been. A *few days* afterwards, Ranthorpe observed the ugly old boots protruding a little at the cupboard-door. To get rid of this eye-sore, he took a chair, placed his trunk upon it, and opened the cupboard, in order to effectually secrete the boots. You may endeavor to imagine his astonishment when, in moving them, he descried two large bags. They were very heavy ; and what do you suppose they contained? ONE HUNDRED BAD HALF-CROWNS EACH. There could be no doubt about their quality. He showed them to his wife, whose astonishment was as great as his own. They began to entertain strange suspicions about the landlord ; and next began to reflect that, after what had happened at the theater, he would probably *suspect them.* They, however, rang the bell, summoned the worthy householder, and showed him the useless and dangerous booty. They were relieved, however, by seeing his broad countenance, at first filled with amazement and distraction, suddenly illuminated with a glance of profound penetration, and a smile of self-satisfied sagacity. "I quite understand it now, ma'am," said their host, addressing Mrs. Ranthorpe. "Some months ago, two young men came one day and took these rooms. They gave me no reference, but offered to pay in advance, which, as I always like to be on the safe side, I allowed them to do. Their hours were very strange ; but they came in and went out very quiet, and gave but very little trouble. Indeed, my missus said they were the best lodgers we had had for this many a day. The money was regular, and, what seems odd now, none of it *bad.* One day they went out together, after they had been in this house eight weeks ; and from that day to this, I have never seen or heard of them. They certainly were very mysterious, and never told what their occupation was. A few clothes they left are up-stairs in a chest of drawers now, and a carpet-

15.

bag and a portmanteau. I did have my suspicions, which I mentioned to the old woman, when I saw that two young men somewhat answering to their description had been tried at the Old Bailey, and sentenced to transportation."

Here ends this *curious case.* But suppose upon his arrest at the theater officers had been sent to search his lodgings, and the two bags, as they would have certainly been, found. His wife could not have been a witness, the possession of a bad half-crown, and the finding of two bags of bad half-crowns in his bed-room, his poverty, his almost friendlessness in London,—must not these facts have inevitably caused his conviction. Of what avail, against all this, witnesses to character? Of what avail the ingenuity and eloquence of counsel? The landlord of the house, so wise *after* the event, would probably have directed his suspicions immediately to his new lodgers, and the fact of Ranthorpe sitting up alone at late hours of the night, to write, and other facts having in them some *scintilla* of suspicion, would have been marshaled against him in compact array by the barrister prosecuting for the Mint. And this would have been a case of purely circumstantial evidence.

XXXII.

Case of Andrew Mirelees.

ON the 14th January, 1749, Andrew Mirelees, a master tanner of Leith, set out from his house about seven o'clock in the morning, to go and receive some money of a customer who lived at Haddingtou, a town about fifteen miles from Edinburgh. He was expected by his family to return the same day. Being a man of regular habits, his wife became half distracted when midnight arrived, and her husband was still absent. About one in the morning, her fears were in some measure relieved by the sound of a horse's feet entering the stable yard. Mrs. Mirelees had a servant who sat up with her. Eagerly rising from their seats, and taking a light in their hands, they hurried out, nothing doubting but that the absent husband and master had arrived. Great indeed was their surprise, and inexpressible the alarm and terror which filled the bosom of the anxious wife, when she beheld the horse without its master, and the poor animal stabbed in many parts,—scarcely able to stand,

and apparently bleeding to death,—an event which soon afterwards took place. The wife and servant instantly concluded that Andrew Mirelees had been robbed and murdered, an idea that derived additional force from the ill repute of a wild and desolate common, across which the latter part of his homeward journey lay, and which had, in "olden times," been noted as the haunt of robbers and murderers.

Filled with the belief that her husband had certainly been robbed and murdered, the afflicted wife went early the next morning into Edinburgh; and upon stating the case to the chief magistrate, he immediately issued a proclamation, with a reward for detecting and apprehending the unknown delinquents. The rumor of the supposed murder was calculated to awaken strong feelings of sympathy for the widow, and abhorrence of the malefactors, and a multitude went out to search the common, expecting to find the body of the deceased. After some time thus employed, the mastiff that had followed Mirelees was found laying dead on a bed of furze, where the poor animal had crept, and bled to death from a number of deep gashes made in its body, in the same manner, and apparently with the same instrument by which the horse had been wounded. The spectacle of the dog laying weltering in its gore, naturally led to the belief that its death had been the result of an attempt to defend its master against the assassins. The search after the corpse was then carried on with renovated zeal, but without success; they could trace the blood from the spot where the stream appeared to have commenced, but the greensward showed no signs or marks of any struggle, such as might have been expected from the horrid transaction which was supposed to have so recently occurred. At such a moment, the discovery of two chairmen, quite drunk, carrying a sedan, in which was a horseman's surtout coat, that was instantly recognized as being that in which Mr. Mirelees had gone out, and much stained with blood,—and also his hat, wig, spurs, and whip, excited a burst of horror and indignation. It was no easy task, on the part of the more sober-minded, to prevent the vehement and ferocious from putting them both to death on the spot, instead of taking them into custody, and leaving their punishment to the regular course of law. What rendered the guilt of the two chairmen so apparent as almost to exclude the possibility of their being innocent was, that in the pocket of one them a large clasp-knife, stained with blood, was found, and the breadth of the blade tallied exactly with the stabs found in the body of the dead mastff.

It was a very fortunate circumstance for the chairman, that during the search of their persons, and of their sedan-chair, Lord Elches, one of the lords of the sessions, or chief judges, passed over the common, being then on his way to Edinburgh from his seat at Carberry. Seeing so many persons collected in so lonely a place, he stopped to make inquiry; and when he had heard the alarming recital, seen the slaughtered mastiff, and the bloodstained garments and bloody knife found upon the chairmen, his lordship instantly ordered the latter to be committed to prison, and strictly forbade every person using the least violence towards their person, on pain of the severest punishment that the law permitted. This admonition, and the certainty that the supposed murderers would be brought to justice, stilled the headstrong passions of the multitude, and in all probability saved two innocent men from being murdered on the spot.

The chairmen were so stupefied, as well as intoxicated, that neither the tremendous charge brought against them, nor the imminent peril of being torn to pieces by an enraged mob, had power to sober them. When they came to their senses, they ap-

peared astonished beyond measure at the heinousness of the charge, and scarcely less grieved and
terrified when they reflected upon the very suspicious appearances which attended their present
situation as prisoners, apprehended on a charge of
having robbed and murdered Mr. Mirelees, whose
blood-stained garments had been found in their possession. When the magistrates asked the prisoners
what defense, if any, they had to offer, they stated
that they had been employed to convey in their
sedan-chair a sick person to Musselburgh, where,
having received more than their fare, they spent it
along with some strangers whom they chanced to
meet with at a public house, in whose society they
had remained boozing till the next morning; and
that, as they were proceeding homewards over the
common, they there found the clothes and the bloody
knife,—circumstances which had raised such cruel
and unfounded suspicions. — This explanation,
though correct, was by no means satisfactory,
and the two prisoners were remanded, and an investigation as to the validity of their defense was
set on foot by the magistracy. The truth of the
first part of the story they told was confirmed;
namely, their having carried a sick person from
Edinburgh to Musselburgh, and also their having

received something more than their fare ; but as to the *strangers* with whom they alleged they had spent their money, and remained in company all night, although there were but few public houses on the way ; yet, whether from fear, or with sincerity, each of the landlords positively denied having seen or entertained them. The unhappy men were therefore fully committed to take their trial for murder. One of them, the father of three children, died a few days afterwards in prison; whether from prior disease, from ill treatment by the mob who met them upon the common, or of a broken heart at so horrid a charge, and no visible means of repelling it, is not stated. In consequence of this calamity, the widow and children were sent to the poor-house, overwhelmed by want, no less than by unmerited ignominy.

A diligent search was perseveringly made to find the body of the supposed murdered man, whose sorrow-stricken wife offered an additional reward of five guineas to any person who could discover where it was concealed ; but all to no purpose. It appeared upon inquiry that Mr. Mirelees had dined at Haddington, where he received twenty-five pounds ; and that, as he said, he set off for home about three o'clock in the afternoon. About half past five he called at an alehouse at Musselburgh, situated on the merge of the heath where the dead mastiff was found, and where the two chairmen declared they had picked up the garments and knife, and drank some brandy and water; but no one could trace him any further, although this place was not more than five miles distant from his own house. The surviving chairman remained in prison, prejudged by the popular voice as being guilty of the murder, and also of having in some unaccountable way concealed or destroyed the body of the man whom he stood accused of having robbed and murdered. In this state of doubt the affair remained about five weeks, when the fullest possible evidence was obtained of the innocence of the two chairmen, by the sudden and unexpected re-appearance in Edinburgh of Mr. Mirelees himself, — in perfectly good health,—not a drop of whose blood had been shed ; nor had he, as was supposed, been stopped or robbed on his way home. For as Mr. Burton, an Edinburgh tradesman, who had been purchasing goods at Sheffield, was returning to Scotland, calling to dine at an inn at Leeds in Yorkshire, as he passed through the kitchen, to his utter amazement he there saw Mr. Mirelees sitting very composedly smoking his pipe. It may well be supposed that Mr. Burton's astonishment was so great, he knew not whether to believe his own eyes, or conclude it was the ghost of Mr. Mirelees whom he thus unexpectedly beheld living, and whom he so firmly believed to have been murdered; but he was soon relieved from doubt and terror by the well-known voice of his old friend Mirelees, saying as he arose, *"Eh! Mr. Burton, how do you do?"* The latter, in almost breathless astonishment, took him by the hand, and instantly communicated all the consequences that had arisen from the hour of his disappearance,—the arrest of the two chairmen upon suspicion of having murdered him; the death of one, and the imminent peril of the other of being condemned as his murderer when brought to trial. At these communications Mirelees appeared alike shocked and surprised; and upon Mr. Burton proposing they should travel post to Edinburgh, in order to save the surviving chairman from further suffering and peril, as well as to relieve the sorrow of Mrs. Mirelees, he readily consented. Upon the arrival of Mirelees alive and well in Edinburgh, it was a matter of some difficulty to persuade his wife to approach him, so strongly was she impressed with the belief it must be his ghost. The tidings of the safe return of the man whom so

many had mourned as dead, and the wild and incoherent account he gave of the cause of his disappearance, instantly changed the current of public
sympathy, and the poor weavers became objects of
general commiseration. Finding himself an object
of suspicion and aversion, Mirelees had the hardihood to make an affidavit the day after his arrival,
of the following tenor—viz: "That soon after he
left Musselburgh, he was met on the road by two
gentlemen in a post-chase, who ordered him to stop,
and he making some resistance, they stabbed his
horse and his dog, and by force dragged him into
the carriage ; that they halted at several towns
upon the way to change horses, but would not
suffer him to come out the chaise, nor did he ever
know where he was till they told him he was at the
Black Swan at York. That they kept him confined
at that inn three days, and afterwards carried him
thence at midnight, and set him down in the midst
of a forest, and he never saw them afterwards ;—
that they did not demand his money, but treated
him with part of whatever they had for themselves."
This affidavit being published, so far was it from
answering his expectations, Mirelees found the
odium he labored under increased by the incredi-
bility of his allegations; the poor chairman was,

however, immediately liberated, and his character
fully restored. If the Chief Justice had not been
absent from Edinburgh, he would, no doubt, have
caused Mirelees to be taken up immediately on his
return ; as it was, as soon as a copy of this extraordinary affidavit reached him, his lordship issued
his warrant for the apprehending of Mirelees as an
impostor. The villain having, however, a keen
sense of the danger he was in from the contempt
and abhorrence which his person and his story
every where experienced, absconded once more,
and was seen at Campvere, a seaport in Dutch
Zeeland, in April, 1756. Knowing himself to be
out of the reach of British jurisdiction, he refused
to make any other confession. It is, however, of
little moment what his motives were for acting in so
strange and so cruel a manner; the great interest
connected with the case being the danger in which
two innocent persons stood of being condemned and
executed as robbers and murderers from the force
of circumstantial evidence.

XXXIII.

Case of Taantje.

In the anxiety of legislators to strike terror into the hearts of servants, by inflicting the most appalling punishments upon domestics who are accused of robbery or murder, much of the injustice of convicting and punishing upon circumstantial evidence, both at home and abroad, has arisen. It is scarcely possible for an accused menial to have a fair trial, so powerful is the prejudice which exists against him; and as each of the jurymen is commonly the master of more than one servant, and naturally anxious to intimidate *them* by the severity of punishment awarded to others, the court and jury might, without injustice, be described as generally feeling a stronger solicitude to prevent the acquittal of a guilty prisoner, than the erroneous condemnation of one that is innocent. When a foreigner is tried in Great Britain for murder, he is permitted to have a jury comprising half its complement of foreigners; and when a domestic servant is to be tried for murder or felony committed in the house or upon the person of a master or mistress, it would be but an act of moral justice to summon upon the jury a moiety of housekeepers who have irreproachably served fourteen years and upwards in the capacity of domestic servants. As long as this concession is wanting, a *servant* cannot be said to be tried by his *peers*. On the contrary, he is tried by a judge and a jury much too prone to take up the worst ·side of the question. If Elizabeth Fenning had been tried before a jury thus composed, it is all but impossible she could have been found guilty upon such vague and dubious evidence as was produced against her. I think it was Paley who said, in some of his essays, "that the evil of an INNOCENT person put to death upon a false charge is often more than counterbalanced by its *beneficial effect* to society, in operating as an example, and thereby *preventing* crime." A truly Turkish axiom this, and disgraceful to his memory.

It has already been observed how tenacious the criminal tribunals of the Netherlands formerly were, and probably are yet, of taking life away ; and also that circumstantial evidence was never permitted to go farther than led to the confinement of the accused during life, or until decisive evidence of guilt or innocence could be obtained. In the first ages of the Belgic republic, the number of criminals was very small, and the patience and diligence with which their rechters or judges sought into the merits of every case, was most praiseworthy and exemplary. But whenever a sentence was once pronounced, it was rigidly executed, *no pardon being ever granted.* As the usual effects of wealth and luxury became apparent, the current of justice grew turbid and impure, the laws more cruel and sanguinary, and that terrible engine of despotism, *the rack*, was resorted to in all cases where *suspicion* predominated, or where the prisoner had the misfortune to be an object of fear and hatred to private and powerful enemies, who might chance to thirst after an opportunity of sacrificing him to their resentment. As commercial wealth increased, public and private morals grew more and more polluted, and the administration of justice more and more corrupt. It was in this state of things that the condemnation of accused persons upon circumstantial evidence, and also upon confessions forced from them by torture, became an ordinary practice.

Amongst the many instances that are recorded in the annals of Belgic jurisprudence of the lamentable effects of ignominious punishments, inflicted by

virtue of sentences founded upon circumstantial
evidence alone, the case of a servant-woman, who
lived in the family of a principal inhabitant of the
city of Delft, is, perhaps, one of the most remarkable. She had lived many years in the family, and
in all that time her conduct had been irreproach-
able. It happened, however, one Sunday, when
the master, mistress, and all the household, alone
excepting this servant, had gone to a place of worship, that the house was robbed, and a small cabi⸱ t
containing jewels and gold coin to a very large
amount stolen and carried away. On the return
of her mistress, she went to deposit some trinkets
that she had worn at church in that repository, as
was her usual custom, which led to the detection
of the theft. And as the lady had taken the jewels
from the cabinet but two hours before, when the
other valuables were all safe, it proved that the
crime had been committed whilst the master,
mistress, and family were at church.

When Taantje was questioned respecting the
admission of any person into the house during
their absence, she asserted in the most positive
manner that no one had come in or gone out. She
appeared extremely affected at the incident, looked
pale, wept and trembled, all which symtoms were

construed as unequivocal marks of guilt. When further questioned, she merely repeated her first declaration, namely, that she had not opened the door to any one during their absence,—that it had not been opened,—that she had not committed the robbery, was not privy to it, and constantly ended her discourse by appealing to a just God to attest her innocence, and bring the ral criminals to punishment.

A neighbor deposed that during the time the family were at church he heard the back-door open and shut very gently, and some steps as of a person going out. These facts Taantje positively contradicted, alleging that those persons must have been deceived ; that no person could have come in, or gone out, unknown to her, and she had not the least consciousness or belief that any person had been concealed in the house.

The chief man-servant made oath that he had, the overnight, as was his usual custom, locked up the lofts or garrets, left the keys outside, and had found them in the same state in the morning. Other servants made oath of having seen the cabinet in the chamber where it usually stood when the family went to church. It was therefore concluded by the magistrates, as well as by her master and mistress,

16

that the person who had been heard to *quit* the house, during their absence at church, was a confederate of the female servant who had been left in charge ; and that, after Taantje had stolen the cabinet, it was conveyed away by an accomplice.

A Lutheran minister, who visited the family, took great pains to prevent the poor woman being sent to prison. He urged the *possibility* at least of *some* person acquainted with the habits of the family, and the plan of the house, secreting himself, and who might, however improbable it appeared to them, have committed this important robbery, wholly unknown to poor Taantje, whose whole life gave a flat contradiction to the imputation of dishonesty. The good man further argued in her favor from the known sobriety of her demeanor,—her having no lover, no followers, and scarcely any other acquaintance or associates than her fellow-servants. But all was in vain. Useless were the torrents of tears that she shed, or the supplications she uttered. To the usual place of confinement for female felons she was consigned ; and 'he judges by whom the case was heard, making up their minds that she was guilty, and being excessively fearful of *encouraging similar crimes in others*, if they failed to treat her in the most severe manner allowed by law,—condemned her to undergo the torture both ordinary and extraordinary, to wring from her the name and residence of her accomplice. Upon hearing this sentence, the poor woman fell on her knees, supplicating of God, if he saw it good she should suffer unjustly, to endow her with fortitude to meet the agony to which she was doomed, without its forcing her to make a false confession; to forgive her judges, who, she said, knew not what they did ; and to bring the real delinquent to justice, that her character might be vindicated, and her innocence of the crime imputed to her made manifest. In this her utmost distress she was attended and consoled by the benevolent minister;—he stood by her side when she was tortured, and he bore testimony to her constancy in enduring the dreadful punishment, when every joint in her body was, one by one, dislocated, and also her unremitting protestations of innocence ; but every thing was construed as emanating from obdurate wickedness, and refinement of criminality. And the miserable creature, when reduced to a state of incurable decrepitude by a cruel and speculative process, was condemned to twenty years confinement and hard labor in the house of correction at Delft.

Under all these terrible inflictions, so meek, pious, and resigned was the conduct of the innocent sufferer, that the chaplain, keepers, and medical and other visitors of the prison, were struck with admiration, so much so that a powerful opinion became formed that she *must* be innocent. And ultimately, her master, touched with sorrow and remorse, made application for a remission of the unexpired part of the term of her imprisonment, upon the ground that he believed she was innocent of the crime for which she had so cruelly suffered. He was asked if he meant to take her again into his house? to which question he replied in the affirmative; and Taantje, after many years of suffering, was once more restored to her old home;—but she was now a cripple and forced to use crutches to be able to move from one place to another. Her master made her a handsome present towards securing her an annuity for life; and the good priest who had so strongly defended her, exerted himself so successfully, that a benevolent fund was raised sufficient for her frugal support, if circum-stances should occur depriving her of her asylum in her contrite master's house, and he should neg-lect to make provision for her future support.

In this peaceful manner, grateful for the favors

her master's hand bestowed, and freely forgiving all she had suffered through his prosecution, when an event occurred which led to the detection of the real criminal, and relieved poor Taantje even from the shadow of suspicion. It happened thus:

As Taantje, pursuing her former occupation as principal housemaid, went out occasionally into the city, a place of small extent compared to Rotterdam or Amsterdam; and one day, as she was passing through the principal flesh market, a butcher tapped her on the shoulder, and said in a half whisper, and an ironical tone of voice, "*Ah! what a creature is a naked woman!*" She felt as if electrified by those words; the recollections excited by which almost overpowered poor Taantje. Her shattered limbs shook, and she had the utmost difficulty to avoid dropping down upon the pavement; for she was conscious that, as she changed her linen on the Sunday morning when her master's house was robbed, and whilst the family were at church, she had uttered that very exclamation, and never on any other occasion. She also recol lected that this individual had, that very morning, brought some minced veal;* hence it instantaneously

---

* In Holland the butchers chop meat of all kinds, if rquired, like sausage meat. It is called "*Gehaakt Vleesch.*"

struck her that this man had contrived to conceal
himself in the solders or garrets, where he had overheard her utter the words he had then repeated ;
and availing himself of her being entirely undressed,
he crept down the back-stairs, stole the cabinet from
her mistress's room, and let himself out at the back-
door, as before mentioned.

Filled with the belief that her prayer was at
length heard, poor Taantje hastened home, and
seeking her master, in a tremulous tone she related all that had occurred, and every circumstance connected with it. When he had heard the
whole she had to say, he enjoined the strictest
secresy ; and so strongly was he affected by her artless tale, and the pungent recollection of the tremendous injustice he had dealt out to his innocent and
faithful servant, that the tears trickled rapidly down
his furrowed cheeks ; and taking her by the hand,
and kneeling before her, he said he feared neither
God nor his neighbors would forgive his hardhearted-
in having persecuted her as he had done. Poor
Taantje was less able to bear this humility and contrition than she had been his pride and cruelty ;
and with a nobleness of soul that would have reflected honor on the highest station in life, she insisted on his rising, and strove to reconcile him to

himself by admitting and expatiating upon the weight of unfavorable circumstances by which she was then oppressed and borne down.

Without a moment's delay her master hastened to the house of the senior burgomaster, and communicated the singular facts he had just learned from the lips of Taantje. His opinion too was that the butcher was the robber, an idea that was strengthened by the corroborating facts, that when the robbery was committed the suspected individual was a journeyman, and in less than a year afterwards he commenced business on his own account, and had lived ever since in a more expensive manner than his trade seemed competent to support. The magistrates next made inquiries as to his relations and most intimate connections; and when every preliminary step was taken that was deemed expedient, the burgomasters and other magistrates caused the suspected person to be arrested, and his premises searched. The penitent master of poor Taantje and her fellow domestics assisted; and so suddenly was the measure executed, there was neither time nor opportunity to remove or conceal a single article. It was not, however, till after a long and laborious search they found any thing that in the least degree corroborated their suspicions. At last, under the iron hearth of the best bedroom there was found a small box containing many valuables, which were at once identified as the property of Taantje's master and mistress, and which were stolen on the Sunday morning named. And thus, at the distance of fourteen or fifteen years from the time when the robbery was committed, and when the criminal deemed himself in absolute security, his own malignity and stupidity were made the instruments of his detection and punishment. When it was known outside the house, what had occurred within, the populace would have killed the delinquent, and leveled his dwelling with the earth, but for the presence of the burgomasters and magistrates, and their solemn assurance the criminal should be brought to speedy justice. The populace exclaimed in the bitterest terms of reprobation against the master and mistress of the innocent and injured servant, and the judges by whom she had been tortured and condemned. Nor was the tumult quelled till the presiding magistrates appeared in the front of the stadthouse, and again assured the indignant citizens that prompt justice should be done to every party; and that the master and mistress of Taantje had already rendered her every atonement in their power make—had obtained her release from confinement—had supported her in a kind and comfortable manner—and assisted largely in providing for her future support. Lastly, the speedy trial and punishment of the butcher, if found guilty, was that part of the concessions to popular feeling which had the greatest effect in restoring tranquillity. As to the butcher, he evinced the utmost hardihood and callosity of heart till the concealed trinkets and jewelry were found, which he had abstained from selling, lest it should lead to his detection; for, exclusive of the jewels, he had stolen two thousand ducats in gold. When the searchers observed that the hearth-iron seemed as if it were movable, the villain was seen to turn pale; and when the dienaars* found it moved, and began to force it up from its place, the delinquent made an effort to draw his knife, apparently with the design to cut his way throught the hostile group that surrounded him thus, and make his escape, or perish in the attempt; but this effort had been foreseen and guarded against, and ere he could do any mischief, his arm was arrested, the weapon taken from him, — he was bound with strong cords, and conveyed to the strongest dungeon in the city prison amidst the groans and execrations of the populace; where,

---

* Police officers.

seeing certain death before his eyes, his cruel heart
relented, and he made the following confession, viz.

That his master served the master of Taantje with
butcher's meat for his table, which he used to carry
—that the year before the robbery took place he
had courted a servant maid, then living in the house,
through his intimacy with whom he acquired a
knowledge of the upper rooms, and of the lady's
jewels and money being kept in the cabinet he afterwards stole. The girl, he said, supposed he meant
to marry her, and he fully exonerated her from all
knowledge of, or privity to, his design of stealing
the cabinet. Some time afterwards she was discharged, and their intercouse ceased ; and then he
began to devise means of executing his design, but
never had an opportunity till the morning in question, when, having forgot to take some minced veal
home on Saturday evening, as he should have done,
he carried it in a large basket on Sunday morning.
The family were gone to church—Taantje was up
stairs, and setting the meat in the usual place, he
pretended to go directly out, and to shut the door
after him, instead of which he shut himself in, and
pulling off his shoes, crept softly up to the turf
solder or garrets, waiting for Taantje coming up to
the maid's garret to change her dress. The unsus-

pecting woman, unconscious that any human being was near her, being entirely undressed, and contemplating her naked figure, uttered the singular exclamation already noted, which, being plainly overheard by the villain in ambuscade, he immediately sallied forth, and descending by the back stairs, found the doors unlocked, and putting the cabinet into the basket, and covering it with a cloth, the streets being clear, he reached his lodgings unperceived or unnoticed. Upon opening the box, and finding how rich a booty he had obtained, he resolved to conceal the jewels, and pretending that a relation had lent him a small sum of money, to begin business, and commence trade upon his own account. He said he felt great sorrow and compunction for the sufferings of Taantje, the truth of which may be questioned, since he never offered her the least consolation or relief in the midst of her sufferings. And when a conviction of her innocence operated so powerfully in her favor as to induce a subscription in her behalf, the miscreant had not the grace to dedicate to her use any part of the ill-gotten store he had obtained at the cost of her unmerited disgrace and sufferings.

As to Taantje, her meekness and humility remained unaltered after this complete vindication of her character. Her master was so bowed down by the odium occasioned by his severe proceedings against her, which his subsequent benevolence could not remove, nor the soothing discourse of Taantje mitigate, that he retired to Utrecht with his wife and family. The delinquent was condemned to be broken alive on the wheel. According to the custom of the Dutch, his sentence was pronounced under the canopy of heaven, and not in any edifice, or under any roof; a custon derived from ages very remote, and intended to show that the judges wished their actions should be open and solemn, as if transacted in the presence of the deity. And so vivid were the recollections of Taantje of the horrible tortures she had endured, that on the day of his execution she seemed as if she was again extended on the rack, and her joints all dislocated, one by one. Next, before the highest tribunal in the state, the proceedings of the local tribunal were revised, the result of which was that the presiding judges were all removed from their stations, declared disqualified ever to act again in that awful capacity, and the city was condemned to pay the poor sufferer a considerable fine, because the magistracy had not caused the real thief to be apprehended and his premises searched, when it was proved that he had been on the premises during the absence of the family on the morning of the robbery, and due pains had not been taken to ascertain if he had not concealed himself in the house, and committed the robbery for which the female in question had been falsely accused and unjustly punished.

XXXIV.

Case of a German Boor.

AMONG cases, foreign and domestic, whose moral tendency demonstrates the cruelty and folly of trusting so far to appearances, however strong, as to take away life, or declare a man infamous, this case of a poor husbandry laborer, who about half a century since was beheaded at Haarlem, not more than ten miles distant from Amsterdam, and a city celebrated as the birth-place and residence of Laurens Coster, conveys an excellent moral. This poor man was a Westphalian boor or clown, who was pursuing his way to Amsterdam in search of more profitable labor than his own country afforded. It happened that the party of emigrants with whom he had traveled, stopped to drink at a road-side house in Haarlem wood, where he soon became so completely intoxicated that they laid him under a tree asleep, and left him to get along as he could when he became sober.

Great was his terror, and inexpressible his amazement, when, upon awaking, the poor wanderer saw about him a number of men, dressed in blue, and wearing silver-hilted swords, and hearing himself accused of having robbed and murdered a merchant; and greater still was his horror and affright on seeing that the blade and haft of his knife were besmeared with blood—that his right hand was bloody, and that in his pockets were found property which was known to have belonged to the murdered man. The terror and confusion he manifested, and which was so natural to his condition as an innocent man, were interpreted as unequivocal proofs of guilt. His protestations and supplications were alike disregarded. His country, and his poverty, combined to render him a subject of reproach and derision; for the indigent German laborers were no less subject to insult and to wrong in Holland, than the poor Irish are in England. After many months close confinement the unhappy man was condemned to die by being beheaded,* after having been put to the tor-

---

* About the year 1803, a Dutchman, by trade a pork butcher, residing near the Admiralty, in Amsterdam, murdered his wife, and then strove to conceal himself by flight He was however taken, tried, and condemned to die by the sword. When the criminal was brought upon the scaffold, he could not be induced to kneel down. with his eyes covered, and his head erect, and arms pinioned. but plunged so violently it was found impossible to behead, without first killing him. It caused no small confusion to the judges, who, in Holland, are com pelled to witness the execution of the sentences they pronounce. At

ture to make him confess his crme and his accomplices.

The probability of the assassins having found the
poor German drunk and fast asleep, of having
stained his knife and hand with blood, and put
into his pockets a part of the spoil they had taken
from the merchant they had just murdered; and
the improbability that a person capable of committing such a crime falling asleep by the highway
side, his hands and arms besmeared with blood, and
the property in his pockets, were all overlooked.
The companions of the accused appeared in his
behalf, and they proved he was dead drunk, and
neither able to stand or go when they left him in
the wood. The public prosecutor contended that he
had arisen in a state of frenzy—had robbed and
murdered the merchant, and being unable to proceed, had staggered back to the tree where they had
deposited him, and was there taken. The result was,

---

length, after the loss of half an hour's time, the executioner put a cord
round his neck, and he submitted quietly enough to be hung. A Mr.
Humphries, a well known London *collector* of books and prints, under
the signature "*Londonienis*" wrote a humoious article, which was in
serted in the Rotterdam paper, in which, having heard that the criminal was a staunch *republican*, he said, he was resolved to go out of
the world with his head on, and that he continued to the last, like the
Batavian republic, "*one and indivisible.*" It was the only capital execution that occurred in Amsterdam, a city containing 300,000 inhabit
ants, in the course of three years.

the poor man was condemned to die, and suffered death by beheading.

The fate of the poor German was forgotten, when, upon a gang of desperate robbers and murderers being detected and apprehended in Gelderland, and just as they were led out to execution, two of them confessed having committed the crime for which the poor German had suffered a wrongful death at Haarlem. The criminals, in their joint confession, stated that as they were waiting the arrival of the merchant in a herberg or inn in Haarlem wood, whom they knew would pass along near about that time, on his way from the Lemmer to Amsterdam— that they noticed the German boors, and the very drunken state of one of them whom the rest of his comrades left dead drunk under an oaken tree; that after they had murdered the traveler, and plundered his person, events which took place only a very short distance from the spot where the unfortunate German lay asleep, one of the banditti suggested the horrible expedient of staining his hands, his garments, and his knife, with the yet reeking gore of the slain; and putting into his pockets a few of the least valuable trinkets found upon him. And so hardened were those wretches, it appears they were present at his execution. On this account it is

17

said Haarlem city lost the privilege of ever more having its own executioner, a proper stigma upon the negligence and prejudice which led to the execution of an innocent person.

XXXV.

Case of a Dutch Servant Maid.

ANOTHER instance may be cited of a diabolical project, devised and executed by a vindictive lady, residing at Vlissingen, in Zealand. She had a servant girl against whom she took up so vehement a hatred that nothing less than her total destruction could appease her. Animated by this savage feeling, she found a key which opened the girl's box, into which she placed a small gold cup, some silver spoons, pieces of lace, and other articles which she could identify as her property ; and then went before the magistrates, making oath that she had lost the cup, a necklace, and other jewels, as well as some small pieces of plate, and obtained permission to search her box and person, The poor girl was thunderstruck at the accusation. Confident of her innocence of the imputed crime, she openly accused her mistress of perjury, eagerly led the police officers to the box, which she opened with short-lived ex-·ultation, for, at the bottom, and carefully folded up in her garments, various articles belonging to her mistress were found, but neither the gold cup, nor diamond ear-rings and necklace. If a huge serpent had sprung from the box and coiled itself in her bosom, the affrighted maid could not have expressed more horror; she shrieked, rather than said, "My mistress put it there—my mistress put it there—I am innocent! I am innocent!" These exclamations were, however, attributed to artifice, and she was committed to prison, tried, and condemned to be flogged on the public scaffold, brand-marked, and imprisoned twelve years in the Spin house, which sentence was rigidly executed. The excellent character of the girl, and some dark spots in the character of the mistress, coming to the ears of Ploos Van Amstel, who was, in his day, the Garrow of Amsterdam, he visited the prison, and hearing a most favorable report of the unhappy girl's conduct, he saw and spoke to her, whose firm, plausible, modest, consistent manner, impressed that celebrated lawyer with a strong belief that the mistress had acted as the prisoner declared. He therefore set confidential agents to work, to dive into her character, and he found it compatible with the girl's allegations. In the course of his researches he met with a poor char-woman, who made oath that she had seen the identical cup in the possession of the

lady, long after the punishment of the girl, and
that the prosecutrix seemed greatly confused at the
disclosure, and hastily put it out of sight. Upon
the strength of this positive testimony the public-
spirited advocate went to the presiding burgomaster
and told him his suspicions, and exhibited his
proofs, as he found a similar mistrust pevailing in
the bosom of that magistrate, and had little difficulty
in attaining the requisite authority. To prevent
any suppression of truth by bribery or other influence, the burgomaster connived at the lawyer
himself, dressed as an inferior officer of justice,
assisting in executing the measures that were resolved to be taken, in order, if possible, to detect
the cup of gold and diamond ornaments in the
possession of the prosecutrix. Whilst two parties
of police officers, each headed by a magistrate, examined the town and country house of the suspected
lady, Ploos Van Amstel proceeded to the humbler
dwelling of a female relative who subsisted upon
the bounty of the prosecutrix, and whose conduct
in bearing testimony against the prisoner, and supporting the charges urged against her, had subjected
her to many censures, and much opprobrium. The
female who had sworn she had seen a cup which
appeared to be gold, and exactly resembling the one

said to have been stolen by the prisoner, told the lawyer this female was then in the lady's house, and she thought the gold cup was more likely to be in her custody than the lady's. The police officers contrived to enter the house before they were perceived, and whilst the person of the female and her servant were secured, Ploos Van Amstel proceeded up to her bed-room; and there, in a recess formed for concealing smuggled goods, of which he had received private intelligence, he found a small box, in which were the identical cup and the jewels for stealing which the servant girl had been falsely accused and erroneously condemned, and suffered an infamous and terrible punishment. The surprise, terror, and confusion of the guilty woman in whose custody these articles were found, and whose false and suborned evidence had materially contributed to the condemnation of the accused, was excessive. She saw at one glance the abyss that yawned to swallow her, and forgetful of every thing but the hope of escaping, she arraigned the prosecutrix of having prevailed upon her to aid in her infernal projects against her servant maid.

Acting as a notary, Ploos Van Amstel took minutes of her confessions, which the magistrate witnessed, as well as the inferior officers. The magistrates then went with the dienaars, to lodge the woman in the same prison where the poor girl was confined. Ploos Van Amstel proceeded to the town house of the prosecutrix, having in his possession the golden cup, the ear-rings, and the necklace, and the written confession.

When he arrived he found, of course, that the search had been unsuccessful ; and the prosecutrix, too confident in a fallacious security, was menacing the magistrates with a prosecution for defamation, and was ordering the officers to quit her house. When she saw Ploos Van Amstel arrive, she fiercely exclaimed, "What other ruffian is come to ransack my dwelling?" "It is only Ploos Van Amstel, madame," said the magistrate, "who has been to examine a secret recess in the house of ———." In an instant, as if by the touch of magician's wand, all her arrogance vanished. and she would have falled senseless on the floor but for the humanity of the gentleman whom she had so insolently accosted. When then she opened her eyes, and recognized the well known features of that popular advocate, bearing in his hands the identical property she thought she had secured against every danger, her shrieks were piercing—her distress, indescribable —she tore her hair, threw herself at his feet, and

offered to resign half her fortune to the poor servant,
and to quit the country for ever, if she could be
exempted from public shame and punishment. But
her depravity had been so rampantly displayed, and
her conduct marked by such fiend-like cruelty, that
the lawyer soon put an end to every hope, by
ordering the officers to place her in a coach that
was waiting, and convey her to prison to be dealt
with according to law. At the same time the magistrates put their seals on the doors of the principal
apartments, and left their officers in possession of
the house. Having thus fully accomplished the
object of his search, and having obtained an order
of release for the innocent sufferer, that she might
appear as an evidence against the newly made
prisoners, the active and benevolent lawyer went
to the public prison, where dressed in the female
felon's garb, and pursuing her daily task of spinning
an allotted quantity of flax, he found the pale,
desponding, emaciated captive.

Ploos Van Amstel was too judicious to make
the injured woman at once aware of the complete
revolution that had occurred in her fortune. He
began by telling her that the detection and punishment of her cruel and merciless mistress were events
very near at hand, and subsequently her own restora-

tion to liberty and character was not only possible, but probable. She was at first incredulous; but when her deliverer assured her that he was *certain* of her complete triumph, and made her acquainted with his name and avocation, she was so violently affected as to be near fainting, and falling on her knees, her first action was to thank God that had raised her up a friend to make manifest her inno- cence. A heavy flood of tears succeeded; and when this seasonable relief of an overcharged heart had so far re-composed her agitated bosom, as to enable her to converse rationally. the jailer's wife walked in and invited the astonished sufferer to go with her into her house; and there she was requested to retire to a private room, to take off the prison dress, and put on the respectable apparel that was pro- vided for her. Scarcely knowing what she did, and dubious if the whole was not a flattering dream, and fearful she should awake, and still. find herself a wretched prisoner, she obeyed. So excessive, how- ever, was the tremor that seized her nerves, it was deemed advisable to have her blooded. When she returned, dressed as a tradesman's daughter, she was apprised of her full liberation, and of the de- tection and confinement of her proud and unrelent- ing mistress; and as a confirmation of her good fortune, her deliverer showed her the cup and the jewels she had wickedly and falsely been accused of stealing. Such was the result of the wicked machinations of a rich lady, against a poor servant girl. The city was fined in a very large sum by the States-general; and the servant maid, enriched and vindicated, became the wife of an opulent and respectable man; and the prosecutrix and her accomplice were condemned to *fifty years'* hard labor and close confinement, being the longest term of confinement allowed in Holland, from an affected abhorrence of condemning any one to perpetual incarceration.

XXXV.

Case of a Negro Murderer.

A NEGRO, who had run away from from his master in South Carolina, arrived in London in an American ship. Soon after landing, he became acquainted with a poor, honest laundress, in Wapping, who washed his linen. This poor woman usually wore two gold rings on one of her fingers, and it was said she had saved a little money, which induced this wretch to conceive the design of murdering her, and taking her property. She was a widow, and lived in an humble dwelling with her nephew. One night her nephew came home much intoxicated, and was put to bed. The negro, who was aware of the circumstance, thought this would be a favorable opportunity for executing his bloody design. Accordingly, he climbed up to the top of the house, stripped himself naked, and descended through the chimney to the apartment of the laundress, whom he murdered—not until after a severe struggle, the noise of which awoke her drunken nephew in the adjoining room, who got up and hastened to the rescue of his aunt. In the mean time the villain had cut off the finger with the rings; but before he could escape, he was grappled with by the nephew, who, being a very powerful man, though much intoxicated, very nearly overpowered him; when, by the light of the moon, which shone through the window, he discovered the complection of the villain, whom (having seldom seen a negro) he took for the devil. The murderer then disengaged himself from the grasp of the nephew, and succeeded in making his escape through the chimney. But the nephew believed, and ever afterwards delared, that it was the devil with whom he had struggled, and who had subsequently flown into the air and disappeared. The negro, in the course of the struggle, had besmeared the young man's shirt in many places with the blood of his victim; and this joined with other circumstances, induced his neighbors to consider the nephew as the murderer of his aunt. He was arrested, examined, and committed to prison, though he persisted in asserting his innocence, and told his story of the midnight visitor, which appeared not only improbable, but ridiculous in the extreme. He was tried, convicted, and executed, protesting to the last his total ignorance of the murder, and throwing it wholly on his black antagonist, whom he believed to be no other than Satan. The real murderer was not suspected, and returned to America with his little booty ; but he, after a wretched existence of ten years, on his death-bed confessed the murder, and related the particulars attending it.

XXXVI.

Case of Erroneous Execution for Murder.

A GENTLEMAN having been reveling abroad, was returning home late at night, but overcome with wine he fell down in the street, and lay there in a state of insensibility. Soon after, two persons, who were passing, having quareled, one of them, observing that the drunkard had a sword by his side, snatched it away, and with it ran his adversary through the body. Leaving the instrument sticking in his wound, he ran off as fast as he could. When the watchman of the night came in the course of his rounds to the scene of the tragedy, and saw one man laying dead, with a sword in his body, and another lying near him in a state of drunkenness, with his scabbard empty, he had no doubt whatever that the crime and the offender were both before him ; and seizing the drunkard he conveyed him to prison.

Next morning he was examined before a mag. istrate ; and being unable to remove the strong pre.

sumptious which circumstances established against him, he was committed for trial. When tried, he was found guilty, and immediately executed for the murder of which he was perfectly innocent.

The real criminal was some time after condemned to death for another offense ; and in his last moments confessed how he had made use of the reveler's sword to execute his own private wrongs.

XXXVII.

Murder of a Father.

A MAN was tried for and convicted of the murder of his own father. The evidence against him was merely circumstantial, and the principal witness was his sister. She proved that her father possessed a small income, which with his industry enabled him to live with comfort; that her brother, who was his heir at law, had often expressed a great desire to come into possession of his father's effects; and that he had long behaved in a very undutiful manner to him, wishing, as the witness believed, to put a period to his existence by uneasiness and vexation; that on the evening the murder was committed, the deceased went a short distance from the house to milk a cow he had for some time kept, and that witness also went out to spend the evening and to sleep, leaving only her brother in the house; that returning home early in the morning, and finding that her father and brother were both absent, she was much alarmed, and sent for some of the neighbors to consult with them, and to receive advice what should be done ; that in company with these neighbors she went to the hovel in which her father was accustomed to milk the cow, where they found him murdered in a most inhuman manner ; that a suspicion immediately falling on her brotner, and there being then some snow upon the ground, in which the footsteps of a human being, to and from the hovel, were observed, it was agreed to take one of her brother's shoes, and to measure therewith the impressions in the snow ; this was done, and there did not remain a doubt that the impressions were made with his shoes. Thus confirmed in their suspicions, they immediately went to the prisoner's room, and after a diligent search they found a hammer in the corner of a private drawer with several spots of blood upon it.

The circumstance of finding the deceased and the hammer, and the identity of the footsteps, as described by the former witness, were fully proved by the neighbors whom she had called ; and upon this evidence the prisoner was convicted and suffered death, but denied the act to the last.

About four years after, the sister who had been chief witness was extremely ill ; and understanding that there were no hopes of her recovery, she

18.

confessed that her father and brother having offended her, she was determined they should both
die ; and, accordingly, when the former went to
milk the cow, she followed him with her brother's
hammer and in his shoes ; that she felled her father
with the hammer, and laid it where it was afterwards found ; that she then went from home to
give a better color to the horrid transaction, and
that her brother was perfectly innocent of the crime
for which he had suffered.

She was immediately taken into custody, but
died before she could be brought to trial.

XXXVIII.

Case of Youth Betrayed.

A few years ago the green of a rich bleacher in the north of Ireland had been frequently robbed at night to a very considerable amount, notwithstanding the utmost vigilance of the proprietor and his servants to protect it, and without the slightest clue being furnished for the detection of the robber.

Effectually and repeatedly baffled by the ingenuity of the thief or thieves, the proprietor at length offered a reward of one hundred pounds for the apprehension of any person or persons de tected robbing the green.

A few days after this proclamation, the master was at midnight raised from his bed by the alarm of a faithful servant, "there was somebody with a lantern crossing the green." The master started up from his bed, and flew to the window; it was so. He hurried on his clothes, and armed himself with a pistol; the servant flew for his loaded musket, and they cautiously followed the light. The person with the lantern (a man) was, as they ap proached, on tip-toe, distinctly seen stooping and groping on the ground; he was seen lifting and tumbling the linen. The servant fired; the robber fell. The man and master now proceeded to examine the spot. The robber was dead; he was recognized to be a youth of about nineteen, who resided a few fields off. The linen was cut across; bundles of it were tied up; and upon searching and examining farther, the servant, in the presence of his master, picked up a pen-knife, with the name of the unhappy youth engraved upon the handle. The evidence was conclusive; for in the morning the lantern was acknowledged by the afflicted and implicated father of the boy to be his lantern. Defense was dumb.

The faithful servant received the hundred pounds reward, and was, besides, promoted to be the confidential overseer of the establishment.

The faithful servant, this confidential overseer, was shortly afterwards proved to have been himself the thief, and was hanged at Dundalk for the murder of the youth whom he had cruelly betrayed.

It appeared, upon the clearest evidence, and by the dying confession and description of the wretch himself, that all this circumstantial evidence was preconcerted by him, not only to screen himself from the imputation of former robberies, but to get the hundred pounds reward.

The dupe, the victim, he chose for his diabolical purpose was artless, affectionate and obliging. The boy had a favorite knife, a pen-knife, with his name engraved upon its handle. The first act of this fiend was to coax him to give him that knife as a keepsake. On the evening of the fatal day the miscreant prepared the bleach green, the theater of this melancholy tragedy, for his performance. He tore the linen from the pegs in some places, he cut it across in others; he turned it up in heaps; he tied it up in bundles as if ready to be removed, and placed the favorite knife, the keepsake, in one of the cuts he had himself made.

Matters being thus prepared, he invited the devoted youth to supper, and as the nights were dark, he told him to bring the lantern to light him home. At supper, or after, he artfully turned the conversation upon the favorite knife, which he affected with great concern to miss, and pretending that the last recollection he had of it, was using it on a particular spot of the bleach green, described the spot to the obliging boy, and begged him to see if it was there. He lit the lantern which he had been desired to bring with him to light him home, and with alacrity proceeded upon his fatal errand.

As soon as the monster saw his victim was completely in the snare, he gave the alarm, and the melancholy crime described was the result.

Could there have been possibly a stronger case of circumstantial evidence than this? The young man seemed actually caught in the act. There was the knife with his name on it; the linen cut, tied up in bundles; the lantern acknowledged by his father. The time, past midnight. The master himself present, a man of the fairest character; the servant, of unblemished reputation.

XXXIX.

Case of Martin Guerre.

MARTIN GUERRE was, at the age of eleven, married in January, 1539, to Mademoiselle Bertraude del Rols, of Artigues, of the same age. A certain provision was made for the wedded pair, and in the ninth year of their marriage a third member was added to the group, by the birth of a boy, who received the name of Sanxi.

But a cloud now gathered over the domestic sky. Martin was tempted to appropriate to his own use some wheat belonging to his father, and fearing the latter's displeasure, absented himself from home until the matter should blow over. Eight days were assigned — between Monsieur and Madame Guerre — as the probable period for this; but as many *years* actually did elapse before Martin was again seen, and during the whole of that time no token of his existence cheered his wife and child.

At length, one winter's evening, a traveler, claim- ing to be Martin, suddenly presented himself, and declared that he had returned a penitent man, re-

solved to atone by every office of affection and con-
jugal duty for the anxiety and distress he had
occasioned.

Not the least question of the visitor's being indeed Martin Guerre seems to have occurred to anybody. His own four sisters, his uncle, and every
member of his wife's family then at hand, acknowledged him without an instant's hesitation.
And no wonder ; for not only was the newly-ar
rived identical in form and feature with Guerre,
but he showed himself familiar with circumstances
which could be known only to the latter.

Madame Guerre, whose attachment to her lord
had never wavered or diminished in his absence,
received his representative with every token of the
fondest affection ; returning to her quiet wifely
habits as before, and in the period of three years
during which they lived together, presenting the
supposed Martin with two children, one of whom,
however, died in infancy.

Whether or not the wife ever suspected that
she was the victim of a daring imposture can never
be ascertained. It was deemed impossible that some
or other of those almost imperceptible yet positive
differences, that must always exist between man
and man, should not have at times awakened her

suspicions. The probability is that they did so; and that her continued acquiescence in this singular connection was the result partly of personal liking for the man who enacted his *role* of husband with a tenderness and fidelity the original did not, and partly from a conviction that, impostor as he might be, her peace and respectability would be best consulted by keeping her own counsel and his.

What circumstance prompted the first attempt to investigate the matter was not distinctly known. It was, however, at the pressing instance of Pierre Guerre, an uncle of the missing man, and other connections of the family, that Bertrande was at length induced to invoke the vengeance of the law on her pretended spouse. He was thereupon arrested, and before the Court of Rieux Bertrande accused him of falsely and treacherously personated her husband, Martin Guerre, and demanded that he should be condemned to do penance in the usual public form, should pay a fine to the king, and make compensation to herself in the sum of ten thousand livres.

The accused made an eloquent defense, maintaining stoutly his identity with Martin Guerre. He then explained the causes of his prolonged absence, giving a minute and circumstantial history

of the seven or eight years, during which he had
served as a soldier, passing afterwards into the service of the king of Spain. Consumed with the desire once more to see his wife and son, he had at
length wandered back, browned and bearded, to
the village he had left a smooth - cheeked boy.
Pierre Guerre, that very uncle who now sought his
ruin, was the first to recognize him, and only
changed in his demeanor when he—the accused—
requested an account of the moneys he had, as
agent for Martin Guerre, administered in his absence. His uncle had even attempted his life, and
it was only through the energetic interposition of
his wife that he had been protected from mortal injury.

In the severe interrogatory to which he was subjected, he replied without hesitation and with unfailing accuracy to every question of family history ;
naming the time and the place of the birth of Martin Guerre, his father, mother, brothers, and sisters, and even more distant relations ; the day,
month, and year of his own marriage ; the parties
present, or otherwise associated with the marriage ;
the dresses of the guests, and a multitude of special
incidents which occurred on that and the preceding
day. He spoke of Sanxi, his little son, and next

his departure, journeyings, the cities he had visited in France and Spain, and the acquaintance he had made there ; furnishing the names and addresses of those who could most readily confirm his narrative ; and unquestionably leaving a very strong impression in his favor on the minds of his hearers.

The testimony of his wife Bertrande corroborated all the statements of the accused, so far as they came within her knowledge ; but she positively denied his identity with her husband.

The court now ordered that an inquiry should be instituted into the conduct of Bertrande during the absence of her husband, and into the character and repute of the witnesses who so persistently pursued the accusation. The result was satisfactory.

On the resumption of the trial there were summoned no less than one hundred and fifty witnesses. Of these, *forty* declared on oath that the accused was unquestionably the long-missing Martin Guerre They had been his intimate companions in his boyhood and youth, and their conviction was strengthened by the recollection of certain marks or scars, which time had not effaced.

On the other hand, a great body of witnesses as positively declared that the accused was *not* Guerre, but one Arnaud du Tilh, called "Pansette," with whom some, at least, among them had been acquainted from the cradle. The remaining witnesses, sixty in number, affirmed that so close was the resemblance they dared not pronounce an opinion.

The court now ordered that young Sanxi Guerre should be produced and compared with his alleged father. A formal report declared that there existed no resemblance ; a second report averred that, on being compared with the sisters of Guerre, the boy's face exhibited an unmistakable likeness.

Greatly to the public surprise, the process resulted in the conviction of the accused. As Arnaud du Tilh, he was pronounced guilty of the alleged offense, and sentenced to decapitation. Appeal being made on his behalf to the parliament of Toulouse, the higher court decided that the matter had been insufficiently weighed, decreed a new trial, and ordered that Pierre Guerre and Bertrande should be successively confronted with the accused.

The confrontation, however, produced nothing, though it is recorded that the bearing of the accused, calm and confident, contrasted favorably with the downcast looks of his opponents.

Thirty new witnesses now appeared upon the

scene. Of these, ten declared him to be the true Martin Guerre, seven or eight decided in favor of Arnaud du Tilh, and the remainder refused definitely to give any opinion on the matter.

On summing up the testimony, it resulted that forty-five witnesses declared the accused to be no Martin Guerre, but Arnaud du Tilh. Among these were several who had passed years in the latter's company, while the character of these deponents sufficed to place their evidence beyond suspicion.

The principal witness was maternal uncle of Du Tilh, one Carbon Bareau, who at once recognized his nephew, and seeing him in fetters, burst into tears at witnessing the disgrace he had brought upon the family. Other witnesses had been present when Arnaud du Tilh had executed certain deeds, &c., and these instruments were produced in corroboration.

All of them agreed in describing Martin Guerre as taller and darker than the accused, slender in body and limb, round - shouldered, with a high, divided chin, pendent lower lip, and squat (*camus*) nose, having the trace of an ulcer on one cheek, and a scar on the right eyebrow. Now, Arnaud, the accused, was short and stout, having neither humpy shoulders nor squat nose. It was singular enough, however, that both the marks referred to as indicative of Martin Guerre were perceptible in the face of Arnaud.

The shoemaker of Martin Guerre deposed that the dimensions of his foot exceeded by one quarter that of the accused. Another witness alleged that Guerre was a skillful swordsman and wrestler. The accused was a novice in either art. Jean Espagnol, of Tonges, swore that the prisoner had revealed himself to him as Arnaud, but enjoining secrecy, and declaring that Martin Guerre had made over to him the whole of his possessions. Pelegrin de Liberos deposed that the accused had given him two handkerchiefs, to be delivered to Jean du Tilh, *his brother.*

Two other witnesses declared that a soldier from Rochefort, passing through Artigues, and hearing the accused called Martin Guerre, denounced him as an impostor; he himself having lately known the real Martin in Flanders, where he had lost a leg at the battle of St. Laurent, before St. Quentin. It is indicative of the wife's good faith in the process, that she had, through great difficulties, obtained a legal verification of the soldier's testimony.

Finally, numerous persons declared that Arnaud

du Tilh had from boyhood been a *mauvais sujet* of the worst description ; a drunkard, a swearer, an atheist and blasphemer ; a man, in short, "quoted and signed to do a deed of shame" such as that now imputed to him.

Such was the formidable case set up against the "claimant." Let us now hear his answer.

Nearly forty credible witnesses asserted that he was actually Martin Guerre, whom the greater part had known from infancy. Among these were his four sisters, with the husbands of two of the latter. Friends who had been present at his marriage with Bertrande de Rols confirmed their testimony ; and the housekeeper who, on the nuptial night, bore to the new-married pair the little collation, called in courtly circles *media noche*, among burgesses *reveillon*, positively identified the accused as the bridegroom.

A great number of witnesses averred that Martin Guerre had two teeth in the left lower jaw broken, a drop of extravasated blood in the left eye, the nail of the left forefinger missing, and three warts on the left hand, one being on the little finger. *All these peculiarities existed in the accused.*

It was, moreover, proved that the prisoner, on

arriving at Artigues, recognized and saluted as old
friends all those who had been intimate with
Guerre; that in conversation with his wife he recalled to her memory incidents which could have
been only known to herself and husband; and it
was stated, by way of illustration, that Madame
Guerre having mentioned that she had preserved
certain chests unopened, he desired her to fetch
from one of them a pair of white pantaloons folded
in taffeta. The garment was found as he had described.

With regard to the dissimilarity in appearance
between the men, it was urged that a very considerable change must of necessity have occurred
in Martin Guerre; nor was there anything remarkable in the slender stripling returning, after so long
an absence, a stout and sturdy man; an alteration
which, to the eye, would naturally diminish his
stature.

The want of resemblance between Sanxi Guerre
and the accused was pronounced to be of little
value. How many sons might not be classed in
the same category? The report of the soldier from
Rochefort, being but mere hearsay, could not be
accepted, the law expressly refusing credence to
such testimony.

The indifferent character attributed to Arnaud du Tilh could not affect the accused, who claimed to be another man, Martin Guerre; and it was at least in evidence that his course of life during the four years that had elapsed since his return had been without reproach.

Lastly, the marvelous accuracy with which the accused assumed and maintained the character he claimed, transcended, his supporters alleged, human ingenuity. . His acquaintance with dates, incidents, conversations, &c., &c., in the actual life of Guerre, was as inexhaustible as it was shown, by irrefragable testimony, to be correct.

Such was the conflict of reason and of evidence with which the judges of Toulouse were called upon to deal. All sources of information seemed to be now fairly exhausted. It was necessary to arrive at some conclusion; and the court were upon the very point of pronouncing the accused to be Martin Guerre, when there occurred an event so unexpected, so singularly timed, and so decisive, that the spectators may be excused for regarding it as a direct interposition of Heaven to overrule man's erring judgment, and avert a cruel wrong. The veritable husband — Martin Guerre — suddenly stumped into court, on the wooden leg described

19

by the Rochefort witness, and demanded to be heard.

Arrested and interrogated, he denounced the impostor—whose history he gave in detail—and demanded to be confronted with him. It was done; and a singular scene ensued. The accused -- Arnaud du Tilh — in his turn denounced the rival husband, boldly declaring that he was willing to be condemned if he did not on the spot convict the latter of fraud and machination.

Maintaining the same arrogant tone, he then proceeded to cross - examine the other as to certain domestic incidents which ought to be within his knowledge. The answers were delivered with hesitation ; and the impostor, if such he were, certainly displayed a more intimate acquaintance with Martin Guerre's domestic history than did that gentleman himself.

On examining the peculiar marks deposed to by the witnesses on the part of Guerre, these were found duly existing in the newly arrived man, although less apparent than in the other.

The first claimant was now withdrawn, and the second — he of the wooden leg — underwent a close interrogatory touching many domestic particulars which had not hitherto been submitted to either.

To these he replied with unfailing accuracy. But once more justice was at fault; for Martin Guerre the second, interrogated in his turn, replied with the like precision.

In despair the court now directed that the four sisters, the two brothers-in-law, and uncle of Martin Guerre, the brothers of Arnaud du Tilh, and the chief witnesses who asserted the latter to be Guerre, should appear together, and decide, once for all, which was the real man.

All obeyed excepting the brothers of Du Tilh, whom the court, with a consideration at that period somewhat rare, forbore to compel to give testimony which would probably affect the life of their relative.

The eldest sister of Guerre, who entered first, paused for an instant as if thunder-stricken ; then, bursting into tears, fell on Martin's breast, and acknowledged him to be her brother. The rest followed suit ; the witnesses hitherto most inflexibly against him passing one by one into the same view.

Last of all came Bertrande de Rols. No sooner had her eyes lit upon Guerre than, weeping and trembling, she threw herself at his feet — foot, rather — entreating pardon for having suffered herself to be betrayed by artifice into so great a fault. She laid part of the blame upon her sisters-in-law, who had so readily accepted the imposture, but more upon her own warm love for her absent husband, and that eager longing for his actual return which had contributed to the self-deceit. She averred that no sooner had she become conscious of her error than, but for the dread of God's anger, she would have concealed her grief and dishonor in the grave. In place of this she determined on revenge, and, as all the world knew, had pursued to the death the destroyer of her fame and peace.

The woman's natural manner, her beauty and her tears, sensibly affected the whole auditory, save only Martin Guerre himself. The stern reasoner declined to be moved by her passionate and soul-stirring words.

"Dry your tears, madam," he said, coldly. "They cannot and they ought not to move my pity. The example of my sisters and uncle can be no excuse for *you*. A wife must know her husband better than the very closest connections, and such an error as yours can only be made by one willfully blind. You—you alone—are answerable for what has befallen me."

The judges in vain attempted to soften the man's bitterness.

The records of this most extraordinary case do not describe what was the demeanor of the convicted impostor at the moment of discovery.

The court decreed that Arnaud du Tilh, called " Pansette," had been convicted of the several crimes of imposture, falsehood, substitution of name and person, adultery, rape, sacrilege, detention (*plagiat*),* and larceny, and condemned him to do penance before the church of Artigues, on his knees, in his shirt, with head and feet bare, a halter round his neck, and a burning taper in his hand, asking pardon of God and the king, Martin Guerre, and Bertrande de Rols, his wife ; that he should then be handed over to the common executioner, who should conduct him through the most public ways to the house of Martin Guerre, in front of which, upon a scaffold purposely prepared, he should be executed by hanging, and his body burned. All his effects were forfeited to the crown. The decree bears date September 12th, 1560.

While under condemnation in the prison at

---

* Holding possession of a person who properly belongs to another.

Artigues, Arnaud made a full confession, declaring that the imposture had first suggested itself to him on his being mistaken by intimate friends of Martin Guerre for that individual himself. From them and others he gleaned all necessary particulars of the past life and ways of the man he proposed to personate.

XL

CASE OF AN APPRENTICE.

IN the year 1723, a young man who was serving his apprenticeship in London to a master sailmaker, got leave to visit his mother, to spend the Christmas holidays. She lived a few miles beyond Deal, in Kent. He walked the journey, and on his arrival at Deal, in the evening, being much fatigued, and also troubled with a bowel complaint, he applied to the landlady of a public house, who was acquainted with his mother, for a night's lodging. Her house was full, and every bed occupied; but she told him that if he would sleep with her uncle, who had lately come ashore, and was boatswain of an Indiaman, he should be welcome. He was glad to accept the offer, and after spending the evening with his new comrade, they retired to rest. In the middle of the night he was attacked with his complaint, and wakening his bedfellow, he asked him the way to the garden. The boatswain told him to go through the kitchen; but, as he would find it difficult to open the door into the yard, the latch being out of order, he desired him to take a knife out of his pocket, with which he could raise the latch. The young man did as he was directed, and after remaining near half an hour in the yard, he returned to his bed, but was much surprised to find his companion had risen and gone. Being impatient to visit his mother and friends, he also arose before day, and pursued his journey, and arrived home at noon.

The landlady, who had been told of his intention to depart early, was not surprised; but not seeing her uncle in the morning, she went to call him. She was dreadfully shocked to find the bed stained with blood, and every inquiry after her uncle was in vain. The alarm now became general, and on further examination, marks of blood were traced from the bedroom into the street, and at intervals, down to the edge of the pier-head. Rumor was immediately busy, and suspicion fell, of course, on the young man who slept with him, that he had committed the murder, and thrown the body over the pier into the sea. A warrant was issued against him, and he was taken that evening at his mother's house. On his being examined and searched, marks of blood were discovered on his shirt and trousers, and in his pocket were a knife and a remarkable silver coin, both of which the landlady swore positively were her uncle's property, and that she saw them in his possession on the evening he retired to rest with the young man. On these strong circumstances the unfortunate youth was found guilty. He related all the above circumstances in his defence ; but as he could not account for the marks of blood on his person, unless that he got them when he returned to the bed, nor for the silver coin being in his possession, his story was not credited. The certainty of the boatswain's disappearance, and the blood at the pier, traced from his bedroom, were two evident signs of his being murdered; and even the judge was so convinced of his guilt, that he ordered the execution to take place in three days. At the fatal tree the youth declared his nnocence, and persisted in it with such affecting asseverations,

that many pitied him, though none doubted the
justness of his sentence.

The executioners of those days were not so
expert at their trade as modern ones, nor were
drops and platforms invented. The young man
was very tall ; his feet sometimes touched the
ground, and some of his friends who surrounded
the gallows contrived to give the body some support as it was suspended. After being cut down,
those friends bore it speedily away in a coffin, and
in the course of a few hours animation was restored,
and the innocent saved. When he was able to
move, his friends insisted on his quitting the country and never returning. He accordingly travelled
by night to Portsmouth, where he entered on
board a man-of-war, on the point of sailing for a
distant part of the world ; and as he changed his
name, and disguised his person, his melancholy
story never was discovered. After a few years of
service, during which his exemplary conduct was
the cause of his promotion through the lower
grades, he was at last made a master's mate, and
his ship being paid off in the West Indies, he, with a
few more of the crew, were transferred to another
man-of-war, which had just arrived short of hands
from a different station. What were his feelings

of astonishment, and then of delight and ecstasy, when almost the first person he saw on board his new ship was the identical boatswain for whose murder he had been tried, condemned, and executed, five years before! Nor was the surprise of the old boatswain much less when he heard the story.

An explanation of all the mysterious circumstances then took place. It appeared the boatswain had been bled for a pain in his side by the barber, unknown to his niece, on the day of the young man's arrival at Deal; that when the young man wakened him, and retired to the yard, he found the bandage had come off his arm during the night, and that the blood was flowing afresh. Being alarmed, he rose to go to the barber, who lived across the street, but a press-gang laid hold of him just as he left the public house. They hurried him to the pier, where their boat was waiting: a few minutes brought them on board a frigate, then underway for the East Indies, and he omitted ever writing home to account for his sudden disappearance. Thus were the chief circumstances explained by the two friends, thus strangely met. The silver coin being found in the possession of the young man, could only be explained by the conjecture,

that when the boatswain gave him the knife in the
dark, it is probable that as the coin was in the
same pocket, it stuck between the blades of the
knife, and in this manner became the strongest
proof against him.

XLI.

CASE OF A JEWELLER.

A JEWELLER, possessed of a good character and considerable wealth, having occasion, in the way of his business, to travel a considerable distance from the place of his abode, took with him a servant on whose honesty he thought he might safely rely, in order to take . care of his property, and guard his person. The trader also carried with him a considerable sum of money, and an assortment of valuable jewels, to the possession of which large property the servant was privy. It is to be supposed it was the temptation thus casually presented, which operating most powerfully on an avaricious mind, that induced him suddenly to contemplate the murder of his too confiding master. Watching an opportunity in a lonely place, he drew a pistol that was put into his hands to defend his unsuspecting master, and shot him from behind through the head: the murdered man fell from his horse, and expired without a groan. The wretch then rifled his person, and tying a heavy stone round the neck of the corpse, and dragging it to an adjacent water, threw it in. He then made off to a part of England where he supposed himself and his master were alike unknown. There he began to trade, at first in a very petty way, that his obscurity might screen him from suspicion. Assuming the appearance of a thriving man by the natural result of a successful trade, in the course of years he became a man of wealth and local consequence, and married a young woman of respectable fortune and connexions. In the further progress of a prosperous career, he was chosen common-councilman, then alderman, and lastly, mayor. In that important office he conducted himself in a becoming manner, neither overstraining the laws to reach offenders, nor relaxing them so far as to encourage crime. At this period a case occurred of so peculiar a nature, and so exactly analogous to his own, it wholly unhinged his mind, and led to his sudden debasement.

Amongst the prisoners tried on capital charges was a servant-man for the murder of this very master whom the mayor had murdered many years before. The evidence was apparently complete,—

the jury brought in a verdict of guilty. During the course of this trial the mayor appeared to be unusually disordered; he turned pale, and shook in every limb as the circumstances of the murder were recited. At length, before the recorder pronounced sentence, he rose from his seat, threw off his scarlet gown as mayor, and going to the bar or dock where the prisoner stood, spake thus to those who had sat with him on the bench:

"You see before you, gentlemen, a striking instance of the just awards of heaven. This day, after thirty years' concealment, presents to your eyes the real criminal, and not the man who stands by my side."

It was at first supposed his mind was suddenly disordered,—but, coolly and deliberately, to the amazement of all who heard him, he told his real name, place of birth, his various servitudes till engaged by Mr. ——, the jeweller; the temptation that assailed him; the murder, robbery, and disposal of his master's body, aggravating the ingratitude and cruelty of his conduct in murdering a man who had raised him from poverty and misery, and reposed unlimited confidence in him. He explained the artful manner in which he had hitherto eluded justice: "But," said he, "the mo-

ment this unhappy prisoner appeared before me,
charged with the very same crime, conscience set
before my eyes such a picture of my former guilt,
and I became so conscious of my crime, I could not
consent, by any further concealment, to pass sentence against a fellow-creature wholly innocent of
the crime. I have, therefore, for his safety, accused myself; nor can I feel any relief from the
tortures of an awakened conscience, but by requiring that this man may be discharged, and proceedings be instituted against myself instead."

The magistrates found themselves bound to
commit him to prison ; and in the due course of
law he was convicted and executed.

XLII.

CASE OF A FARMER.

MANY years since, a farmer who resided near Southam in the county of Warwick, was murdered on his return from the market held in that place. The next morning a man went to his anxious wife, and asked her if her husband had come home the preceding night. Full of terror, she answered in the negative, and expressed the most lively fears as to the cause of his absence. "Your alarm," said the visitor, "cannot equal mine. Last night, as I lay in bed, quite awake, the ghost of your husband appeared to me, pointed to several ghastly stabs in his body, told me he had been murdered by * * *, (naming the individual,) and his carcase thrown into a marl-pit." The poor woman believed all he said,—the pit was searched, the body was found, the denounced person was apprehended, committed for trial, and tried at the ensuing assizes held at Warwick. The Lord Chief-Justice Raymond presided : the same individual appeared as prosecutor, and an ignorant, credulous jury, would have found the prisoner guilty upon such vague evidence, just as rashly as the justice of peace had committed him, if the Judge had not checked them; who addressed the jury in these words : " I think, gentlemen, you seem inclined to lay more stress on the supposed evidence of an apparition than it will bear. I cannot say I give much credit to these kind of stories; but be that as it may, we have no right to follow our private opinions here. We are now in a court of law, and according to law we must proceed; and I know not of any law that requires us to give credit to the evidence of apparitions; nor yet, if it did, doth the ghost appear to give evidence. Crier," said the judge, " call in the ghost !"—The crier called the ghost by the name of the deceased three times, but to no purpose. "Gentlemen of the jury," continued the judge, "the prisoner at the bar, as you have heard by undeniable witnesses, is a man of the most unblemished character. It has not appeared in the course of this trial, or the preceding examinations, that there was any quarrel or private grudge between him and the deceased. I do believe him to be perfectly innocent; and as there is no evidence against him, either positive or circumstantial, he must be acquitted. But from many circumstances which have arisen during the trial, I do strongly suspect that the person who said he had seen the apparition was himself the murderer; in which case he might easily ascertain the pit, the stabs, &c., without any supernatural assistance. Upon such grounds of suspicion, I think myself justified in committing him to close confinement till the matter can be further inquired into." The wretch turned pale, and trembled as the judge directed his looks towards him. He was instantly seized, and the innocent prisoner released. The premises of the 'ghost-seer' were immediately searched; property belonging to the deceased was found and identified; and such other strong proofs were forthcoming, that he confessed his guilt, was tried, and executed at the following assizes.

XLIII.

CASE OF AN INNKEEPER.

ABOUT a century since, an innkeeper residing in
Oxford, not far from St. Ald's Bridge, leading to
Abingdon, had a gentleman call at his house, who
was known to be very rich, and to have, at that
time, a bag of gold coin in his travelling-bags or
portmanteau.   About midnight the wretch went
with a dark lantern and a sharp knife into his bed-
room, and creeping softly towards the bed, was
struck with horror and dismay at seeing the blood
pouring from his throat, and the gentleman writhing in the agonies of death; and on looking at his
saddle-bags, he saw they were open!   Just as the
disappointed and terrified villain was retiring, two
persons, armed with swords and pistols, rushed
into the room, having been alarmed by the groans
of the murdered man, and the noise made by the
murderer.   Seeing the landlord in that plight, they
instantly seized him; and although none of the

property was found upon his person, nor were his knife or hands bloody, he was condemned to be hung and gibbeted. Some years later, the person who had anticipated the murderous intentions of this villain was condemned to die on the gallows for another horrid crime, and prior to his death he made a full and circumstantial confession of having concealed himself in the inn, knowing this gentleman would be there; and that he cut his throat whilst he was asleep, and carried off the bag of gold. And thus, by an extraordinary chance, both those wretches died upon the gallows; but though guilty as far as intention went, yet the innkeeper, in the eye of the law, was innocent, and consequently juridically murdered on the strength of circumstantial evidence.

XLIV.

CASE OF A GERMAN VIOLIN-MAKER.

A GERMAN violin-maker, in London, intending to return home, had bought his wife a silver coffee-pot, which was left standing on the table in his chamber. Some one knocked at the door, and two Jews entered. One bespoke a violin; the other, while he was conversing, snatched up the coffee-pot, and ran. The German looked round, and missed the coffee-pot, but the other Jew said to him, "Do not be uneasy, my friend; go with me, and I will make my comrade give you back your coffee-pot. It is only some trick; he is a mad-headed fellow." The poor German went with the Jew, who brought him into a chamber, where were four other Jews, and his coffee-pot on the table. He took it, and said, "God be praised, I have found it once more." The Jews answered not a word; and the German returned home with the coffee-pot. Forthwith went the five Israelites to the justice, and swore that the German had entered their chamber and stole thereout a silver coffee-pot. A constable attended them to the German's house. The Jew said, "That is my coffee-pot." "Yes, that is yours," say the others. The German was taken into custody, and being destitute of witnesses, was hung upon the evidence of the five Jews.

XLV.

CASE OF THE ARMSTRONGS.

ABOUT the commencement of the present century there stood near the centre of a rather
extensive hamlet, not many miles distant from a
northern seaport town, a large, substantially-built,
but somewhat straggling building, known as Craig
Farm (popularly Crook Farm) House.   The farm
consisted of about one hundred acres of tolerable
arable and meadow land; and belonged to a farmer
of the name of Armstrong.   He had purchased it
about three years previously, at a sale held in pursuance of a decree of the High Court of Chancery,
for the purpose of liquidating certain costs incurred
in the suit of Craig *versus* Craig, which the said
high court had nursed so long and successfully, as
to enable the solicitor to the victorious claimant to
incarcerate his triumphant client for several years in
the Fleet, in " satisfaction " of the charges of victory
remaining due after the proceeds of the sale of Craig

Farm had been deducted from the gross total. Farmer Armstrong was married, but childless; his dame, like himself, was a native of Devonshire. They bore the character of a plodding, taciturn, morose-mannered couple; seldom leaving the farm except to attend market, and rarely seen at church or chapel, they naturally enough became objects of suspicion and dislike to the prying, gossipping villagers, to whom mystery or reserve of any kind was of course exceedingly annoying and unpleasant.

Soon after Armstrong was settled in his new purchase, another stranger arrived, and took up his abode in the best apartments of the house. The new-comer, a man of about fifty years of age, and evidently, from his dress and gait, a seafaring person, was as reserved and unsocial as his landlord. His name, or at least that which he chose to be known by, was Wilson. He had one child, a daughter, about thirteen years of age, whom he placed at a boarding-school in the adjacent town. He seldom saw her; the intercourse between the father and daughter being principally carried on through Mary Strugnell, a widow of about thirty years of age, and a native of the place. She was engaged as a servant to Mr. Wilson,

and seldom left Craig Farm except on Sunday af-
ternoons, when, if the weather was at all favorable,
she paid a visit to an aunt living in the town ;
there saw Miss Wilson ; and returned home usually
at half-past ten o'clock—later, rather than earlier.
Armstrong was occasionally absent from his home
for several days together, on business, it was
rumored, for Wilson ; and on the Sunday in the
first week of January, 1802, both he and his wife
had been away for upwards of a week, and were
not yet returned.

About a quarter past ten o'clock on that evening, the early-retiring inhabitants of the hamlet
were roused from their slumbers by a loud and
continuous knocking at the front door of Armstrong's house ; louder and louder, more and more
vehement and impatient, resounded the blows upon
the stillness of the night, till the soundest sleepers
were awakened.   Windows were hastily thrown
open, and presently numerous footsteps approached
the scene of growing hubbub.   The unwonted
noise was caused, it was found, by Farmer Armstrong, who, accompanied by his wife, was thunder-
ing vehemently upon the door with a heavy black-
thorn stick.   Still no answer was obtained.   Mrs.
Strugnell, it was supposed, had not returned from

town : but where was Mr. Wilson, who was almost always at home both day and night ?   Presently a lad called out that a white sheet or cloth of some sort was hanging out of one of the back windows. This announcement, confirming the vague apprehensions which had begun to germinate in the wise heads of the villagers, disposed them to adopt a more effectual mode of obtaining admission than knocking seemed likely to prove.   Johnson, the constable of the parish, a man of great shrewdness, at once proposed to break in the door.   Armstrong, who, as well as his wife, was deadly pale, and trembling violently, either from cold or agitation, hesitatingly consented, and crowbars being speedily procured, an entrance was forced, and in rushed a score of excited men.   Armstrong's wife, it was afterwards remembered, caught hold of her husband's arm in a hurried, frightened manner, whispered hastily in his ear, and then both followed into the house.

"Now, Farmer," cried Johnson, as soon as he had procured a light, " lead the way up-stairs."

Armstrong, who appeared to have somewhat recovered from his panic, darted at once up the staircase, followed by the whole body of rustics. On reaching the landing-place, he knocked at Mr.

Wilson's bed-room door. No answer was returned. Armstrong seemed to hesitate, but the constable at once lifted the latch ; they entered, and then a melancholy spectacle presented itself.

Wilson, completely dressed, lay extended on the floor a lifeless corpse. He had been stabbed in two places in the breast with some sharp-pointed instrument. Life was quite extinct. The window was open. On further inspection, several bundles containing many of Wilson's valuables in jewellery and plate, together with clothes, shirts, silk hand-kerchiefs, were found. The wardrobe and a secretary-bureau had been forced open. The assassins had, it seemed, been disturbed, and had hurried off by the window without their plunder. A hat was also picked up in the room, a shiny, black hat, much too small for the deceased. The constable snatched it up, and attempted to clap it on Armstrong's head, but it was not nearly large enough. This, together with the bundles, dissipated a suspicion which had been growing in Johnson's mind, and he roughly exclaimed, " You need not look so scared, farmer ; it's not you ; that's quite clear."

To this remark neither Armstrong nor his wife answered a syllable, but continued to gaze at the corpse, the bundles, and the broken locks, in bewildered terror and astonishment. Presently some one asked if anybody had seen Mrs. Strugnell ?

The question roused Armstrong, and he said, " She is not come home ; her door is locked."

" How do you know that ?" cried the constable, turning sharply round, and looking keenly in his face. . " How do you know that ?"

" Because—because," stammered Armstrong, " because she always locks it when she goes out."

" Which is her room ? "

" The next to this."

They hastened out and found the next door was fast.

"Are you there, Mrs. Strugnell ?" shouted Johnson.

There was no reply.

" She is never home till half-past ten o'clock on Sunday evenings," remarked Armstrong in a calmer voice.

" The key is in the lock on the inside," cried a young man who had been striving to peep through the key-hole.

Armstrong, it was afterwards sworn, started as if he had been shot ; and his wife again clutched his arm with the same nervous, frenzied gripe as before

"Mrs. Strugnell, are you there?" once more shouted the constable. He was answered by a low moan. In an instant the frail door was burst in, and Mrs. Strugnell was soon pulled out, apparently more dead than alive, from underneath the bed-stead, where she, in speechless consternation, lay partially concealed. Placing her in a chair, they soon succeeded—much more easily indeed than they anticipated—in restoring her to consciousness. Nervously she glanced round the rude circle of eager faces that environed her, till her eyes fell upon Armstrong and his wife, when she gave a loud shriek, and muttering, "They, they, are the murderers!" swooned, or appeared to do so, again instantly.

The accused persons, in spite of their frenzied protestations of innocence, were instantly seized and taken off to a place of security; Mrs. Strugnell was conveyed to a neighbor's close by; the house was carefully secured; and the agitated and won-dering villagers departed to their several homes, but not, I fancy, to sleep any more for that night.

The deposition made by Mrs. Strugnell at the inquest on the body was in substance as follows:

"On the afternoon in question she had, in accordance' with her usual custom, proceeded to town. She called on her aunt, and took tea with her, and afterwards went to the independent chapel. After service, she called to see Miss Wilson, but was informed that, in consequence of a severe cold, the young lady had gone to bed. She then immediately proceeded homewards, and consequently arrived at Craig Farm more than an hour before her usual time. She let herself in with her latch key, and proceeded into her bedroom. There was no light in Mr. Wilson's chamber, but she could hear him moving about in it. She was just about to go down-stairs, having put away her Sunday bonnet and shawl, when she heard a noise, as of persons entering by the back way, and walking gently across the kitchen floor. Alarmed as to who it could be, Mr. and Mrs. Armstrong not being expected home for several days, she gently closed her door and locked it. A few minutes after, she heard stealthy steps ascending the creaking stairs, and presently her door was tried, and a voice in a low, hurried whisper said, ' Mary, are you there? She was positive it was Mr. Armstrong's voice, but was too terrified to answer. Then Mrs. Armstrong—she was sure it was she—said also in a whisper, as if addressing her husband, 'She is never back at this hour.' A minute or so after

there was a tap at Mr. Wilson's door. She could
not catch what answer was made; but by Armstrong's reply she gathered that Mr. Wilson had
laid down, and did not wish to be disturbed.
He was often in the habit of lying down with
his clothes on. Armstrong said, ' I will not disturb
you, sir; I'll only just put this parcel on the table.'
There is no lock to Mr. Wilson door. Armstrong stepped into the room, and almost immediately she heard a sound as of a violent blow, followed by a deep groan, and then all was still.
She was paralyzed with horror and affright.
After a lapse of a few seconds, a voice—Mrs. Armstrong's, undoubtedly—asked in a tremulous tone,
if 'all was over?' Her husband answered, 'Yes:
but where be the keys of the writing-desk kept?
' In the little table-drawer,' was the reply. Arm-
stong then came out of the bedroom, and both
went into Mr. Wilson's sitting apartment. They
soon returned, and crept stealthily along the passage to their own bedroom on the same floor.
They then went down-stairs to the kitchen. One
of them—the woman, she had no doubt—went out
the backway, and heavy footsteps again ascended
the stairs. Almost dead with fright, she then
crawled under the bedstead, and remembered no

more till she found herself surrounded by the villagers.

In confirmation of this statement, a large clasp-knife belonging to Armstrong, and with which it was evident the murder had been perpetrated, was found in one corner of Wilson's bedroom; and a mortgage deed, for one thousand pounds on Craig Farm, the property of Wilson, and which Strugnell swore was always kept in the writing-desk in the front room, was discovered in a chest in the prisoner's sleeping-apartment, together with nearly one hundred and fifty pounds in gold, silver, and county-bank notes, although it was known that Armstrong had but a fortnight before declined a very advantageous offer of some cows he was desirous of purchasing, under the plea of being short of cash. Worse perhaps than all, a key of the back-door was found in his pocket, which not only confirmed Strugnell's evidence, but clearly demonstrated that the knocking at the door for admittance, which had roused and alarmed the hamlet, was a pure subterfuge. The conclusion, therefore, almost universally arrived at throughout the neighborhood was, that Armstrong and his wife were the guilty parties; and that the bundles, the broken locks, the sheet hanging out of the window, the shiny, black hat, were, like the knocking, mere cunning devices to mislead inquiry. The case excited great interest in the county.

The trial proceeded. The cause of the death was scientifically stated by two medical men.

Next followed the evidence as to the finding of the knife in the bedroom of the deceased; the discovery of the mortgage deed, and the large sum of money in the prisoners' sleeping apartment; the finding the key of the back-door in the male prisoner's pocket; and his demeanor and expressions on the night of the perpetration of the crime. In his cross-examination of the constable, several facts were elicited by the counsel for the prisoners. Their attorney had judiciously maintained the strictest secresy as to the nature of the defence, so that it now took the prosecution completely by surprise. The constable, in reply to questions by counsel, stated that the pockets of the deceased were empty ; that not only his purse, but a gold watch, chain, and seals, which he usually wore, had vanished, and no trace of them had as yet been discovered. Many other things were also missing. A young man of the name of Pearce, apparently a sailor, had been seen in the village once or twice in the company of Mary Strugnell; but he did not notice what sort of hat he generally wore; he had not seen Pearce since the night the crime was committed; had not sought for him.

Mary Strugnell was the next witness. She repeated her previous evidence with precision and apparent sincerity. A subtle and able cross-examination of more than two hours' duration followed; and at its conclusion, the case for the prosecution was so damaged, that a verdict of condemnation appeared to be out of the question. The salient points dwelt upon, and varied in every possible way, in this long sifting, were these:—

"What was the reason she did not return in the evening in question to her aunt's to supper as usual?"

"She did not know, except that she wished to get home."

"Did she keep company with a man of the name of Pearce?"

"She had walked out with him once or twice."

"When was the last time?"

"She did not remember."

"Did Pearce walk with her home on the night of the murder?"

"No."

"Not part of the way?"

" Yes; part of the way."

" Did Pearce sometimes wear a black, shiny hat?"

" No—yes; she did not remember."

"Where was Pearce now?"

" She didn't know."

" Had he disappeared since that Sunday evening?"

"She didn't know."

" Had she seen him since?"

" No."

" Had Mr. Wilson ever threatened to discharge her for insolence to Mrs. Armstrong?"

" Yes; but she knew he was not in earnest."

"Was not the clasp-knife that had been found always left in the kitchen for culinary purposes?"

" No—not always; generally—but not this time that Armstrong went away, she was sure."

" Mary Strugnell, you be a false sworn woman before God and man!" interrupted the male prisoner, with great violence of manner.

The outbreak of the prisoner was checked and rebuked by the judge, and the cross-examination soon afterwards closed. The jurors, having deliberated for something more than half an hour, returned into court with a verdict of " guilty " against both prisoners, accompanying it, however, with a strong recommendation to mercy!

"Mercy!" said the judge. "What for? On what ground?"

The jurors stared at each other and at the judge : they had no reason to give! The fact was, their conviction of the prisoners' guilt had been very much shaken by the cross-examination of the chief witness for the prosecution, and this recommendation was a compromise which conscience made with doubt.

The usual ridiculous formality of asking the wretched convicts what they had to urge why sentence should not be passed upon them was gone through; the judge, with unmoved feeling, put on the fatal cap; and then a new and startling light burst upon the mysterious, bewildering affair.

"Stop my lord!" exclaimed Armstrong with rough vehemence. "Hear me speak! I'll tell ye all about it; I will indeed, my lord. Quiet, Martha, I tell ye. It's I, my lord, that's guilty, not the woman. God bless ye, my lord; not the wife! Doant hurt the wife, and I'se tell ye all about it. I alone am guilty; not, the Lord be praised, of murder, but of robbery!"

"John! John!" sobbed the wife, clinging passionately to her husband, "let us die together!"

"Quiet, Martha, I tell ye! Yes, my lord, I'se tell ye all about it. I was gone away, wife and I, for more nor a week, to receive money for Mr. Wilson, on account of smuggled goods—that money, my lord, as was found in the chest. When we came home on that dreadful Sunday night, my lord, we went in the back way; and hearing a noise, 1 went up-stairs, and found poor Wilson stone-dead on the floor. I were dreadful skeared, and let drop the candle. I called to wife, and told her of it. She screamed out, and amaist fainted away. And then, my lord, all at once the devil shot it into my head to keep the money I had brought; and knowing as the keys of the desk where the mortgage writing was kept was in the bed-room, I crept back, as that false-hearted woman said, got the keys, and took the deed; and then I persuaded wife, who had been trembling in the kitchen all the while, that we had better go out quiet again, as there was nobody in the house but us—I had tried that woman's door—and we might perhaps be taken for the murderers. And so we did; and that's the downright, honest truth, my lord. I'm rightly served, but God bless you, doant hurt the woman—my wife, my lord, these thirty years. Five-and-twenty years ago, come May, which I shall never see, we buried our two children. Had they lived, I might have been a better man; but the place they left empty was soon filled up by love of cursed lucre, and that has brought me here. I deserve it; but oh, mercy, my lord! mercy, good gentlemen!"—turning from the stony features of the judge to the jury, as if they could help him—" not for me, but the wife. She be as innocent of this as a new born babe. It's I! I! scoundrel that I be, that has brought thee, Martha, to this shameful pass!" The rugged man snatched his life-companion to his breast with passionate emotion, and tears of remorse and agony streamed down his rough cheeks.

It was evident that the man had uttered the whole truth. It was apparently one of those cases in which a person liable to suspicion damages his own cause by resorting to a trick. No doubt, by his act of theft, Armstrong had been driven to an expedient which would not have been adopted by a person perfectly innocent. And thus, from one thing to another, the charge of murder had been fixed upon him and his hapless wife. The judge was quite undisturbed. Viewing the harangue of

3

Armstrong as a mere tissue of falsehood, he coolly pronounced sentence of death upon the prisoners. They were to be hanged on Monday. This was Friday.

On Monday morning a chaise-and-four drove rapidly up to the hotel, where the prosecuting lawyer was stopping, and out tumbled Johnson, the constable. His tale was soon told. On the previous evening, the landlady of the Black Swan, a road-side public-house about four miles distant from the scene of the murder, reading the name of Pearce in the report of the trial in the Sunday county paper, sent for Johnson to state that that person had on the fatal evening called and left a portmanteau in her charge, promising to call for it in an hour, but had never been there since. On opening the portmanteau, Wilson's watch, chains, and seals, and other property, were discovered in it. Instantly, for there was not a moment to spare, in company with Armstrong's counsel, the judge was sought, and with some difficulty they obtained from him a formal order to the sheriff to suspend the execution till further orders. Off the constable started, and happily arrived in time to stay the execution, and deprive the already-assembled mob of the brutal exhibition they so anxiously awaited.

On inquiring for Mary Strugnell, it was found that she had absconded on the evening of the trial. All search for her proved vain.

Five months had passed away; the fate of Armstrong and his wife was still undecided, when a message was brought to the counsel for the prosecution, from a woman said to be dying in St. Bartholomew's hospital. It was Mary Strugnell; who, when in a state of intoxication, had fallen down in front of a carriage, as she was crossing near Holborn Hill, and had both her legs broken. She was dying miserably, and had sent to make a full confession relative to Wilson's murder. Armstrong's account was perfectly correct. The deed was committed by Pearce, and they were packing up their plunder when they were startled by the unexpected return of the Armstrongs. Pearce, snatching up a bundle and a portmanteau, escaped by the window; she had not nerve enough to attempt it, and crawled back to her bed-room, where she, watching the doings of the farmer through the chinks of the partition which separated her room from the passage, concocted the story which convicted the prisoners. Pearce, thinking himself pursued, too heavily encumbered for rapid flight, left the portmanteau as described, intending to call for it in the morning, if his fears proved groundless. He, however, had not courage to risk calling again, and made the best of his way to London. He was now in Newgate under sentence of death for a burglary, accompanied by personal violence to the inmates of the dwelling he and his gang had entered and robbed. The deposition of the dying wretch was put into proper form; and the result was, after a great deal of petitioning and worrying of authorities, a full pardon for both Armstrong and his wife.

XLVI.

CASE OF GEORGE MANNERS.

A MISS LASCELLES, of Middlesex, England, formed a matrimonial engagement with one George Manners. Her elder brother, Edmund Lascelles, who acted towards her as a guardian, their parents being dead, strongly objected to the proposed union, but was either unable or unwilling to give any satisfactory reasons for his objections. His conduct towards his sister was extremely violent and harsh ; and finally, to appease him, she consented to postpone for an indefinite period the proposed marriage. All correspondence between Mr. Manners and Miss Lascelles was not, however, stopped, and they only decided to wait for a more auspicious season.

One evening, about six o'clock, Mr. Manners suddenly appeared at the residence of Miss Lascelles and her brother. Mr. Lascelles was absent ɩt the time. Mr. Manners complained bitterly that their happiness should be sacrificed to the passionate freak of the brother, and urged Miss Lascelles to leave the house, go to the residence of a relation, and there be married. The plan she willingly agreed to; but as a condition, made Mr. Manners promise to wait and make one last effort with her brother. Mr. Lascelles returned about nine o'clock, and immediately assailed his sister with insults and reproaches. At the request of Mr. Manners, she left the room, and the two men had a stormy interview, lasting about twenty minutes. Then the door opened, and Mr. Manners was heard to say:

"Good night, Mr. Lascelles, I trust our next meeting may be a different one:" and immediately afterward, Mr. Lascelles appearing to have refused to shake hands on parting, in a half laughing way—"Next time, Lascelles, I shall not ask for your hand—I shall take it."

About an hour later, Mr. Lascelles also went out, and about eleven o'clock the house was aroused by two men carrying his dead body into the kitchen, followed by George Manners with his hands and clothes dabbled with blood. Death appeared to have been caused by two instruments, a bludgeon and a knife; and what appeared most singular, the *right hand, on which was a sapphire ring, was gone.* As Mr. Manners had been heard to speak the words, "he would not ask Lascelles' hand, but take it," suspicion at once pointed to him, and he was accordingly arrested, and committed for examination.

On the inquest, the following testimony was given by James Crosby, a farm laborer:

"I had been sent into the village for some medicine for a sick beast, and was returning to the farm by the park, a little before eleven, when near the low gate I saw a man standing with his back to me. The moon was shining, and I recognized him at once for Mr. George Manners of Beckfield. When Mr. Manners saw me, he seemed much excited, and called out, 'Quick! help! Mr. Lascelles has been murdered.' I said, 'Good God! who did it?' He said, 'I don't know; I found him in the ditch; help me to carry him in.' By this time I had come up and saw Mr. Lascelles on the ground, lying on his side. I said, 'How do you know he's dead?' He said, 'I fear there's very little hope; he has bled so profusely. I am covered with blood.' I was examining the body, and as I turned it over I found that the right hand was gone. It had been cut off at the wrist. I said, 'Look here! Did

you know this ?' He spoke very low, and only said,
' How horrible !' I said, ' Let us look for the hand ;
it may be in the ditch.' He said, ' No, no ! we are
wasting time. Bring him in, and let us send for
the doctor.' I ran to the ditch, however, but could
see nothing but a pool of blood. Coming back, I
found on the ground a thick hedge-stake covered
with blood. The grass by the ditch was very much
stamped and trodden. I said, ' There has been a
desperate struggle.' He said, ' Mr. Lascelles was
a very· strong man.' I said, ' Yes ; as strong as
you, Mr. Manners. He said, ' Not quite ; very
nearly, though.' He said nothing more till we
got to the hall ; then he said, ' Who can break it
to his sister ?' I said, ' They will have to know.
It's them that killed him has brought this misery
upon them.' The low gate is a quarter of a mile,
or more, from the hall."

Miss Lascelles was also forced to testify to the
interview before mentioned, and also to the parting
words between the two men.

George Manners was fully committed to stand
his trial at the ensuing assizes.

Upon the trial the same evidence was produced,
and the jury found the accused guilty. A few days
before the time set for his execution some circum-

stances directed the search for the missing hand—which was still being prosecuted by the friends of Mr. Manners—to the cellar of a barn belonging to one Parker, a small farmer in the neighborhood; and as a reward of their diligence, the missing hand was there found, together with a rusty knife. Parker was at once arrested, and confessed his guilt. The wretched man said, that being out on the fatal night about some sick cattle, he had met Mr. Lascelles by the gate; that Lascelles had begun, as usual, to taunt him; that the opportunity of revenge was too strong, and he had murdered him. His first idea had been flight; and being unable to drag the ring from the hand which was swollen, he had cut it off, and thrown the body into the ditch. On hearing of the finding of the body, and of George Manners' position, he determined to brave it out, with what almost fatal success we have seen. He dared not sell the ring, and so buried it in his barn.

XLVII.

CASE OF ARTHUR MELLON.

MRS. MELLON was a very gay, fashionable woman, who devoted her time and thoughts to the requirements of "society." Her husband, a man of a quiet, studious temperament, found but little pleasure in the constant round of balls, fêtes, dinner parties, and all the numerous diversions of fashionable dissipation, into which his wife led him; and the usual result in such cases followed, a brief period of married life. First a coldness, which was followed by frequent quarrels. These discords were aggravated by the wife's lack of discretion and the husband's jealousy; and finally became a subject of gossip in the circle in which they moved. Suddenly Mrs. Mellon was taken sick, and died, with strong symptoms of poison. There was an inquest, and the chemists who examined the body discovered arsenic. It was easily proved that Mr. Mellon had frequently quarrelled with her, and was very jealous. That he had purchased a quantity of arsenic just before her death, and a package of arsenic was found in his desk. When she was first taken sick he insisted on nursing her himself. Every circumstance pointed strongly to Mr. Mellon as the murderer. He was found guilty by the coroner's jury, and committed to prison to be tried for his life.

Upon the trial the prosecution established such a strong case of circumstantial evidence based on the frequent quarrels between the prisoner and his deceased wife, the purchase of the arsenic, the discovery of arsenic in his desk, and his nursing of his wife to the exclusion of every one else, that conviction seemed an assured fact. The last witness called for the prosecution, was a medical gentleman, who had assisted at the examination of the body. The prisoner's counsel put the following questions :

Q. Have you ever known, or is it a matter of authentic record, that arsenic is taken in small doses as a cosmetic, to improve the complexion ?

A. It is sometimes used for that purpose.

Q. Is it also administered as a medicine for certain diseases ?

A. Yes, undoubtedly.

Q. Now, sir, is it not a fact well known to medical science, that arsenic, taken for some time in
small doses may accumulate in the system, so as to
produce violent and even fatal action ?

A. It is possible.

Q. Are there not cases of such cumulative
action ?

A. Yes.

Q. One question more. If a person in the habit
of taking arsenic, either as a medicine or a cosmetic, were to die suddenly from any cause, would
not arsenic be found in the liver and other viscera
by a chemical analysis ?

A. There is no doubt that it would.

Q. That will do, sir.

The defence called but one witness, a maid who
had waited on Mrs. Mellon, but had left her service some time before her death, and who was only
found a day before the trial.

She testified to having lived more than two
years with Mrs. Mellon ; to the uniform kindness
and affection of her husband ; and to the nature of
their domestic difficulties. She was sure that he
loved " the very ground she trod upon," and that
if he was sometimes jealous and out of temper, they always made it up ; and she was sure

that he would not have harmed her for the world.

Q. Was it within your knowledge, witness, that the deceased lady ever gave her husband any ground for jealousy?

A. No, your honor, not that ever I saw; but she was very handsome, and liked to be admired.

Q. Witness, you say she was very handsome. Did your mistress ever take anything for her complexion?

A. Yes, sir; sure an' she did often.

Q. Do you know what it was?

A. It was a white powder, like.

Q. A white powder that she rubbed on her skin?

A. No, your honor; it was a powder that she swallowed.

Q. What did she call it?

A. I never heard any name for it.

Q. How do you know that she took it for her complexion, and not as a medicine for some disease?

A. Because she told me in a joking way, that if I would take some, it would make me as white and pretty as she was.

Q. Where did she keep this white powder?

A. In a little drawer of her writing desk.

Q. Is that writing desk portable, **witness?** inquired the judge.

A. Is it what, your lordship?

Q. Can it be brought into court?

A. Aisily enough, your lordship.

Q. The court will take a recess while this desk is produced.

Two officers went with the witness and returned with the writing-desk, in an inner and concealed drawer of which was discovered an ounce glass-stoppered bottle, about a third full of a white powder. It was identified as the bottle from which Mrs. Mellon took her cosmetic; and a chemist pronounced it to be ARSENIC.

The jury did not require the eloquence of counsel nor the judge's luminous charge to bring in a verdict of " *Not guilty.*"

XLVIII.

CASE OF BOYNTON.

A YOUNG man named Boynton had been for some days staying at the house of a friend on a plantation on the Mississippi River. One morning the deceased, the master of the house, was found murdered in a rice break; by his side was seen Boynton's pistols, and in Boynton's hat, in the room where he was then sleeping, was found a paper which was known to have been a short time before in the pocket of the deceased. On this evidence Boynton was convicted and executed; persisting, to the end, in his ignorance of the perpetrator of the murder, and breaking wildly from the sheriff, when the hour of execution arrived, proclaiming his innocence with an earnestness that shook the confidence of the bystanders in his guilt.

Not many months after, a man who had been prowling about the neighborhood at the time, was

arrested, tried, and sentenced in another State for
a murder, subsequently occurring; and when on
the gallows, he confessed that he had been the
perpetrator of the murder for which Boynton had
suffered; that he had taken the pistols from Boynton's pillow, and had in return placed a paper from
the dead man's pocket in Boynton's hat.

XLIX.

CASE OF A BOOKBINDER.

IN 1694 a few copies of a libel entitled the "Ghost of M. Scarron," were circulated in Paris and Versailles. The pamphlet was adorned with an engraving which parodied the monument raised by Marshal Lafeuillade, on the Place des Victoires, to the glory of his master. Instead of having four statues chained at his feet, the King was represented chained between four women; La Vallière, Fontanges, Montespan, and Maintenon.

It was among the princes of the blood and at the court that the "old woman," as the Palatine Princess called her, had most enemies. This hatred defeated the vigilance of the police; before the prefect, M. de la Reynie, knew of the existence of the work, the King found a copy under his napkin at breakfast, and Madame de Maintenon received another copy at the same time and in the same way. This outrage, inflicted, as it were, in the

4

midst of his palace, exasperated Louis XIV.
M. de la Reynie, the prefect of police was immediately called to Versailles; the King bitterly
upbraided him for what he called his guilty indif-
ference, and ordered him to discover the authors
of the libel and to punish them without pity.

Either the persons who had given cause for
royal anger were very powerful and clever, or the
means of action of a lieutenant of police were limited, for the best agents of M. de la Reynie were
unsuccessful. Still the King was as angry as ever;
he even seemed as vexed at the failure of his
agents as at the insult, and whenever he saw the
lieutenant he did not spare his reproaches to that
unfortunate official.

At length chance smiled on M. de la Reynie,
who saw his disgrace fast drawing near. One
morning he was carelessly listening to the complaint of an artisan, from whose dwelling 5,000
livres had been stolen the day before. The poor
fellow obviously took the lieutenant for Providence
itself, and, supposing that he could get his money
restored, he was loud in his lamentations. While
he was speaking, the secretary of the lieutenant
entered and hurriedly handed a letter to this magistrate, begging him to read it at once. The lieu-

tenant had scarcely glanced at the paper than he jumped in his arm-chair with every sign of strong excitement. At his bidding the secretary went in quest of a police officer, while M. de la Reynie was feverishly writing a few lines on a piece of parchment bearing the seal of the State.

His emotion was so great that he altogether forgot the presence of a third party; and he did not notice that the despoiled artisan, who was standing within a yard of him, could read every word he was writing. The man was looking on with the candid confidence of one who is so convinced of the importance of his business that he cannot doubt but that the magistrate is engrossed by it; but the secretary, who had returned with an officer, roughly pulled him back.

M. de la Reynie looked up, and appeared disagreeably surprised by the presence of the artisan.

"Write down your name," said he, in a harsh voice; "your affair shall be seen to."

Profound astonishment appeared on the face of the man; he hesitated for a few seconds, went to the table, took up a piece of paper and a pen, and then turning round: "Allow me to observe, monseigneur," said he, "that I have had the honor to acquaint you with my name and occupation; and

further, that you remembered my words so well
that I was marvelling at the strength of your
memory when, a moment ago, I saw you writing
my name down as correctly as I could do."

M. de la Reynie bit his lip, and made a sign to
his secretary to draw closer to the artisan.

"Your name is Jean Larcher," said he to the
latter.

"It is, monseigneur."

"You are a bookbinder of the Rue des Lions-
Saint-Paul."

"Moseigneur is quite right," answered poor Jean
Larcher, who was smiling, while he crumpled in
his fingers the piece of paper he was about to write
upon.

M. de la Reynie was smiling also, although in a
different way. He took the police officer aside,
whispered a few words in his ear, and then intro-
ducing him to the bookbinder : "This gentleman,"
said he, "will accompany you to your house ; he
will do all in his power to discover your thief, and
we shall take care that you meet with such justice
as is due to you."

The lieutenant laid stress on these last words,
and the bookbinder, astounded at meeting with so
gracious a reception from a high magistrate, could

hardly find words to express his thanks and gratitude. He left the residence of the lieutenant of police without any other apparent escort than that obligingly tendered by M. de la Reynie. On the way the police officer questioned the bookbinder, who furnished him with all the information he had already given to the lieutenant, not omitting to give the topography of his house, concerning which his companion seemed particularly interested. Master Jean Larcher was overjoyed at the great attention shown by M. de la Reynie's man : he did not doubt but that his five thousand livres would soon be returned to him, and he insisted on regaling his companion with the best wine they could procure in a wine shop.

After this halt they went in the direction of the Rue des Lions-Saint-Paul. Soldiers and policemen were standing around the bookbinder's house. The good man manifested more satisfaction than surprise at this military display. He observed to his companion that if his house had been as well guarded on the preceding night, so many good people would not have to be troubled now. The house inhabited by Larcher was narrow, but rather deep. It consisted of a ground floor composed of two rooms, one on the street side which was used as a shop and a dining-room, the other being a workshop. An alley led to a staircase which communicated with the first floor, composed of two more rooms. One of these was Master Larcher's bedroom : the other contained the books and papers reserved for binding. To this last room the police officer asked to be taken. But while Larcher was showing the cupboard wherein his money had been secreted, M. de la Reynie's man took quite another direction, and climbing up to the top of another cupboard, he brought down a small bundle of pamphlets upon which a com-missaire, who suddenly turned up, pounced like a vulture.

Master Larcher, greatly astonished that so much attention should be given to what appeared to him of no import concerning his own business, was pulling the officer by the sleeve to show him how the cupboard had been forced open. But this last gentleman's manners toward him had considerably changed; he hardly listened to the man who, a few moments before, was treated by him as an intimate friend.

However, the commissaire began to question the bookbinder. He showed him the pamphlets, and asked if they were his property.

In his impatience, Master Larcher answered with some rashness that all that was in the house belonged to nim or to his clients. The commissaire then untied the bundle, took a copy of the pamphlet, thrust it under Larcher's eyes, and asked where it came from.

When he read the title of the pamphlet, 'M. Scarron's Ghost,' of which he as well as others, had heard, he turned white, trembled, took his head in his hands, and for a few moments remained quite stupefied. He, however, recovered his powers of speech, and swore that he had no knowledge of the presence of the fatal pamphlets in his shop, and that he now saw them for the first time. M. de la Reynie's people shrugged their shoulders disdainfully. In vain did he repeat his assertions and try to exculpate himself by reminding them that he himself had brought the police to his house with the calmness of a faultless conscience. The officers told him he could explain himself before his judges; and they prepared to take him away.

In a corner of the apartment, Jean Larcher's wife, concealing her face in her apron, was weeping and giving every token of violent grief. As Larcher was crossing the threshold, he begged the officer with whom he had been at first on friendly terms, to allow him to say farewell to the woman he hardly hoped to see again. Hardened as he was, the policeman could not refuse this slight favor; he signed his men to relent, and the unfortunate husband exclaimed, " Marian, Marian !" But Madame Larcher's sobs became more violent, and she did not seem to hear her husband's call. Those who stood around her pushed her towards the prisoner; she hesitated, and then rushing into Larcher's arms she embraced him with many demonstrations of grief and tenderness.

Jean Larcher appeared alone at the bar. He was tortured three times, and he suffered with more firmness than might have been expected of a poor man already advanced in years. He constantly refused to name his accomplices. When questioned, he said that the death of one innocent man was enough for his judges, and that he had no wish that, through him, the latter should have to answer for more blood.

Sentenced to be hanged, he was led to the gibbet on Friday, November 19, 1694, at six o'clock in the evening. He was seated in a cart with a man named Rambult, a printer of Lyons, convicted of a similar crime. Larcher was fidgety, and seemed filled with thoughts not relating to his approaching end. He however behaved with courage, and died protesting his innocence.

Before dying he earnestly begged Sanson the executioner to take a scapulary he had, and to give it to his son if he claimed it. Some years after, Sanson had an opportunity of accomplishing the poor man's wish. It led to a fearful tragedy, and at the same time to the demonstration of the bookbinder's innocence. The scapulary contained the name of a man who was Master Jean Larcher's assistant. Nicolas Larcher, the son, who had been in England, discovered that his mother had, immediately after the execution, married the man designated by his father as a culprit. Seized with frenzy, he broke into their house in the dead of the night, and murdered both his mother, who confessed her crime, and her second husband. The young man was arrested, but died in prison of brain fever.

L.

THE CASE OF JESSIE M'LACHLAN.

MR. JOHN FLEMING, an accountant, had a house
at No. 17, Sandyford Place, Glasgow. He had
also a cottage at Dun.on, where his family passed
the summer, and where he was in the habit of
staying from Friday till Monday. Jessie M'Lachlan, the prisoner, had been in his service some
years before the occurrence in question, but at the
time of the murder was living with her husband, a
sailor, in Glasgow. On Friday, July 4th, 1862,
Mr. Fleming went to Dunoon with his son, leaving
at his house in Glasgow his father, Mr. James
Fleming, a man of eighty-seven, but still active
enough to collect rents, and able to read without
spectacles, and his servant Jessie M'Pherson, a
woman of thirty-five. On the Monday afternoon,
Mr. John Fleming and his son returned to Sandyford Place. When they went in, they found the
old man in the passage, and the son said some-

thing to him about some meat which he had sent in for dinner. The old man answered, " There's no use sending anything in for dinner, as the servant has run off, and there's no one to cook it." He also told his grandson that her door was locked. Upon this, Mr. John Fleming went down-stairs, found the servant's door locked, and opened it with a key belonging to the pantry. In the room he found the dead body of Jessie M'Pherson, and went at once for the doctors and the police, leaving everything as he found it. The state of the room and of the body were minutely described by Mr. Fleming, Dr. Watson, Dr. Joseph Fleming, and Dr. M'Leod, and by the police officers M'Call and Campbell. The result of their evidence is as follows:

The room was on the same floor as the kitchen, and had two windows looking out into the area. When the door was opened the blinds were down and half the shutters shut. The bed stood with its side against the wall, the foot towards the door, and the head towards the window. The body was lying at the foot of the bed, with the feet towards the window, and the head in a slanting direction towards the door. It was naked from the small of the back downwards. On the upper part of the

body were a shift and a woollen shift, and over it
had been thrown a dark cloth or shawl. It had
upon various parts, as many as forty wounds, both
cuts and bruises, of every variety of importance.
The most serious wound was behind the right ear,
where the great vessels of the neck were destroyed,
and the skull was much injured. There were besides this wounds which divided the bridge of the
nose. On the scalp and forehead there were
wounds which divided the flesh and passed into,
but not through, the skull ; and there were many
other cuts of less importance on the hands, arms,
and other parts of the body. They appeared to
have been inflicted with an instrument edged but
blunt, and their depth showed that they were not
given by a strong person, but either by a woman
or a weak man. The jawbone, however, was cut
through in two places, which would require considerable force. The bedclothes were disarranged,
and stained in places with blood ; and a sheet
which had been washed, and was marked with
blood, was found rolled up in a corner of the room.
The pillows, also, were bloody. It was suggested,
as an inference from these circumstances, that the
bed had been slept in. Opposite the bed, and
near the fireplace, were three bloody footprints of

the left foot. They appeared to be prints of a small, naked foot, with a high instep. There was also a basin behind the door, containing some bloody water.

Along the lobby from the kitchen to the bed-room there was a mark, described by Dr. M'Leod as a trail, which looked as if it had been rubbed over but not washed. In the kitchen itself were what he and Dr. Fleming described as " evidence of a severe conflict." The floor, which was made of a blue stone, had been partially washed, and in the washed part stains remained, which were apparently blood-stains. There were also impressions, "which," said Dr. M'Leod, " I was then convinced, and am now convinced, had been confused footmarks. If I might be allowed to express what I mean by footmarks, I may state they were a sort of twists of portions of the heels upon the floor, with the ball of the foot in other cases marked also upon the stone. There were also marks of blood on many other parts of the kitchen and other places adjacent to it. In a drawer in the kitchen was found a cleaver with marks of blood on it. The cleaver might have produced the injuries found on the body. From all these facts, the medical witnesses, who, by the Scotch law, are

allowed to state inferences in their report, inferred
that the deceased had been murdered, probably
within three days, by some instrument like a
cleaver ; that there had been a struggle, and that
most of the wounds had been inflicted whilst the
deceased was lying prostrate, by a female or a
weak man standing over her ; and that the body
had been drawn along the lobby to the room in
which it was found, the face downwards, and the
legs dragging along the ground. On searching
the house, nothing was found to throw light upon
the subject ; but some silver and a quantity of
plated articles were missed.

Such being the *corpus delicti*, the next question
was, Who had committed the crime? The prose-
cutors, of course, maintained that the prisoner was
the guilty person. She not merely denied her
guilt, but pleaded specially, in a manner which the
Scotch criminal law apparently admits, though it is
unknown to our own system, that old Mr. Fleming
had committed the murder. The evidence on the
part of the prosecution was to the following effect :
—Old Mr. Fleming, according to his own account,
returned to Sandyford Place, after a walk, about
eight o'clock on the Friday evening. He had his
tea in the kitchen with the deceased, choosing to

sit there because there was no other fire in the house. He stayed by the kitchen fire till about half-past nine, and then went to bed. At four in the morning he " was waukened wi' a lood sqeel; efter that followed ither twa sqeels—no sae lood as the ither; but it was a verra odd kind of sqeel I heard." " All was by i' the coorse of a minute's time." He jumped out of bed looking at his watch, saw that it was just four A.M., and, hearing nothing more, went to bed, and stayed there till he rose at about nine. He then went down, and being surprised at not having seen the servant, who generally brought him porridge before he got up, knocked at her door three times, and tried it, but got no answer. As he went to the door, he found a passage window into the area standing open, and closed it. He gave a minute account of the way in which he passed the Saturday, Sunday, and Monday morning, till his son arrived, mentioning the persons who called, and the places to which he went. If this evidence were true, it would follow that the murder was committed at about four o'clock on the Saturday morning, the time when he heard the cries.

As it was the case for the prisoner, that Fleming had himself committed the murder, he was cross-examined at great length, in order to bring out facts suspicious in themselves, or assertions which could be contradicted by others. The first point to which the prisoner's counsel addressed themselves was the old man's statement, that he had lain in bed till nine. He was at first confident in the correctness of this statement, and added that the first person who came to the house on the Saturday was the servant at the next house, who wanted to borrow a spade. But after a great deal of questioning, in the course of which he appears to have become much confused, he admitted that a man came with milk between eight and nine, that he refused to take any in, and that the door-chain was not up. He was then pressed to give a reason why he did not let the servant open the door, the obvious suggestion being that he then knew that she was dead. His answer was that he had been over the house just before the milkman called, and, finding no one, naturally answered the door on hearing a knock. Both the milkman and his boy (called as witnesses for the prisoner) said they called at about 7.45, and the boy added that he saw the old man dressed, and that he took the chain off when he spoke to him. Thus, the contradiction resolved itself entirely into a mistake about time, and a defect of memory about the chain. If the old man got up earlier than he thought, the whole thing came to nothing.

He was further pressed to explain why he did not get up when he heard the cries. His answer was, because they stopped. He said that he did not send for the police in the morning because it did not occur to him. " I was looking for her back every other minute, always expecting that she had gone away with some of her friends. I thought she would come back. It never occurred to me trouble, or murder, or anything of the kind." . .

. . " I looked for her always coming back, and thought that if there had been anything,—drink, or anything—going, that she might have been enticed out with friends, yet she would be back." No other evidence whatever against old Fleming, and nothing that could even attract suspicion, was discovered in any other part of the inquiry. One or two trifling circumstances were brought forward, but they were so slight that they proved nothing except the closeness of the scrutiny to which the matter had been subjected. A bag was found in old Fleming's room, which had a small mark of blood upon it; but the mark was a very small one, and might have been caused by any trifling acci

dent. There was also a little blood on one or two
of his shirts; but the same observation applied to
them. Two or three witnesses, called for the prisoner, deposed to having heard the deceased use
expressions which, it was suggested, implied that
she had some cause to complain of his conduct.
Mary M'Pherson said that Jessie M'Pherson had
told her that "her heart was broken with the
old man. He was so inquisitive that the door-bell
never could ring but he had to know who it was."
A Mrs. Smith said that she asked Jessie M'Pherson
how she was in Fleming's family? She said, "I
don't feel very happy or comfortable; for Fleming
is just an old wretch—an old devil." She added,
"I cannot tell you the cause, because Sandy"
(Mrs. Smith's husband) "is with you." Whether
"the cause" meant the cause of Fleming's being
an old wretch, or the cause of her looking ill, on
which Mrs. Smith had made a remark, does not
appear. Another witness, Elizabeth Brownlie,
spoke of Jessie M'Pherson having observed that
the old man remarked everything, and said that
she spoke of him on one occasion as "the old
devil." That he was rather too inquisitive about
her proceedings appears to have been the only
definite complaint she made of him. All this,

which, in an English court, could not have been given in evidence, is a long way from the point, and far too minute to build any inference upon in a matter of such importance.

Such was the evidence as it affected Fleming. If his evidence were believed, it proved, as against the prisoner, that the murder was committed by some other person than himself, at four on the Saturday morning. The great point was to show that the prisoner was that person. When apprehended, she was, according to the Scotch practice, examined at length before the sheriff substitute. She said that she last saw Jessie M'Pherson on the 28th June (a week before the murder); that she was not in or near Fleming's house on the 4th July; that on that evening she went out with a Mrs. Fraser, and came home and let herself in by a latch-key at about a quarter-past eleven. On the stairs one John M'Donald met her. She then went to bed with her child. When she got up she went out for some coals; and when she came back she found that a Mrs. Campbell, who lodged in the house, had dressed her child in her absence. The greater part of this was contradicted by Mrs. Campbell, her fellow-lodger. She said that she saw the prisoner dressed to go out about ten; that

when she was dressed, Mrs. Fraser came in, and
shortly afterwards she heard the outer door shut.
She then went to bed, and lay awake some time,
to be ready to let in M'Donald, the lodger, and
also Mrs. M'Lachlan.   M'Donald (at the time of
the trial in the East Indies) came in about eleven,
but the witness saw nothing of Mrs. M'Lachlan till
nine in the morning.   She woke at half past five,
heard the child crying, found it in bed alone, and
dressed it.   It afterwards fell asleep, and she put
it into the bed again.   She said there was no latch-
key (check-key the witness called it), and never
had been one, and that in consequence she and the
prisoner had to let each other in.   Upon the matter of the latch-key the witness was confirmed by a
Mrs. Black, who proved that on the Saturday the
prisoner asked her, amongst other things, to "call
at a smith's to get a check-key sorted for her front
door."   About five in the afternoon she asked a
Mrs. Adams to come in at nine or ten to look after
her child, as she was going to see Jessie.   Mrs.
Adams said, "I asked her why she went so late?
She said then that it was the time she has got
alone, as the old man went to bed about that time."
It thus appears that the whole of her statement as
to where she was on the night of the crime was

proved to be false, and that on that night she was absent from home, and that she intended to go and see the deceased.

The next point was of the greatest importance. In her declaration before the sheriff, the prisoner said that on the Friday evening, about a quarter-past eight, old Fleming brought a parcel to her house containing plate, which he directed her to pawn in the name of M'Kay or M'Donald. She was to raise 3*l.* 10*s.* on the plate, or more if she could get it. Fleming said that he wanted some money to go to the Highlands. She accordingly went on the Saturday, in the middle of the day, to a pawnbroker, named Lundie, and borrowed from him 6*l.* 15*s.* on the plate, which she pledged in the name of M'Donald, as suggested by old Fleming. At a quarter to three old Fleming called at her house for the money, and on receiving it offered her 5*l.* for having done the errand. She refused, but took 4*l.* in notes given by the pawnbroker, with which she paid her rent to a Mr. Caldwell. She added, that at that time she had in the house 5*l.* 10*s.* of her own, being the re-mainder of a sum of 11*l.* 10*s.* given her by her brother some time before. It was true that she pledged the plate at the time, and place, and for

the amount stated; but James Fleming denied
totally that part of the evidence which related to
him, and several very strong observations occur
upon it.   If he had intended to steal his son's plate,
there could be no possible reason why he should
make Mrs. M'Lachlan an accomplice.   He had
every opportunity of pledging or disposing of it
by himself, if he were so inclined.   There was no
proof at all that he wanted to go to the Highlands.
If he had, he would not have given the woman 4*l.*
out of 6*l.* 15*s.*, for such a service as pledging the
plate; and besides, he had at the time no less than
180*l.* of his own in two banks—150*l.* in one, and
30*l.* in the other; this was proved by the bankers'
clerks.   It is incredible that under such circumstances he should act in the manner described by
the prisoner.   There was also strong evidence to
show that the prisoner's circumstances at the time
in question were not as she represented them to be.
It was true that her means were good for a person in her station in life.   Her husband made 30*s.*
a week, and they had only one child, and her
brother was in the habit of giving her money after
every voyage that he made; but notwithstanding
this, a Mrs. Adams proved that on the forenoon of
the Friday the prisoner sent her to pawn a look-

ing-glass for 6*s*., with which she was to take a cloak out of pawn. This was done, and it is hardly likely that it would have been done if she had had 5*l*. 10*s*. in ready money in the house at the time. Mrs. Adams also proved that on the Saturday the prisoner sent her to another pawnbroker's (Clark's) to get her husband's clothes out of pawn, and gave her 2*l*. for that purpose, of which she paid 1*l*. 16*s*. 6*d*.; and that on the Monday she sent her again to Clark's for other clothes, with 16*s*., of which she paid 15*s*. 9*d*. She also paid her rent, or part of it (it is not stated which, but 4*l*. 19*s*. was due,) to a Mr. Railton, on the Saturday, between eleven and twelve. Mr. Railton was sure of the time, because he had to go to the Royal Bank before twelve, and it was paid before he went to the Royal Bank. The result is, that before the Saturday morning her husband's clothes and other articles were in pawn; her own cloak was in pawn, and she had to raise money on a looking-glass to redeem the cloak; and she owed nearly 5*l*. for rent, for which application (though not pressing application) had been made. On the Saturday she took all the things out of pawn, and paid the rent nearly three hours before the time when, according to her statement, old Fleming gave her the 4*l*. She thus

paid in the course of the Saturday morning either
7*l*. 11*s*. 3*d*. or 6*l*. 12*s*. 3*d*., according as she paid
the whole or only part of the rent, at a time when,
according to her own account, she had only 5*l*. 10*s*.
in the house. It is hardly possible to draw from
all this any other inference than that she was almost destitute on the Friday, stole the plate on the
Friday night, and pawned it for her own use on
the Saturday. If this be true, it is all but conclusive, especially when it is taken in conjunction with
the incredible story about old Fleming.

The evidence, however, goes much beyond this.
On the Saturday the prisoner bought a tin box,
which she brought away from the shop on the
following Tuesday, and which appears, from the
evidence of a great number of witnesses through
whose hands it passed, to have been taken to Ayr
first, and afterwards to have been brought by the
prisoner's husband to Greenock, to the house of
Mrs. Reid, his sister. It contained several dresses.
which were identified as the property of Jessie
M'Pherson, by persons who were well acquainted
with them. The prisoner's account of the matter
was that Jessie M'Pherson sent her these dresses
on the Friday; some to be mended, and others
to be dyed. But when she heard of the murder

she felt frightened at having the property in her possession, and sent them down first to a Mrs. Darnley, at Ayr, and then by her husband to her sister-in-law, at Greenock, that they might be out of the way. She added that, when her husband heard of her having the clothes, he wished her to go to the procurator-fiscal on the subject, but she was frightened. The whole of this story is highly improbable, though, from the nature of the case, it could not be contradicted by independent evidence. It involves an admission that she had the clothes of the murdered woman in her possession and tried to conceal them.

Besides the evidence as to the clothes of the deceased woman, important evidence was given as to the condition of the clothes of the prisoner. On the Saturday she sent a girl named Sarah Adams (the daughter of the woman who took the goods out of pawn) to the Glasgow station of the Hamilton Railway with a box, which was to be sent to Hamilton, and was sent to Hamilton accordingly, addressed to Mrs. Bain to be left till called for. On the following Tuesday or Wednesday the prisoner called at the Hamilton station, and took the box away in her own name. She then went to the house of a friend named Chassels,

remained there for some time, had some tea, and
left the house carrying a bundle, which was probably composed of the contents of the box, as she
got Mrs. Chassels' son to take the box itself, which
was empty, to a saddler's to be mended. She was
seen shortly afterwards by some other witnesses
carrying a bundle, on the road to a place called
Meikleairnock; and a little girl, called Margaret
Gibson, pointed out to her a place called Tommylin Park where she could get some water to drink.
She saw her go in the direction of the park. In
the afternoon a little boy, a younger son of Mrs.
Chassels, met her returning into Hamilton. He
did not see that she was carrying anything, but
she gave him a handkerchief, which she said she
had picked up, and which was like the one in
which the bundle had been wrapped. On the
Sunday, Margaret Gibson was in the Tommylin
Park, and saw some flannel clothing "thrust in at
the root of the edge." She pulled it out, and
found it all over blood. She was frightened and
ran away, but came back on the Monday with
another girl, called Marion Fairlee. She afterwards found some wincey and a number of pieces
of coburg. A flannel petticoat was also found in
the neighborhood. These articles were identified

by Mrs. Adams as part of the prisoner's clothes. She knew the petticoat from having washed it.

The prisoner's account of the transaction was that she went down to Hamilton to see a friend whose name (she had been lately married) she believed to be Bain, but whom she could not find. She did not explain why she took clothes with her, though she owned she did take clothes, but not those that were found. She also denied giving the handkerchief to young Chassels. It is superfluous to point out the lame and unsatisfactory character of this account. It is, indeed, no account at all.

There was a further point about the prisoner's dress. She had a brown merino dress which had flounces. Jessie M'Pherson also had a brown merino dress which had no flounces. On the Saturday, when Mrs. Rainy got the prisoner's own brown merino dress out of pawn, the prisoner had on another brown merino dress which she took off, saying she would have it dyed black, and putting on her own dress. She had the other dress dyed black, and it was identified as Jessie M'Pherson's by two witnesses, who were perfectly familiar with her clothes.

The prisoner had also some crinoline wires, which she gave to Mrs. Adams on the Saturday, saying that her child had burnt the petticoat to which they belonged. These wires, on being microscopically examined, were found to be stained with blood.

The only remaining piece of evidence against the prisoner was that when she went out with Mrs. Fraser, on the Friday night, she gave her a glass of rum. Mrs. Campbell, her lodger, saw her go to a press in her (Mrs. Campbell's) kitchen, which contained a bottle and a hand-basket. On the following Monday she missed the bottle, and a bottle of similar size, shape, and color, and with a smell of rum about it, was found at the house at Sandyford Place after the murder.

It should be added with regard to the bloody footprints on the bedroom floor, that the prisoner had a high instep, and that her feet were about the size of the marks, and might have made them. They could not have been made by the deceased, whose feet were larger ; nor by old Fleming, whose feet were not only larger, but also too flat. One of the marks was very perfect, because it was so close to the window that the person who made it must have been standing, and must therefore have made a full impression. It should also be borne in mind, that the prisoner knew the house at No. 17,

Sandyford Place, as she had been formerly in service there herself.

This was the case against the prisoner. The evidence in her favor consisted entirely of the testimony of a policeman named Colin Campbell, who deposed that on the Saturday night he saw two women come out of 17, Sandyford Place, by the front door, about half-past eight or a quarter to nine. He saw them well. They stood about five minutes, and one went away and the other turned back. He added that he heard the door shut, and saw a woman running to shut it. He was quite sure that the prisoner was not one of the women. He was sure of the day, because he posted a letter to his father that night; and he appears to have been sure of the house, because he was coming out of No. 18, and they out of No. 17.

This evidence demolished the whole case of the prosecution; because, according to old Fleming, there was no living woman in the house on the Saturday evening to shut the door, and no one came to the house that night, except a young man named Darnley, who wanted to see Jessie M'Pherson.

LI.

CASE OF A GIRL AT LIEGE.

IN the year 1764, a citizen of Liege was found dead in his chamber, shot in the head. Close to him lay a discharged pistol, with which he had ap parently been his own executioner. Firearms are the chief manufacture of that city; and so common is the use of pistols at that place, that every peasant who brings his goods to the markets there, is seen armed with them : so that the circumstance of the pistol did not, at first, meet with so much attention as it might have done in places where those weapons are not in such common use. But, upon the researches of the proper officer of that city, whose duty, like that of our coroner, it is to inquire into all the circumstances of accidental deaths, it appeared that the ball, which was found lodged in the head of the deceased, could never, from its size, have been fired out of the pistol which lay by him; thus it was clear that he had been murdered; nor were they long in deciding who was the murderer! A girl, of about sixteen, the niece of the deceased, had been brought up by him, and he had been always supposed to have intended to leave her his effects, which were something considerable; but the girl had then lately listened to the addresses of a young man whom the uncle did not approve of, and he had, upon that occasion, several times threatened to alter his will, and leave his fortune to some other of his relations. Upon these and some other concurrent circumstances, such as having been heard to wish her uncle's death, &c., the girl was committed to prison, and subjected to the torture; but failing to confess, was discharged.

Some years afterwards, her innocence became manifest, by the confession of the real assassins, who, being sentenced to the wheel for other crimes, confessed themselves the authors of this of which the girl had been suspected; and that, several pistols having been discharged at the deceased, they had, intending that it should appear a suicide, laid a pistol near him, without noticing that it was not the same by which he fell.

LII.

CASE IN THE REIGN OF QUEEN ELIZABETH.

A person was arraigned before Sir James Dyer, Lord Chief Justice of Common Pleas, upon an indictment for the murder of a man who dwelt in the same parish with the prisoner.

The first witness against him deposed, that on a certain day, mentioned by the witness, in the morning, as he was going through a close, which he particularly described, at some distance from the path, he saw a person lying dead, and that two wounds appeared in his breast, and his shirt and clothes were much stained with blood; that the wounds appeared to the witness to have been made by the puncture of a fork or some such instrument, and looking about he discovered a fork lying near the corpse, which he took up, and observed it to be marked with the initials of the prisoner's name; here the witness produced the fork in court, which the prisoner owned to be his.

The prisoner waived asking the witness any questions.

A second witness deposed, that on the morning of the day on which the deceased was killed, the witness had risen very early with an intention of going to a neighboring market town, which he mentioned; that as he was standing in the entry of his own dwelling house, the street door being open, he saw the prisoner come by, dressed in a suit of clothes, the color and fashion of which he described; that he (the witness) was prevented from going to market, and that afterwards the first witness brought notice to the town of the death and wounds of the deceased, and of the prisoner's fork being found near the corpse; that upon this report the prisoner was apprehended, and carried before a justice of peace; that he, this witness, followed the prisoner to the justice's house, and attended his examination, during which he observed the exchange of clothes the prisoner had made since the time he had seen him in the morning; that on the witness charging him with having changed his clothes, he gave several shuffling answers, and would have denied it; that upon witness mentioning this circumstance of change of dress, the justice granted a warrant to search the

6

prisoner's house for the clothes described by the witness as having been put off since the morning; that this witness attended and assisted at the search; that after a nice search of two hours and upwards, the very clothes the witness had described, were discovered concealed in a straw bed. He then produced the bloody clothes in court, which the prisoner owned to be his clothes, and to have been thrust in the straw bed with the intention to conceal them on the account of their being bloody.

The prisoner also waived asking this second witness any questions.

A third witness deposed to his having heard the prisoner deliver certain menaces against the deceased, whence the prosecutor intended to infer a proof of malice prepense. In answer to this the prisoner proposed certain questions to the court, leading to a discovery of the occasion of the menacing expressions deposed to; and from the witness's answer to those questions, it appeared that the deceased had first menaced the prisoner.

The prisoner being called upon for his defence, addressed the following narration to the court, as containing all he knew concerning the manner and circumstances of the death of the deceased. "He rented a close in the same parish with the deceased, and the deceased rented another close adjoining to it; the only way to his own close was through that of the deceased; and on the day the murder in the indictment was said to be committed, he rose early in the morning, in order to go to work in his close with his fork in his hand, and passing through the deceased's ground, he observed a man at some distance from the path, lying down as if dead or drunk; he thought himself bound to see what condition the person was in; and on getting up to him he found him at the last extremity, with two wounds in his breast from which much blood had issued. In order to relieve him, he raised him up, and with great difficulty set him on his lap; he told the deceased he was greatly concerned at his unhappy fate, and the more so as there appeared reason to think he had been murdered. He entreated the deceased to discover if possible who it was, assuring him he would do his best endeavors to bring him to justice. The deceased seemed to be sensible of what he said, and in the midst of his agonies attempted to speak to him, but was seized with a rattling in his throat, gave a hard struggle, then a dreadful groan, and vomiting a deal of blood, some of which fell on his (the prisoner's) clothes, he expired in his arms. The shock he felt on account of this accident was not to be expressed, and the rather as it was well known that there had been a difference between the deceased and himself, on which account he might possibly be suspected of the murder. He therefore thought it advisable to leave the deceased in the condition he was, and take no further notice of the matter; in the confusion he was in when he left the place, he took the deceased's fork away instead of his own, which was by the side of the corpse. Being obliged to go to his work, he thought it best to shift his clothes, and that they might not be seen, he confessed that he had hid them in the place where they were found. It was true he had denied before the justice that he had changed his clothes, being conscious this was an ugly circumstance that might be urged against him, being unwilling to be brought into trouble if he could help it. He concluded his story with a most solemn declaration, that he had related nothing but the exact truth, without adding or diminishing one tittle, as he should answer for it to God Almighty."

Being then called upon to produce his witnesses, the prisoner answered with a steady, composed countenance and resolution of voice. "He had no witnesses but God and his own conscience."

The judge then proceeded to deliver his charge, in which he pathetically enlarged on the heinousness of the crime, and laid great stress on the force of the evidence, which, although circumstantial only, he declared he thought to be irresistible, and little inferior to the most positive proof. The prisoner had indeed cooked up a very plausible story; but if such or the like allegations were to be admitted in a case of this kind, no murderer would ever be brought to justice, such deeds being generally perpetrated in the dark, and with the greatest secrecy. The present case was exempted in his opinion from all possibility of doubt, and they ought not to hesitate one moment about finding the prisoner guilty.

The foreman begged of his lordship, as this was a case of life and death, that the jury might withdraw; and upon this motion, an officer was sworn to keep the jury locked up.

This trial came on the first in the morning, and the judge having sat till nine at night expecting the return of the jury, at last sent an officer to inquire if they were agreed on their verdict.

Some of them returned for answer, that eleven of their body had been of the same mind from the first, but that it was their misfortune to have a foreman, who having taken up a different opinion from them, was unalterably fixed in it. The messenger had no sooner gone, than the complaining members, alarmed at the thought of being kept under confinement all night, and despairing of bringing their dissenting brother over to their own way of thinking, agreed to accede to his opinion, and having acquainted him with their resolution, they sent an officer to detain his lordship a few minutes, and then went into court, and by their foreman brought in the prisoner not guilty.

His lordship could not help expressing the greatest surprise and indignation at this unexpected verdict; and after giving the jury a severe admonition, he refused to record the verdict, and sent them back again with directions that they should be locked up all night without fire or candle. The whole blame was publicly laid on the foreman by the rest of the members, and they spent the night in loading him with reflections, and bewailing their unhappy fate in being associated with so hardened a wretch. But he remained inflexible, constantly declaring he

wou'.' suffer death rather than change his
opin/. ι.

As ,oon as his lordship came into court next
morning, he sent again to the jury, on which the
eleven members joined in requesting their foreman
to go into court, assuring him they would abide
by their former verdict, whatever was the consequence; and on being reproached with their
former inconstancy, they promised never to desert
or recriminate upon their foreman any more.

Upon these assurances they proceeded again
into court, and again brought in the prisoner not
guilty. The judge, unable to conceal his rage at a
verdict which appeared to him in the most
iniquitous light, reproached them severely, and
dismissed them with the cutting reflection "That
the blood of the deceased lay at their doors."

The prisoner, on his part, fell down on his knees,
and with uplifted eyes and hands to God, thanked
him most devoutly for his deliverance; and
addressing himself to the judge, cried out, "You
see, my lord, that God and a good conscience are
the best witnesses."

The circumstance made a deep impression on
the mind of the judge; and as soon as he had
retired from court, he entered into conversation

with the high sheriff upon what had passed, and particularly examined him as to his knowledge of the foreman of the jury. The high sheriff answered his lordship, that he had been acquainted with him many years; that he had a freehold estate of his own of above £50 a-year; and that he rented a very considerable farm besides; that he never knew him charged with an ill action, and that he was universally beloved and esteemed in his neighborhood.

For further information, his lordship sent for the minister of the parish, who gave the same favorable account of his parishioner, with this addition, that he was a constant churchman and a devout communicant.

These accounts increased his lordship's perplexity, from which he could think of no expedient to deliver himself, but by having a conference in private with the only person who could give him satisfaction; this he requested the sheriff to procure, who readily offered his service, and without delay brought about the desired interview.

Upon the foreman of the jury being introduced to the judge, his lordship retired with him into a closet, where his lordship opened his reasons for desiring that visit, making no scruple of acknowledging the uneasiness he was under on account of the verdict, and conjuring his visitor frankly to discover his reasons for acquitting the prisoner. The juryman returned for answer, that he had sufficient reasons to justify his conduct, and that he was neither afraid nor ashamed to reveal them; but as he had hitherto locked them up in his own breast and was under no compulsion to disclose them, he expected his lordship would engage upon his honor to keep what he was about to unfold to him a secret, as he himself had done. His lordship having done so, the juryman proceeded to give his lordship the following account: " The deceased being the tythe-man where he (the juryman) lived, he had, the morning of his decease, been in his (the juryman's) grounds, amongst his corn, and had done him great injustice by taking more than his due, and acting otherwise in a most arbitrary manner. When he complained of this treatment, he had not only been abused with scurrilous language, but the deceased had struck at him several times with his fork, and had actually wounded him in two places, the scars of which wounds he then showed his lordship. The deceased seemed bent on mischief, and the farmer having no weapon to defend himself, had no other

way to preserve his own life but by closing in with
the deceased, and wrenching the fork out of his
hands; which having effected, the deceased
attempted to recover the fork, and in the scuffle
received the two wounds which had occasioned his
death. The farmer was inexpressibly concerned
at the accident which occasioned the man's death,
and especially when the prisoner was taken up on
suspicion of the murder. But the assizes being
just over, he was unwilling to surrender himself
and to confess the matter, because his farm and
affairs would have been ruined by his lying so long
in jail. He was sure to have been acquitted on his
trial, for he had consulted the ablest lawyers upon
the case, who all agreed that as the deceased had
been the aggressor, he could only have been guilty
of manslaughter, at most. It was true he had
suffered greatly in his own mind on the prisoner's
account; but being well assured that imprisonment
would be of less consequence to the prisoner than
himself, he had suffered the law to take its course.
In order, however, to render the prisoner's confinement as easy to him as possible, he had given
him every kind of assistance, and had wholly supported his family ever since. And to get him
clear of the charge laid against him, he had pro-

cured himself to be summoned on the jury, and set at the head of them; having all along determined in his own breast rather to die himself, than to suffer any harm to be done to the "prisoner."

His lordship expressed great satisfaction at this account ; and after thanking the farmer for it, and making this farther stipulation, that in case his lordship should survive him, he might then be at liberty to relate this fact; that it might be delivered down to posterity, the conference broke up.

The juryman lived fifteen years afterwards ; the judge inquiring after him every year, and happening to survive him, delivered the above relation.

LIII.

AN INNOCENT SUFFERER.

ABOUT the year 1766, a young woman who lived
as servant with a person of very depraved habits in Paris, having rejected certain dishonorable
proposals that he made her, became the object
of his revenge. He clandestinely put into the
box where she kept her clothes, several things
belonging to himself and marked with his name;
he then declared that he had been robbed,
sent for a constable, and made his depositions. The
box was opened, and he claimed several articles as
belonging to him.

The poor girl being imprisoned, had only tears
for her defence; and all that she said to the interrogatories was, that she was innocent. The judges,
who in those days seldom scrutinized any case
very deeply, pronounced her guilty, and she was
condemned to be hanged. She was led to the
scaffold, and very unskilfully executed, it being

the first essay of the executioner's son in this horrid profession. A surgeon bought the body; and as he was preparing in the evening to dissect it, he perceived some remains of warmth; the knife dropped from his hand, and he put into bed the unfortunate woman he was going to dissect. His endeavors to restore her to life succeeded. At the same time he sent for an ecclesiastic, with whose discretion and experience he was well acquainted, as well to consult him on this strange event, as to make him witness of his conduct.

When the unfortunate girl opened her eyes and saw the figure of the priest (who had features strongly marked) standing before her, she thought herself in the other world. She clasped her hands with terror and exclaimed, " Eternal Father! you know my innocence; have mercy on me!" She did not cease to invoke the ecclesiastic, and it was long before she could be convinced that she was not dead, so strongly had the idea of punishment and death impressed her imagination.

The accuser was unexpectedly confronted with his victim. Terrified by the sudden appearance of one whom he believed dead, his courage failed him, and falling on his knees, he confessed his atrocious crime.

LIV.

CASE OF BLAKE.

ABOUT the time of the breaking out of the American Revolution, there stood on the road between Albany and Schenectady, a fantastic old building, whose walls had been reared by the sturdy hand of some Dutch architect. From the lowest branch of a large sycamore in front of this house, hung a sign-board, indicating that it was a place of public entertainment. It was called the Blue Horse, and was noted throughout the surrounding country.

It was about five o'clock in the afternoon of a bright day in autumn, that a group of some half a dozen men were collected in the bar room, gossiping on the events of the day. A hot dialogue between two of the party was fast verging into a quarrel.

" Come, come — stop this, Wickliffe," said an old man, " this dispute is mere nonsense."

The person whom he addressed, was a short,

square-built man, with a dark sallow face, a black eye, a low wrinkled forehead, and lips that worked and twitched, baring his teeth like a mastiff preparing to bite. He was an ugly looking fellow.

He turned slowly to the old man, and snapping his fingers in his face, said with an oath, " This quarrel with that boy, is my affair, not yours; don't meddle with what don't concern you."

The opponent of Wickliffe, a young fellow of three or four and twenty, replied:

" Well, Wickliffe," said he, " if you will quarrel, I wont. I'll say no more about this matter." Turning away, he paid no more attention to his opponent.

At last, however, Wickliffe muttered something between his teeth, which drew forth the cry of " Shame ! shame !" from those around him.

" What's that you say ?" said the young man, advancing.

" Nothing, nothing," replied several. " Don't mind him, Harry."

Harry Blake's face became deadly pale.

" Wickliffe, I did not hear what you said, but I dare you to repeat it. If you *do*, and there is one word in it that should not be, this hour will be the bitterest of your life."

His adversary did not seem inclined to give up
the dispute, but repeated, in different language,
the insult he had offered before. Hardly were the
words out of his mouth when Blake was upon him.
He lifted him from his feet, and flung him across
the room against the opposite wall. Wickliffe lay
for a moment stunned, but on recovering, sprang
to his feet, and shaking his hand at Blake, said,
"My boy, you may take your measure for a
coffin ; after this, you will need one."

He then left the room, and Blake would have
rushed after him, but for being restrained by those
present.

They detained him some time, reasoning with
him on the absurdity of quarrelling with a man of
Wickliffe's stamp. But at last he left them—for
he had five miles to ride home—and mounting his
horse, was soon galloping along the road.

Soon after, two more of the loiterers in the bar
room prepared to start on their homeward way.
Their road lay in the same direction as Blake and
Wickliffe had taken. They were riding quietly
along, when on a sudden, a loud cry, from a little
distance, fell upon their ears. In a moment it was
repeated.

"There's foul play here," said one, named

Walton. "Some one begging for mercy. Did you hear the name?"

"No."

"I did, and it was Harry. Can Harry Blake be settling scores with Wickliffe?"

"I hope not."

A dozen leaps of their horses brought them round the copse of trees, which had shut out a sight that made them shudder. Within twenty yards of them, extended on his back, stone dead lay Wickliffe. Bending over him was Blake grasping a knife, which was driven to the haft into his bosom.

"Good God! Harry Blake taken red-handed in a murder!" exclaimed Grayson. "Don't stab him again! Oh! Harry what have you done!"

Walton sprang from his horse, and flung himself upon Blake, exclaiming, "I charge you with murder!"

Blake stared. "Me with murder? Are you mad? Why, I didn't kill him!"

"It wont do," said Walton. "I saw you with the knife in your grasp—in his bosom—and him dead. This is a sad ending of this afternoon's quarrel."

"Will you hear me?" said Blake, earnestly;

"and you, Grayson, who are older and less im-
petuous than Walton, listen to me. I came here
but a moment. before yourself, hearing some one
calling for help. I found Wickliffe dead, with this
knife in his bosom, and was endeavoring to pull it
out, when you came up. That is the truth, so
help me, God!"

Grayson shook his head. "Would that I could
believe you, Harry; but as I hope to be saved, I
saw you stab him—I did."

Harry clasped his hands, and said, "And you in-
tend to swear to that, and charge me with this
deed?"

"There is no help for it, as I see," said Grayson.
"You know I am a magistrate, and must do my
duty. God grant you may prove yourself innocent,
but unless my eyes deceive me, I saw you stab that
man."

"If that is your belief, God help me!" said
Blake; "if I am charged with murder, such a fact,
sworn to, would hang me. But you have not
looked round for traces of any other murderer. He
may be hid somewhere about here."

After a fruitless search for some time, finding
only footprints corresponding with Blake's, they
mounted their horses, rode to the nearest magis-

trate, delivered Harry over in due form to the law, and prepared to remove the body of Wickliffe.

When Harry Blake was first imprisoned, he bore stoutly up against his fate. But stone walls, and close, pent up chambers, with their stifling, stagnant air, and their murky twilight, are sure to mildew the heart, and break down strength and hope.

In due time the day of trial arrived. The counsel for the prosecution dwelt briefly, but clearly, on the facts already known. The quarrel, the threat, the ride home, the discovery with the murdered man, the footprints in the road, corresponding with the prisoner's, the testimony of Grayson that he saw Blake stab Wickliffe, was conclusive; and the jury, — after the Judge's charge, —without leaving their seats, returned a verdict of " guilty."

The day of the execution came. Among the multitude collected to witness the sight, was Grayson. He implored him to confess. " No, I cannot, for I am innocent." These were Blake's last words, and in a few moments his earthly career was ended.

About three months after the execution, the judge who presided at the trial, received a note

from a prisoner under sentence of death, requesting to see him without delay, as his sentence was
to be carried into effect on the day following. On
his way thither, he overtook Gravson going to
the same place, having received a like summons.
They were at a loss to understand it. Arrived,
they entered the cell together.

The prisoner was seated at a wooden table. He
was tall, gaunt, with sunken eyes, and hollow
cheeks.

"You," he said, turning to the judge, "presided
at the trial of young Harry Blake."

"I did."

"And you," turning to Grayson, "swore you
saw him stab Wickliffe. On your testimony, principally, he was hung."

"I did. I saw him with my own eyes!"

The prisoner uttered a low, sneering laugh, and
turning to the judge first, and then to the witness,
said, "You sentenced an innocent man; and you
swore to a falsehood. Harry Blake did not kill
Wickliffe. He was as innocent of the sin of murder
as you were — more so than you are now.
You have blood and perjury on your soul, for *I*
murdered William Wickliffe!" And in a few words
he described the scene, his hiding place, and all.

" God have mercy on me !" exclaimed Grayson, as he fell senseless to the floor.

It is needless to go into the details of the prisoner's confession, which was so full and clear that it left no doubt on the mind of the judge that he was guilty of Wickliffe's murder, and that Harry Blake was another of those who had gone to swell the list of victims to Circumstantial Evidence.

LV.

CASE IN WARWICK.

THE following instructive case is mentioned by Sir Edward Coke: "In the county of Warwick," says he, "there were two brethren; the one having issue a daughter, and being seized of lands in fee, devised the government of his daughter and his lands until she came to the age of sixteen years, to his brother, and died. The uncle brought up his niece very well, both at her book and needle, etc. When she was about eight or nine years of age, her uncle, for some offence, correcting her, she was heard to say, ' Oh ! good Uncle, kill me not !' After which time the child, after much inquiry, could not be heard of. Whereupon the uncle, being suspected of the murder of her, the rather that he was her next heir, was upon examination, anno 8 Jac. Regis, committed to the jail for suspicion of murder; and was admonished by the justices of assize to find out the child, and thereupon bailed until the next assizes. Against which time, for that he could not find her, and fearing what would fall out against him, he took another child, as like unto her, both in person and years, as he could find, and apparelled her like unto the true child, and brought her to the next assizes; but upon view and examination she was found not to be the true child; and upon these presumptions he was indicted, found guilty, had a judgment, and was hanged. But the truth of the case was, that the child, being beaten over-night, the next morning, when she should go to school, ran away into the next county; and being well educated, she was reared and entertained of a stranger; and when she was sixteen years old, at which time she should come to her land, she came to demand it, and was directly proved to be the true child."

LVI.

CASE OF A FARMER AND HIS SON.

A FARMER was tried under the special commission for Wiltshire, in January, 1831, upon an
indictment which charged him with having
feloniously sent a threatening letter, which was
alleged to have been written by him. That the
letter was in the prisoner's handwriting was
positively deposed by witnesses who had had ample
means of becoming acquainted with it; the letter in
question, and two others of the same kind to other
persons, together with a scrap of paper found in
the prisoner's bureau, had formed one sheet of
paper; the ragged edges of the different portions
exactly fitting each other, and the water-mark
name of the maker, which was divided into three
parts, being perfect when the portions of paper
were united.

The jury found the prisoner guilty, and he was
sentenced to be transported for fourteen years.

The judge and jury having retired for a few minutes, during their absence the prisoner's son, a youth about eighteen years of age, was brought to the table by the prisoner's attorney, and confessed that he had been the writer of the letter in question, and not his father. He then wrote on a piece of paper from memory a copy of the contents of the anonymous letter, which, on comparison, left no doubt of the truth of its statement. The writing was not a verbatim copy, although it differed but little; and the bad spelling of the original was repeated in the copy. The original was then handed to him, and on being desired to do so, he copied it, and the writing was exactly alike.

Upon the return of the learned judge the circumstances were mentioned to him, and two days afterwards the son was put upon his trial and convicted of the identical offence which had been imputed to the father. It appeared that he had access to the bureau, which was commonly left open. The writing of the letter constituted in fact the *corpus delicti ;* there having been no other evidence to inculpate the prisoner as the sender of the letter, which would, however, have been the natural and irresistible inference if he had been the writer.

The correspondence of the fragment of paper found in the prisoner's bureau with the letter in question, and with the two others of the same nature sent to other persons, was simply a circumstance of suspicion, but foreign, as it turned out, to the *factum* in question ; and considering that other persons had access to the bureau, its weight as a circumstance of suspicion seems to have been overrated.

LVII.

CASE OF A YOUTH.

A YOUTH was convicted of stealing a pocket-book containing five one-pound notes, under very extraordinary circumstances. The prosecutrix left home to go to market in a neighboring town, and having stooped down to look at some vegetables exposed to sale, she felt a hand resting upon her shoulder, which, on rising up, she found to be the prisoner's. Having afterwards purchased some articles at a grocer's shop, on searching for her pocket-book in order to pay for them, she found it gone. Her suspicion fell upon the prisoner, who was apprehended, and upon his person was found a black pocket-book, which she identified by a particular mark, as that which she had lost, but it contained no money. Several witnesses deposed that the prisoner had long possessed the identical pocket-book, speaking also to particular marks by which they were enabled to identify it; but some discrepancies in their evidence having led to the suspicion that the defence was a fabricated. one, the jury returned a verdict of guilty, and the prisoner was sentenced to be transported. During the continuance of the assizes, two men who were mowing a field of oats through which the path lay by which the prosecutrix had gone to market, found in the oats, close to the path, a black pocket-book containing five one-pound notes. The men took the notes and pocket-book to the prosecutrix, who immediately recognized them; and the committing magistrate dispatched a messenger with the articles found, and her affidavit of identity, to the judge at the assize town, who directed the prisoner to be placed at the bar, publicly stated the cicumstances so singularly brought to light, and directed his immediate discharge. The prosecutrix must have dropped her pocket-book, or drawn it from her pocket with her handkerchief, and had clearly been mistaken as to the identity of the pocket-book produced upon the trial.

LVIII.

CASE OF ABRAHAM THORNTON.[1]

ABRAHAM THORNTON was tried at the Warwick Autumn Assizes, 1817, before Mr. Justice Holroyd, for the alleged murder of Mary Ashford, a young woman, who was found dead in a pit of water,

---

[1] This was the famous "Wager of Battle" case. So much dissatisfied were the friends of Mary Ashford, and the community of that district, that an ancient law, which had become almost obsolete, was resorted to in order to obtain a new trial. According to this ancient law, a relative or friend of the deceased could appeal a case in which the person accused of the murder was acquitted, to the King's Bench; and the brother of Mary Ashford took such an appeal, and on this process was issued by which Thornton was again taken into custody and carried to London, that he might personally appear and answer to the suit. And here his counsel also resorted to the ancient law to save him. By the same law, indeed, which had come down from feudal times, it appeared that Thornton had a right to repel the appeal by a "wager of battle," or, in other words, a challenge to single combat between the parties. Greatly to the astonishment of the judges, the bar, and all who were spectators, and, indeed, to the whole civilized world, Thornton availed himself of this right, and in the court threw down his glove, according to ancient custom, as a challenge to the appellant. Here was an unlooked-for turn in the case; but upon a full examination, it appeared the law,

about seven o'clock in the morning, with marks of violence about her person and dress, from which it was supposed that she had been violated, and afterwards drowned. The deceased's bonnet and shoes and a bundle were found on the bank of the pit. Upon the grass, at the distance of forty yards, there was the impression of an extended human figure, and a large quantity of blood was upon the ground near the lower extremity of the figure, where there were also the marks of large shoe toes. Spots of blood were traced for ten yards in a direction leading from the impression to the pit, upon a footpath, and about a foot and a half from the path upon the grass on one side of it. When the body was found, there was no trace of any footstep on the grass, which was covered with dew not otherwise disturbed than by the blood; from which circumstance it was insisted

---

however repugnant to the ideas of the nineteenth century, was still unrepealed, and must be observed; and after long arguments by counsel, the court decided that the right of defence in this way was coeval with the right to appeal such a case. But young Ashford was a mere stripling, while Thornton was an athletic man, and a personal combat, with such odds against him, gave little promise of any better success in establishing the guilt of the accused, than was had at the first trial. Ashford therefore declined the combat, and by the law the appeal could not be sustained. The ancient law which had slept so long unnoticed in the vast accumulations of English law, was soon after repealed.

that the spots of blood must have fallen from the body while being carried in some person's arms. Upon the examination of the body, about half a pint of water and some duckweed were found in the stomach, so that the deceased must have been alive when immersed in the water. There were lacerations about the parts of generation, but nothing which might not have been caused by sexual intercourse with consent. Soon after the discovery of the body, there were found in a newly harrowed field adjoining that in which the pit was situated the recent footmarks of the right and left footsteps of the prisoner and also of the footsteps of the deceased, which, from the length and depth of the steps, indicated that there had been running and pursuit, and that the deceased had been overtaken.

From that part of the harrowed field where the deceased had been overtaken, her footsteps and those of the prisoner proceeded together, walking in a direction towards the pit and the spot where the impression was found, until the footsteps came within the distance of forty yards from the pit, when from the hardness of the ground they could be no longer traced. The marks of the prisoner's running footsteps were also discovered in a direction leading from the pit across the harrowed field; from which it was contended that he had run alone in that direction after the commission of the supposed murder. The mark of a man's left shoe was discovered near the edge of the pit, and it was proved that the prisoner had worn right and left shoes. On the prisoner's shirt and breeches were found stains of blood, and he acknowledged that he had had sexual intercourse with the deceased, but alleged that it had taken place with her own consent.

The defence set up was an *alibi*, which, notwithstanding these apparently decisive facts, was most satisfactorily established. The prisoner and the deceased had met at a dance on the preceding evening at a public house, which they left together about midnight. About three in the morning they were seen talking together at a stile near the spot, and about four o'clock the deceased called at the house of Mrs. Butler, at Erdington, where she had left a bundle of clothes the day before. Here she appeared in good health and spirits, changed a part of her dress for some of the garments which she had left there, and quitted the house in about a quarter of an hour. Her way home lay across certain fields, one of which had been newly harrowed, and adjoined that in which the pit was situate. The deceased was successively seen after leaving Mrs. Butler's house by several persons, proceeding alone in a direction towards her own home, along a public road where the prisoner, if he had rejoined her, could have been seen for a considerable distance; the last of such persons saw her within a quarter of an hour afterwards, that is to say, before or about half-past four.

At about half-past four, and not later than twenty-five minutes before five, the accused was seen by four persons, wholly unacquainted with him, walking slowly and leisurely along a lane leading in an opposite direction from the young woman's course towards her home. About a mile from the spot where the prisoner was seen, he was seen by another witness about ten minutes before five, still walking slowly in the same direction, with whom he stopped and conversed for a quarter of an hour; after which, at twenty-five minutes past five, he was again seen walking towards his father's house, which was distant about half a mile.

From Mrs. Butler's house to the pit was a distance of upwards of a mile and a quarter; and allowing twenty minutes to enable the deceased to walk this distance, would bring the time of her arrival at the pit to twenty-five minutes before five; whereas the prisoner was first seen by four persons above all suspicion at half-past four or twenty-five minutes before five, and the distance of the pit from the place where he was seen was two miles and a half. Upon the hypothesis of his guilt, the prisoner must have rejoined the deceased after she left Mrs. Butler's house, and a distance of upwards of three miles and a quarter must have been traversed by him, accompanied for a portion of it by the deceased, and the pursuit, the criminal intercourse, the drowning, and the deliberate placing of the deceased's bonnet, shoes, and bundle, must have taken place within twenty or twenty-five minutes. The defence was set up at the instant of the prisoner's apprehension, which took place within a few hours after the discovery of the body, and was maintained without contradiction or variation before the coroner's inquest and the committing magistrates, and also upon the trial, and no inroad was made on the credibility of the testimony by which it was supported. The various time-pieces to which the witnesses referred, and which differed much from each other, were carefully compared on the day after the occurrence, and reduced to a common standard, so that there could be no doubt of the real times as spoken to by them.

Thus, it was not within the bounds of possibility that the prisoner could have committed the crime imputed to him ; nevertheless public indignation was so strongly excited that his acquittal, though it afforded a fine example of the calm and unimpassioned administration of justice, occasioned great public dissatisfaction.

LIX.

CASE OF JOHN STRINGER.

JOHN STRINGER was tried at the Lent assizes, held at Kingston, in the county of Surry, in the year 1765, before the late Lord Chief Baron Smythe, for the murder of his wife, and found guilty. The trial being on Saturday, he was ordered for execution on the Monday following. The case was thus: Stringer, a man in low circumstances, had brought his wife, who had long been in an ill state of health, from London to Lambeth, for the benefit of the air: here they lived for some time; generally in great harmony; but not without those little quarrels and scuffles, so common with persons in their rank of life. Upon the woman's death, some of the neighboring females, who had been occasionally witnesses to these little accidental bickerings between the husband and wife, took it in their heads that he had murdered her, notwithstanding she had never

been heard to make the least complaint of her husband during the course of her illness ; and the man
was brought to trial in consequence.

Some trifling evidence being given of the little
differences that had arisen between them; and the
opinion of a young surgeon, that some appearances
on the corpse were somewhat the appearances of a
mortification, occasioned by bruises; Stringer, on
these slight circumstances, was convicted and left
for execution !

Mr Carsan, a surgeon of great experience in the
neighborhood, (and still living there,) had, on the
report of the murder, from mere curiosity, examined
the body, and was so clear that there were no
marks of violence thereon, that he had not the
least apprehension of the possibility of Stringer's
being convicted : but hearing of the conviction,
confident of the innocence of the unhappy man,
and actuated by the love of justice and humanity,
he instantly, on the Sunday, waited on, and represented the case to the Archbishop of Canterbury.
His grace gave Mr. Carsan a letter to Baron
Smythe ; who, convinced, by his statement of the
matter, that himself and the jury had been too precipitate in forming an opinion of the guilt of
Stringer, granted an immediate respite ; which gave

Mr. Carson an opportunity of laying the whole
case before his majesty, and he had the satisfaction
of saving an innocent man from an undeserved and
ignominious death.

LX.

A CASE IN MAINE.*

In 1834, while residing in Maine, I went to
Wiscasset to attend the Circuit Court of the United
States. Soon after entering the Court-house a
stranger came to me and said he wished to engage
me. We stepped into a lobby, and I asked him
what the case was ; in reply, he said that his name
was Merriam, that he was postmaster at Camden,
and that he had been bound over on a charge of
abstracting money from the mail. I said, "If
you are bound over, you have had a hearing before a magistrate. What was the evidence in that
hearing ? Tell me as fully as you can." He replied that there were three witnesses against him—
Mr. Mitchell, the postmaster at Portland, Mr.
Pickard, the mail contractor, and the driver of the
stage.

---

* This case is from a report of Peleg Sprague, Esq., and his statement is
given verbatim.

Mr. Mitchell testified that letters, containing money, having been several times lost from the Eastern mail, he was employed by the Postmaster-General to detect the offenders; that for that purpose he went to Belfast, and there he and Mr. Pickard, the mail contractor, prepared a letter addressed to Gen. McLellan, of Bath, purporting to contain a remittance from a debtor; that into this letter they put a sum of money, in bank bills, and made it up in such a manner as to appear to contain something, and be easily distinguished from other letters; that they put it into the mail-bag, which was taken by the driver into the stage; that they [Mitchell and Pickard] took a chaise, and accompanied the stage, leaving Belfast in the night; that they arrived at a Post-office between Belfast and Camden; that the bag was carried into the office, and in due time brought out, and then examined by all three, Mitchell, Pickard, and the driver, and the letter to McLellan was found in it; that they then proceeded on their way till they came to the Post-office in Camden; that the mail-bag with the letter to McLellan in it was taken into the office, and, after the usual time, was brought out and put into the stage; that they then drove some distance from the village, there stopped, took the bag from the stage and carried it to the chaise, and there they opened the bag, took out all the letters and papers, and placed the letters on one end of the seat of the chaise and the papers on the other, and then they examined the bag; that they took each letter and each paper by itself, and put them back into the bag, and the letter to Gen. McLellan was not there. The bag was then taken by the driver to the stage, and he proceeded on his way. Mitchell and Pickard returned to the village and had the postmaster arrested for abstracting money from the mails.

Mr. Pickard testified to the same facts, confirming Mr. Mitchell in every particular.

The driver also was a witness, and confirmed all that had been testified as to his participation in the business.

In answer to questions, Merriam stated that all three of the witnesses swore that the letter to Gen. McLellan was in the mail-bag when it went into the office at Camden, and was not in the bag, when it came out; and the driver testified that there was no one in the office but the postmaster. I asked my client what evidence he had. He replied that he had not any evidence. I then asked him what he had to say. He answered that all he

could say, was, he was in his office that morning
alone. The mail-bag was brought to him; he
opened it as usual, took out the letters for Camden,
put in those that were to go forward, closed the bag,
locked and delivered it to the driver, who carried it
away, and that was all he knew about it.

Such was the case of my client as presented by
himself. What was my duty? It was true, he
denied that he was guilty, but so can every criminal, and all do who employ counsel. He admitted
that he had not the slightest evidence to offer against
the testimony of three respectable witnesses, and
that he had not a word to say in explanation.
Ought I to have flared up with virtuous indignation, and at once refused to aid a man to escape
punishment who was so palpably guilty? That was
not my course; but after reflecting a few minutes, I
said: "Have you ever caused inquiry to be made
of Gen. McLellan whether he received that letter?"
He replied, "No, I never thought of such a
thing." I then advised him to send a person immediately to Bath and ask Gen. McLellan if he had
any knowledge of such a letter, and also to make
the same inquiry of the postmaster at Bath. He
sent a man accordingly, who in due time returned
and reported that Gen. McLellan said that he did

receive such a letter on a day which he named, and which was a short time only before. When he received the letter he had no recollection of the writer, but supposed it was all right.

The messenger then went to the postmaster, who said that he recollected such a letter, that it came by the Eastern mail, on a day which he named, that he opened the mail-bag himself, and seeing a letter directed to Gen. McLellan, which looked as if it might have money in it, he did not like to have it lying in his office, and sent it by his boy to the General. The time when the letter reached the postmaster of Bath, and Gen. McLellan, as stated by them, was the afternoon of the day on which it passed through Camden. On receiving this intelligence, I went to the District Attorney, Mr. Shepley, stated what information we had obtained, and requested him to subpœna Gen. McLellan and the postmaster at Bath to go before the Grand Jury. He did so, and the result was that no indictment was found, and my client was discharged.

LXI.

CASE OF HENRY UPTON AND JOSEPH SWIFT.

On the night of the 6th of January, 1860, Dr. Matlack's house at Germantown, Pa., was burglariously entered by persons then unknown, and robbed of coats, boots and other clothing.

Thomas Gilbert, Joseph Swift, and Henry Upton, were engaged the same night in cleaning out a cess-pool, not more than a quarter of a mile from the house where the burglary was committed. Marks, as of privy filth, were found on the under side of one of the window-shutters, which had been pried off with a coulter, that was afterwards found in a dry culvert under the railroad, about three hundred yards from the house. Evidence was presented that Gilbert, Swift, and Upton had but one load to take from the well at 12 o'clock, and that they did not get home till at or near three o'clock. Two sets of tracks through the snow were traced by the police from the house robbed across the field, to the house of Gilbert. The boot of Upton, which he had worn that night, was tried by the policeman, and he swore it fitted exactly into one set of the tracks. Also, that the boot was loaded with large nails, which had made a distinct impression in the snow, and in pressing down the boot there-was no change made in the nail prints.

A police officer questioned Gilbert as to where the goods were, and Gilbert told him the street they were in, but could not tell the house. He also said to the officer that Swift did not do it, but that he and Upton did it. The officer believed him to be of sound mind when this statement was made, though he died soon after and before trial, in the same station-house, of delirium tremens. The goods were not found. The defendants, Swift and Upton, were tried and convicted. Reasons were filed for a new trial. A new trial was granted to Swift, and denied to Upton. Upton was sentenced to two years in the penitentiary. About the time Upton was sentenced, the police took a young German, named Peter Miller, into custody, for a burglary in the house of Mr. Powers. They spoke of the arrest and conviction of Swift and Upton in his presence, which induced him to say, "Ha! they got the wrong man that time."

This remark, of course, induced the officers to question him further. He was a little shy at first, but after solicitation, he made full statements, which were verified to the satisfaction of all parties, disclosing the following facts:

On the night of January 6th, a bright moonlight night, Peter Miller walked out of the city along the Germantown Railroad, to Nicetown lane—went west on that lane about three hundred yards, to the farm-house of George Crager, farmer and trucker —went to the wagon-house shed, took out a dirty coulter from a plough, which had probably been last used in ploughing privy filth—took the coulter to Dr. Matlack's, pried off the shutters, went in, stole the goods, came out, and threw the coulter under the culvert, where it was found by the police, and went back to the city with the goods. These facts were proved to the satisfaction of the party robbed, in this way: Miller was taken from the prisoner's dock in the court-room out to Germantown, to Alderman King's office, where he described to Dr. Matlack and Mr. Maule, who lived in the house, the internal arrangement of the parlor and kitchen, the clock on the mantel, and many other things, after which he was taken to the end of Penn street, on which the robbed house stood.

He soon came to a house somewhat resembling it, started towards it, and then stopped, and said, " No, that's not it; " he went on further, then paused— looked—"That's it." Showed just where he got in, how he got out; showed a scratch on the under side of the drawer casing, which the robbed party had not discovered—told them also of things he had taken, which till then they had not missed, but which they found were really gone; told Mr. Maule that he was up in his room in the second story, and described the position of his bed—then went and showed where he had thrown the coulter under the culvert, and then where he had got the coulter from; and upon inquiring of the farmer, he stated that he had missed the coulter a day or two after Miller said he had taken it. There could have been no possible chance of collusion between these parties. Gilbert died a short time after the robbery, and was all the time in custody. Swift and Upton were also in custody till after Miller's arrest for the burglary of Mr. Power's house. These facts satisfied the robbed party, the District Attorney and the Judge who tried the cause, and Upton was pardoned. Miller was arraigned for this same burglary of which Swift and Upton had been convicted and pleaded guilty.

LXII.

CASE IN OHIO.

SEVERAL years since a man residing about seventy miles from Cincinnati, died from the effects of poison, and suspicion resting on a near neighbor, he was arrested and brought to trial. The wife of the deceased made positive oath that the prisoner at the bar was at her house previous to the sickness of her husband, and administered the poison in a cup of coffee, as she had reason to believe. It was also proven that the prisoner purchased poison in Cincinnati, about that time, of the description found in the stomach of the deceased. In defence, the prisoner admitted that he purchased the poison, but declared that he had purchased it for the woman who swore against him, and who said, when she sent for it, that she wished to employ it to exterminate rats; that he gave it into her hand on his return, and was utterly ignorant of when or how it was administered to her husband.—This story, however, availed nothing with the jury. The woman was a religious woman, and her story was entitled to credit. He was accordingly convicted and hung, protesting his innocence to the hour of his death. A few years passed, and the guilty woman confessed, not long before her death, that she was the guilty person, and that the man who was executed knew nothing of the circumstances of the murder.

LXIII.

CASE OF WILLIAMS.

OF instances of mistaken identity we select the following, occurring in Benton, Illinois, in 1866. A skeleton was found in the woods, and the jury of inquest found it to be the skeleton of a young man named Henry Mahorn, who was supposed to have enlisted in the army; but on inquiry it was found that he had not been heard from subsequent to the time of his supposed enlistment, which corroborated the finding of the jury. The clothing attached to the body was identified as having belonged to Mahorn, and certain teeth were found to have been extracted during his lifetime, which teeth were found wanting in the skeleton. A young man named Daniel Williams was last seen in the company of Mahorn, being on their way to enlist as substitutes. Williams returned and reported that Mahorn had enlisted in the 10th Missouri Volunteers. This was found to be false, and Williams

9

was arrested and brought before Judge Duff for trial. The circumstances pointing to the guilt of the prisoner were so strong that nine-tenths of the community were satisfied of his guilt. In the midst of the trial Henry Mahorn appeared in the court room, to the utter astonishment of all, he having enlisted under an assumed name, and being discharged by reason of expiration of time of service, had returned to learn of his supposed death. The prisoner was so overcome at his unexpected .and apparently providential deliverance, that he wept like a child. The Judge at once ordered his release.

LXIV.

CASE OF MORRIS.

In July, 1859, there lived near Pontiac, in Livingston county, Illinois, a farmer and his family, named Murphy. The family lived near Rook's Creek, on the line of the Chicago, Alton and St. Louis Railroad, and their eldest daughter, Mary Murphy, was employed as a domestic in Pontiac, a distance of five or six miles from her home. She had spent Saturday at home, and on Sunday afternoon left her father's house to return to her place of service at Pontiac, following the railroad track, and walking the distance alone. She was afterward, and on the same day, seen within about two miles from Pontiac, going in that direction. This was the last seen of Mary Murphy alive. Her body was found eighteen days later, lying near the railroad track, and bearing evidence of having been murdered.

In Bloomington there lived a negro named

Wiley J. Morris. On the Saturday prior to the Sunday when Mary Murphy was last seen alive, he was engaged in a fight, and Morris whipped his antagonist so badly that he (Morris) left Bloomington, bearing some blood stains on his clothes. He was seen walking on the railroad track toward Pontiac on the fatal Sunday, about one mile behind Mary Murphy when she was last seen alive. He was seen the same evening in Pontiac, when he told that he had been in a fight at Bloomington, and was escaping from the officers. From there he went to Joliet, wearing the blood-stained garment. From Joliet he went to Michigan. After the body of Mary Murphy had been found, the facts concerning Morris were learned, and the theory was formed that he had overtaken the girl on the railroad track and murdered her; and it soon settled into a firm conviction in the minds of the people. Morris was traced up and arrested in Michigan in the early part of 1860, and taken to Bloomington for safe keeping. At the next Grand Jury of Livingston county he was indicted for the murder of the girl, having previously undergone a preliminary examination before Justice Streamer, who held him on the charge of murder without bail. Morris protested his innocence from the moment of his arrest.

He had no money, and had difficulty in obtaining his witnesses and in getting them to attend court from Bloomington, Joliet, and from Michigan. A. E. Harding, of Pontiac, became interested in Morris and became convinced that he was innocent, and he was almost the only person in Pontiac that was not ready to hang him. Mr. Harding agreed to defend him.

The trial came on at the September term, 1860. A jury was selected in the county where the murder was committed. The evidence was all circumstantial, yet the jury partook of the popular prejudice and belief, and eleven were for conviction; but one, Mr. Russ, a cool-headed and clear-minded man, held out, much to the disgust of the detectives, and the disappointment of the people.

A change of venue was applied for by Mr. Harding, in behalf of his client, on account of the prejudice of the people of Livingston county. The court granted the change of venue, and the cause was sent to Kankakee county for trial, and Morris was sent to the Kankakee jail. The cause came on for trial at the April term, 1861; the same Judge presiding that presided over the former trial. The proof did not show that the accused was seen within a mile of the murdered girl. The theory was that

he was walking in the same direction with the girl,
and was walking faster than she was, and had
overtaken her.   The facts were that he was seen a
mile from her by some railroad laborers, and there
was a possibility that he might have overtaken her
at about the place where her body was found.   He
proved that he had a fight at Bloomington on the
Saturday previous, and got the blood on his clothes
that was seen at Pontiac and Joliet.   The people of
Pontiac were so firmly convinced of his guilt that
they brought every witness who knew any fact that
was against the negro.   Many came here as spectators.   The story of the girl's murder was in every
mouth.   Morris was found guilty.   The court refused to disturb the verdict of the jury, and Wiley
J. Morris was condemned to be hung on the third
Friday in May, 1861.

A petition for a reprieve or commutation of
sentence to imprisonment was circulated.   When it
was carried to Springfield, to be laid before the
Executive, the Governor had been called away to
Washington, and did not return to examine the
petition until the day after Morris was hanged.
The last words of Morris, with the cap over his
head, the rope around his neck, his hands tied, and
his feet pinioned, were, " You murder me, you

murder me, you murder me !" and with these words he was launched into eternity.

Many of the citizens of Kankakee will remember C. G. Hilderband. He went from there to Galesburg, and was engaged in the burning of a livery stable and robbing a store or bank, in the winter of 1862. From there he was sent to the penitentiary at Joliet. He escaped in less than a year, and went to Iowa and joined " Hawkeye Bill's " gang. He was incarcerated in the Jeffersonville prison, Indiana and there wrote a history of the crimes that " Hawkeye Bill " and his gang had committed in the West.

After narrating many desperate acts of these desperadoes, he said :

"Three years before this, in the fall of 1859, ' Hawkeye,' in company with Bill Britt, Joe Montana, alias ' French Joe,' a half-breed Indian named Sioux, and Charles Logue, alias ' Big Curtis,' were running some horses from Iowa to Michigan, Hawkeye being along for the purpose of 'doing a job of work ' at Grand Rapids, Mich. They remained in the woods, near Pontiac, Ill., three or four days, resting their horses, and while there committed a terrible crime. Capturing a young woman who was walking on the railroad track one day, they kept her two days, and then murdered her. The name of the young lady was Mary Murphy, and for this crime a negro was arrested, tried, convicted, and hung at Kankakee, Ill. The Sheriff residing at Pontiac, has written a letter corroborating this statement. A short distance east of Pontiac, at Oliver's Grove, the same party committed a similar crime. These three parties, Bill Britt, 'French Joe,' and the half-breed Indian, 'Sioux,' were hung in the West, and Charles Logue, alias 'Big Curtis,' was 'sent up' after this last offence for twenty-three years in the Allegheny prison, Pa., and there died."

The murder mentioned as committed near Oliver's Grove by this gang was the murder of a cattle drover by the name of Patton. This gang made Oliver's Grove, Kankakee, and Beaver Lake, Indiana, regular stopping places while stealing horses and running them East.

LXV.

CASE OF WEATHERWAX.

In June, 1856, Capt. John G. Weatherwax, attended by his cousin, Andrew Weatherwax, sailed from Plattsburgh, N. Y., in a lake boat, for a Canadian port. Having discharged his cargo, he returned to Pike River, which ž just across the line in Canada, to take on a load of wood. During the day the two cousins had a violent quarrel, each threatening the other. About eight o'clock in the evening the quarrel was at its height, and a dull heavy thud was heard, as of some dull instrument, crashing through a skull, and then all was still. The next morning the hat of Andrew, and blood near it, was found on the deck of the vessel. The captain of another boat, only a short distance away, also heard the quarrel and blows. Nothing afterwards was seen of Andrew, and Capt. Weatherwax could or would give no account of him. Some time after the body of a man with the skull crushed

in, was taken from the water at the very spot at
Pike River where his boat had been moored.
The body was identified as the body of Andrew
Weatherwax. Capt. Weatherwax was arrested,
and the preliminary examination showed almost
conclusive evidence of his guilt ; but as the murder
was committed in Canada, it was decided that the
Courts of the United States had no jurisdiction
over the matter, and he was discharged. His
counsel advised him to run away, but he would not,
at the same time asserting his innocence. The
story and excitement spread and reached Canada,
and a requisition was made on the government of
the United States for the supposed criminal. He
was again arrested and sent to Montreal for trial,
his counsel, McMasters, going with him. The
evidence was strong, but it is supposed the jury
was tampered with, as the first would not agree
and the second discharged him. He returned to
Plattsburgh, but everybody believed him guilty,
and he was shunned as a murderer. In 1868
Andrew Weatherwax, to the astonishment of all,
returned to Plattsburgh. He stated that he left
his cousin's boat on the night of the quarrel, partly
intoxicated, and, visiting a dram-shop in the town,
got into another quarrel, was arrested and fined,

and not having money to pay, was about to be committed, when a stranger stepped up and offered to pay it if he would enlist as a seaman, which he did on an English vessel, visiting China, Australia, &c. He returned from his wanderings to learn of his supposed death.

LXVI.

CASE OF GOULD.

MANY years ago, John Gould, of Portland, was convicted of the murder of a man named Starbird. They were drunkards. One morning Starbird was found dead near a rum-shop at the head of Central wharf. At the inquest, and on the trial of Gould, the rumseller testified that he and Starbird were in his shop the night before, both of them drunk and quarrelling, and that he turned them out of his shop because they were noisy and fighting. Starbird was found with his head fatally injured.

On the testimony of the rumseller, Gould was convicted of murder, and sentenced to be hanged whenever the Governor should issue his warrant, and he remained many years in State prison. But the rumseller fell sick one day, and just before his death, he confessed that it was he who had killed Starbird by a blow upon the head with an iron weight. Gould was released from prison.

LXVII.

CASE IN ENGLAND.

Not long since a dying felon in an English jail confessed that he was one of two men who had committed a murder for which an innocent person had been executed. A married man had become enamored of a girl and paid court to her, professing to be single. When leaving her father's house after a visit he induced the girl to accompany him some distance on the road. Subsequently her body was found in a canal in the neighborhood, and an examination proved that she had been feloniously assaulted and then killed. Her lover was traced and arrested. At first he denied having been with her at all, but several witnesses had seen the two together in the immediate vicinity of the outrage and murder. Then he shifted his defence, admitted that he had taken her in the woods, but asserted that he had been interrupted by two men who came, attracted by her cries; that he had thereupon escaped, and had never seen her since. The jury found him guilty, and he suffered death on the gallows, protesting his innocence to the last. The dying confession of the real murderer, years after, confirmed the story.

LXVIII.

CASE OF HAMILTON.

A NUMBER of years ago, a small party, consisting of three brothers, with their families, were on their way to settle in the south-western part of Missouri. They had travelled as far as Kentucky, and at the time of which we speak were encamped for the night on the borders of a small stream. Soon after dusk, they were roused by the appearance of two young men on horseback, who had missed their way, and discovering the encampment of the emigrants, deemed it safer to spend the night with them rather than wander in the darkness, uncertain of their way through the thick woods. The young men gave the names of Hamilton and Saunders.

The night passed quietly, and in the early morning the two friends prepared to pursue their journey. As they were about to depart, one of the emigrants advanced towards them and remarked:

"I reckon, stranger, you allow to encamp at Scottville, to-night?"

" Yes," said Saunders, " I do."

" Well, then, I can tell you a chute, that's a heap shorter than the road you talk of taking. And at the forks of Rushing river, there's a smart chance of blue clay, that's miry like, and it's scary crossing at any time."

Supposing he had found a nearer and better road, and one by which a dangerous ford would be avoided, he thanked his informant, and bidding Hamilton good-bye, proceeded on his journey.

Saunders had been passing a few weeks with Hamilton, who was an old college friend ; and on his return home Hamilton had proposed to accompany him a day or two on his way.

Some time after, a vague report was brought to the village, where Hamilton resided, that the body of a murdered man was found near Scottville. It was first mentioned by a traveller, in a company where Hamilton was present, and he instantly exclaimed :

" No doubt it is Saunders ! How unfortunate that I left him !" and then retired, under great excitement. His manner and expressions awakened suspicions, which were unhappily corroborated by a variety of circumstances that were cautiously whispered by those who dare not openly arraign a person of Hamilton's position. He had ridden away with Saunders, who was known to be in possession of a large sum of money. Since his return, he had paid off debts to a considerable amount, and the penknife of Saunders was recognized in his hands.

The effect of the intelligence upon Hamilton was marked. He would sit for hours in a state of abstraction, from which even the smile of love could not awaken him.

He was arrested and committed for trial. Upon the trial the evidence produced was entirely circumstantial; but it seemed to weave a perfect network of corroborating circumstances around the accused. His recent intimacy with the deceased was clearly proved; also the fact that he had accompanied the deceased on his way, and that he had lost the path in a country with which he was supposed to be perfectly familiar: also his conduct on hearing of the death of his friend. It was further proved that Hamilton was seen in possession of a knife known to have belonged to Saunders, and that a breastpin and a pistol, both clearly proved to have belonged to the prisoner, were found near the body of the murdered man. Finally, the sister of Hamilton was called, and she was forced to acknowledge

10

that the clothes worn by her brother on his return from the journey with Saunders, were torn, soiled with earth, and bloody. *The jury rendered a verdict of guilty, without leaving their seats.* He was sentenced to death, but died in prison, protesting with his last breath his innocence.

About a year afterwards, a man who was executed in Tennessee, confessed that he was one of the party of emigrants with whom Saunders and Hamilton had spent the night; that he had murdered Saunders with a pistol, which he had found where the two gentlemen had slept. Perceiving that the two friends were about to separate, and that Saunders, who had incautiously exhibited a large amount of money the evening before, was about to proceed alone, he advised him to take what he represented to be a shorter way; and then intercepted him at the ford.

The truthfulness of the statement made by Hamilton at once became apparent. In some previous conversations, Saunders had learned that Hamilton was financially embarrassed, on account of some heavy losses, and was at the time much pressed for money. Saunders offered to assist him, but Hamilton declined, not being sure of his ability to repay in a reasonable time. At the time of parting, Saunders again mentioned the subject, and learning that five hundred dollars would relieve his friend from embarrassment, insisted upon his accepting that amount, as he had a large sum with him. Hamilton, after some hesitation, accepted the money. Hamilton then unclasped his college pin, and presented it to his friend, as a token of his visit, and their old college associations ; while Saunders, in the same playful spirit, drew from his pocket a silver-hafted penknife, curiously embossed, which his friend had often admired, and presented it as a similar token.

As Hamilton was riding slowly homeward, engaged in thought, and holding his bridle loosely, a deer sprang suddenly from the thicket, and fell in the road, before his horse, which startled and threw him to the ground. In examining the deer, which had been badly wounded, and was struggling on the ground, some of the animal's blood was sprinkled on his clothes, which had also been soiled and torn by his fall. Paying little attention to these circumstances, he returned home. How fearfully they were made to tell against him, has appeared!

LXIX.

CASE OF PIVARDIÈRE.

THE case of M. de Pivardière is one of the most
singular instances of criminal precipitation and
iniquity that the annals of French justice furnish.
Madame de Chauvelin, his second wife, was accused
of having had him assassinated in his castle. Two
servant-maids were witnesses of the murder; his
own daughter heard the cries and last words of her
father: "My God! have mercy upon me." One of
the maid-servants, falling dangerously ill, took the
sacrament: and while she was performing this
solemn act of religion, declared before God that her
mistress intended to kill her master. Several other
witnesses testified that they had seen linen stained
with his blood; others declared that they had
heard the report of a gun, by which the assassination was supposed to have been committed. And
yet, strange to relate, it turned out after all that
there was no gun fired, no blood shed, nobody

killed! What remains is still more extraordinary; M. de la Pivardière returned home; he appeared in person before the judges of the province, who were preparing everything to execute vengeance on his murderer.*

---

* The most singular part of this case followed the appearance of Pivardière. The judges were resolved not to lose their process : they affirmed to his face that he was dead ; they branded him with the accusation of imposture for saying that he was alive ; they told him that he deserved exemplary punishment for coining a lie before the tribunal of justice ; and maintained that their procedure was more credible than his testimony ! In a word, this criminal process continued eighteen months before the poor gentleman could obtain a declaration of the court that he was alive !

LXX.

CASE OF WEBBER.

ON December 29th, 1876, a terrible disaster occurred at Ashtabula, Ohio, on the Lake Shore Railroad. The train fell through a bridge, and as the cars immediately caught fire, and a large number of the passengers were burned, the most of the bodies were so charred as to prevent recognition. Shortly after this accident, Mrs. Webber, who is a poor woman with two children, appeared in the office of a lawyer, in Rochester, N. Y., and stating that she had every reason to believe that her husband had been killed in that disaster, requested him to commence a suit against the railroad company on her behalf. The evidence which she offered to introduce in proof of her husband's sad fate was only of a circumstantial nature, as nothing was ever found of the body, which was supposed to have been consumed in the flames. She had been to Ashtabula, and in the debris of the wrecked train she had found a bunch of keys which she positively recognized as those having been in the possession of her husband. One of these keys, in further proof, she had ascertained exactly fitted the clock in her house, and an Auburn man was ready to swear that he had made such a key for the deceased. Another key fitted a chest which she had in her possession, while still another of the keys fitted the lock on the door. But the strongest proof of all which she had discovered was a piece of cloth, which she had recognized as having been part of her dead husband's coat. The proof by no means stopped here, however. A physician of Rochester, who knew Mr. Webber, testified that he rode to Buffalo on the same train with the deceased on the fatal 29th of December; while another gentleman testified to seeing deceased take the train at Buffalo which went to ruin at Ashtabula. With this all but positive proof that the husband was among the victims of the disaster, the suit was commenced, the funds enabling her to carry it on being supplied by a kind-hearted gentleman. When the railroad company's attorneys were confronted with the proofs of the plaintiff's case, they advised a settlement with her for $4,000. But she wanted $5,000 or nothing, and the company's lawyers concluded to let the matter go before the courts. The investigations concerning the fate of the husband were continued, and it was ascertained that he had been sent by Gen. Martindale, his former superior officer in the army, to the Pension Home in Wisconsin, several days previous to the Ashtabula disaster, and this fact soon brought to light the very important disclosure that a man of his name, answering his description exactly, and who stated that he had a wife and two children in Rochester, was still alive and safe in that institution, and that he was not near Ashtabula at the time of the disaster. The case is a most remarkable one, however, from the fact that no person doubted the truthfulness of the witnesses whose evidence formed the basis on which the suit was commenced.

LXXI.

CASE IN LINCOLN.*

I HAVE been greatly disturbed all my life by executions which were not preceded by confession ; for when I was but thirteen, I saw a poor woman *with her seven children,* fling herself in the snow-covered road of the Minster—close at Lincoln—to intercept the judge's carriage, screaming for mercy, and protesting the innocence of her husband. He had been convicted of sheep stealing, and was sentenced to die on the following morning. He was so executed. In the same city, at the spring assizes, a murderer was convicted, and on the eve of his execution he confessed the perpetration of the crime for which the poor father of these helpless children suffered. Not only had he committed it, but with the aid of an accomplice he had contrived the circumstantial evidence of which a man entirely innocent was made the victim.

---

* We extract the above from Mr. Phillips' Essay on Capital Punishment.

APPENDIX.

WHO IS THE MURDERER?

A PROBLEM IN THE LAW OF CIRCUMSTANTIAL
EVIDENCE.

BY SAMUEL WARREN.

In the summer of the year 1830, there lived at a
place called Eagle's-cliffe, near Yarm, in the North
Riding of Yorkshire, a man of the name of William
Huntley. He was one of the sons of a respectable
farmer who had died about ten years before, leaving behind him a widow and several children, and
considerable property to be divided between them ;
but his will was so imperfect and obscure as to
have led to a Chancery suit, in order to determine
the true distribution of the property according to
his intention—which was, to leave his widow the
interest of a certain sum for her life, and considerable legacies to each of his children, payable as
they became of age. His son William was, in the
year 1830, about thirty-four years of age, and

married, but lived apart from his wife, with whom he had quarrelled. Owing to his being so long kept out of his little property, he became a weaver in order to support himself—and was, in fact, in humble circumstances. In point of personal appearance—a matter deserving particular attention—he was of middling stature; he had a broad squat face; his head was large behind; his forehead a retreating one, with rather a deep indentation between the eyebrows; and he was pitted with the smallpox. But there was one peculiarity in his face—a very prominent tooth on the left side of the under-jaw—which caught every one's eye on first looking at him. It occasioned him to have a sort of " twist of the mouth "—for which he had been always known and ridiculed by his companions, even at school. The solicitor who had the management of the affairs in Chancery was a Mr. Garbutt, residing at Yarm, and still living. He had occasionally assisted the family, and, amongst them, William Huntley, by small advances during the time of their being kept out of their property.

At length, on Thursday, July 22, 1830—which will be a date found of great importance—Mr. Garbutt was enabled to pay over to him the money due under the will; and on that day gave him a sum of £85, 16s. 4d.—the balance due after deducting the above-mentioned advances—in seventeen £5 bank-notes of the bank of Messrs. Backhouse and Company, bankers at Stockton-upon-Tees, and the remainder in silver and copper. He was also entitled to receive other money, which Mr. Garbutt had received instructions from him to endeavor to obtain; and I believe that he would have been entitled to a still further sum on his mother's death. As I have already mentioned, Huntley at this time resided at Eagle's-cliffe, but was in the constant habit of coming over to a small village at a few miles' distance, called Hutton-Rudby, where his mother lived, and also an intimate friend of his, one Robert Goldsborough, (the prisoner), whose house, on such occasions, he was in the habit of making his own—always passing the night there. Goldsborough was about Huntley's age; was a widower, with a couple of children, and in destitute circumstances, having even been in the receipt of parish relief down to within a few months of the period at which this narrative commences. On the day of Huntley's receiving his money, viz. Thursday, the July 22d, he went over to Hutton-Rudby, and stayed there one or two days, principally in company with his friend, Goldsborough. There is some reason to believe that Huntley was desirous of preventing two or three creditors of his from knowing that he had received so considerable a sum of money; and also that he had, about the time in question, intimated to one or two persons a wish to go to America. He appears to have gone frequently to and fro, between Hutton-Rudby and Eagle's-cliffe, during the ensuing week.

At an early hour, five o'clock, on the morning of Friday, July 30th, he was seen coming to Goldsborough's house; again, about three o'clock in the afternoon of that day, walking on the high-road, in company with Goldsborough, and a man named Garbutt; a third time, at eight o'clock in the evening of the same day, sitting in Goldsborough's house; and about ten o'clock that night, he, Goldsborough, and Garbutt, were observed walking together in a cheerful and friendly manner—Goldsborough with a gun in his hand—all bending their steps towards Crathorne Wood, which was close by, apparently on a poaching errand. From that moment to the present, Huntley has never been seen or heard of. The circumstance of his disappearance was noticed as

soon as six o'clock on the ensuing day, Saturday
—and his continued absence rapidly increased the
suspicion and alarm of the neighborhood. A
quantity of stale-looking blood being seen on the
side of the highroad, on the ensuing Monday morning, near the spot where he had been last seen
walking with Goldsborough and Garbutt—and also
a man's recollecting that, between eleven and
twelve o'clock on Friday night, he had heard the
report of a gun in Crathorne Wood, added to the
circumstance of Huntley's having been seen so frequently in Goldsborough's company, down even to
the moment of his sudden disappearance, naturally
pointed suspicion at Goldsborough, and anxious
inquiries were at once made of him by many persons, to know what had become of Huntley. To
one person, a creditor of Huntley's, Goldsborough
said, with an easy, confident air, that he had set
Huntley on the road to Whitby, where he was going to take ship for America. To Whitby instantly
went several persons in quest of the missing man,
but in vain; no such person had been seen or
heard of in that direction, nor was there—nor had
there been for some time—in that port any vessel
bound for America. The disappointed inquirers re-
tnrned to Goldsborough, to announce the fruitless

ness of their search, when he gave another account of Huntley's movements ; namely, that he had set Huntley on the way to Liverpool, there to take ship for America ; and a short time afterwards, to another class of inquirers, he told an entirely different story ; that he had set Huntley on his way to Bidsdale, to see some friends of his residing there. All this kindled still more vivid suspicion against him. Constables and others searched his house, and found in it a watch, and various articles of clothing, belonging to Huntley, but none of which he made the least attempt to conceal.

When asked to account for his possession of them, he gave inconsistent answers. First, he said that Huntley had given them to him ; but, on being reminded how improbable it was that a man so covetous as Huntley should have done so, he said that the fact was that he had lent Huntley money, and, on his going off to America, he had left the articles in question as a security for the repayment of what he owed. In short, Goldsborough was universally supposed to have murdered Huntley. On one occasion he said, without any embarrassment of manner, when taunted on the subject—"You'll all see, by-and-by, whether he's been murdered !" On another occasion, after following to his door a person who had just quitted it, he said to a man standing near—"That gentleman has been here asking after Huntley, but he'll find him neither at my house, nor at Whitby, nor nowhere else." Confident that the missing man had been murdered, the neighbors, and also the constables, searched far and wide after his body. To a party thus engaged, he once went up and said impatiently— "You fools! it's no use searching there! Only you give up, and I'll bring Huntley to you in a fortnight!" From some cause or other, these efforts were shortly afterwards discontinued. About a week or ten days after Huntley's disappearance, Goldsborough was observed sitting opposite a large fire in his house, reading; and a strong smell was perceived as of woollen burning. "Dear me," said a person to him, "you've a large fire for summer time!" He said he could not sleep, so he was sitting up reading. To another person mentioning the smell of woollen burning, he replied— "That he had been burning only some old things which he had pulled from under the stairs." At times he appeared disconsolate, and agitated, and reserved. Again—he was found suddenly in possession of a considerable sum of money—in banknotes, gold and silver—which he rather exhibited with ostentation than concealed, and this as early as within a day or two after Huntley's disappearance ; offering to lend money to some persons, and making various purchases for himself. He remained at his house till towards the close of autumn, when, wearied with the perpetual suspicions and ill-feeling exhibited towards him, he removed to the town of Barnsley, about thirty or forty miles off, and hired a loom of a man at whose house he took up his abode. When asked what his name was, he replied, "*Touch me lightly !*" He brought with him a good stock of clothes—many of them Huntley's—two watches, and plenty of money, with which he was very liberal. He complained of being out of health, and did no work—his chief amusement being the going out to shoot small birds. Some weeks afterwards he went away, and returned in company with a woman whom he said he had married—and that she had brought him a sum of £80 for her fortune. On being asked whence he had come, he replied, " From Darlington "—and passed under the name of Robert Towers.

This mysterious disappearance of Huntley, connected as it was with the circumstances above related with reference to Goldsborough, gradually ceased to be the subject of gossip and speculation.

But it may be asked—Why were not the startling facts of the case made the subject of a formal
judicial inquiry? Let me ask another question,
however—What proof was there that Huntley had
been murdered at all, or that he was even dead?
Was it impossible—or indeed very improbable—
that Goldsborough's account of the matter might
be the true one—viz., that Huntley had gone to
America, and that Goldsborough was purposely
giving contradictory accounts of Huntley's movements, to enable him to elude discovery? There
was, in fact, no *corpus delicti*—the very first step
failed.

No lawyer, on the above facts only, would feel
himself warranted in recommending the prosecution of Goldsborough for murder, with so serious
a chance of an acquittal : in which case, he could
never have been again tried as the murderer, however conclusive might be evidence subsequently
discovered. " However strong and luminous may
be the circumstances, the coincidence of which
tends to indicate guilt," observes a distinguished
writer on the law of evidence, Mr. Starkie, " they
avail nothing, unless the *corpus delicti*—the fact
that the crime has been actually perpetrated—shall
have been first established. So long as the least

doubt exists as to the act, there can be no certainty as to the criminal agent."

Thus, then, matters rested for a period of eleven years—that is, till the 21st June, 1841—when a number of workmen were employed by a respectable farmer, a quaker, named Nellist, in making some alterations in the sides of a *stell, i. e.* a brook or rivulet, dividing a place called Stokesley from another called Seymour. While one of the laboring men, named Robinson, was engaged in cutting into one of the sides of the stell, at a spot where there was a bend or curve in the stream, called Stokesley Beck, and which was about five miles distant from the spot where Huntley, Garbutt, and Goldsborough had been last seen walking together, after turning up two cattle bones, he discovered one belonging to a human body—a shin bone ; and presently, within a space of a yard and a quarter, " the bones of a Christian," as he expressed it : in fact, a complete skeleton, with the exception of the feet. The head lay at a distance of a yard from the shin bone.

Deeming this rather a curious circumstance, he took out the bones carefully, and laid them out at length on the side of the stell. They had lain at a depth of about three feet from the surface ; and had evidently not been deposited there by digging a hole down from the surface, like a grave, but by hollowing out, or digging a hole in the stell-side, and then thrusting in the body, " back-side first and doubled up," to use the words of the witness. The soil was tough and clayey; and the spot lay at a distance of about a hundred yards from the highroad. This stell was, in fact, not an inconsiderable stream, sometimes subject to overflows; and there was a wooden foot-bridge over it, a good way higher up the stream. The skull was removed from the earth carefully, by hand. It was filled with earth, and the lower back part of it appeared to have been broken off.

The bones having been thus carefully laid out, on Robinson's master, Mr. Nellist, arriving at the spot in the evening, he saw them with not a little surprise; and on looking at the skull and jaw-bone, particularly noticed a long projecting tooth on the left side of the lower jaw. With the exception of two or three, all the teeth were in their sockets, and remained in them till the bones, which had been damp when first discovered, began to dry, when some of the teeth fell out, and, amongst others, the remarkable and all-important tooth in question. Before this had occurred, however, Mr. Nellist took home with him, on the same evening, the skull and jaw-bone, and kept them, together with the loose teeth, in a pail. They were shortly afterwards, but before the prominent tooth in question had dropped out, seen by various persons; several of whom, on noticing the tooth, at once said that the skull was Huntley's, whom they had known. Mr. Nellist committed the skull and teeth, a day or two afterwards, to the care of one Gernon, a constable, who put them into a basket; and having heard of the former suspicions against Goldsborough, whom he also ascertained to be then living under another name at Barnsley, set off of his own accord, carrying with him the bones, to take Goldsborough into custody.

On the evening of the 23d of June, he found Goldsborough sitting in his house alone, without his coat, which hung over a chair back. "I have come," said the constable abruptly, "to take you into custody for the murder of William Huntley, eleven years ago,"—on which Goldsborough appeared dreadfully agitated. "Look at this," continued the officer, taking out the shattered skull, and showing it to Goldsborough, "and tell me if it isn't the remains of Huntley?" Goldsborough could not look at it, but his eyes wandered round the room: and with increasing trepidation, and bursting into tears, he

exclaimed, " I am innocent!   They may swear my
life away if they please, but I never had any clothes,
or a watch [the constable had asked him if he had
not a watch belonging to Huntley], or anything belonging to Huntley!   The last time I ever saw him
was on Thursday!"   The constable then took him
into custody, but released him the next morning,
considering the evidence against him not sufficient to
warrant his detention, especially as he had arrested
Goldsborough on his own responsibility only. ·The
whole matter was soon, however, brought under the
notice of the magistrates, and steps were taken at
once to obtain any evidence that might throw light
on this long hidden transaction :— a reward of one
hundred pounds being offered, in the usual terms, to
any one who should give such evidence as would lead
to the discovery and conviction of the murderer of
William Huntley.

Shortly afterwards a man of the name of
Thomas Groundy was heard making such observations as led to his being taken into custody,
and on the 10th of August Goldsborough was again
arrested—having continued ever since in the same
house in which he had formerly been seized, at
Barnsley—on the charge of having murdered William Huntley ; Thomas Groundy being charged as

an accessory after the fact. The magistrates having heard all the evidence which had been collected, were of opinion that it was expedient for the ends of justice to permit Groundy to turn king's evidence, as it is called—*i. e.* to be relieved from the charge against himself, in order to give evidence impeaching his fellow-prisoner. That was done; and the following is a *verbatim* copy of his deposition —every syllable of which is worthy of notice, in consequence of an extraordinary circumstance which occurred shortly after it had been taken :—

" Thomas Groundy being charged before us as an accessory after the fact to the murder by Robert Goldsborough of William Huntley, and being, after the hearing of all the evidence on the part of the prosecution, in the exercise of our discretion, admitted by us at this stage of the proceedings to give evidence against the said Robert Goldsborough, on his oath saith—

"On the Wednesday after William Huntley was missing, Robert Goldsborough came to me, and asked me if I would help him with a bag to Stokesley—he was going to America; and I told him I would go, and we went by Neville's hindhouse, and then we kept no road, and we went down to yon wood beside the stone bridge. He took me to a bag which was laid upon the ground in the wood, and I laid hold of it, and I found like a man's head, and I asked him what it was—and he stopped about five minutes before he spoke, and he then said—'it is a bad job, it is Huntley—as he was waiving *(qu. walking)* by me, I shot him.' Then I fell frightened, and wanted to go home, and Goldsborough said—'If you mention it I'll give you as much.' And I said I would not mention it, and I wanted to make off, and I made off. That the body was in the wood, within two or three hundred yards from the bridge. It is quite a lonely place. It was a rough place in the wood. Goldsborough never said anything more to me about it, and I was frightened, and durst not mention it to him. It was about hay-time. I knew William Huntley. He had a long tooth, and used to twist his mouth." Sworn, &c., 14th August, 1841.

" The mark of

" THOMAS ✗ GROUNDY."

Two or three hours afterwards, Groundy hanged himself!—He had been placed in a room in York Castle, only to await the arrival of his sureties, who were to be bound with him for his appearance to give evidence at the trial, and had not been left

On being placed at the bar, he rested his arms on the iron bar, with his hands clasped together—never removing the gloves he wore. This was the attitude which he preserved, with scarce any variation, during the whole of his two days' trial. He pleaded "Not Guilty," with an air of modest firmness and sadness, eyeing each of his jurymen as they were sworn, and also the judge in his imposing ermine robes, and the counsel immediately beneath him, with anxious attention. He appeared to me a man of firm nerves, or rather perhaps of slow feeling, who had made up his mind to the worst. Was he not an object of profound interest? Had he really done the deed which now, after so many years' concealment, was to be dragged into the light of day? Had he shot dead the companion walking beside him in unsuspicious sociality, rifled the bleeding body, and then thrust it, in the dead of the night, into the earth?—or was he standing there as innocent of the crime imputed to him, as the judge who was to try him, yet long blighted by unjust suspicion, and now desparing of a fair trial—the miserable victim of blind and cruel prejudice —to be convicted, within a few days hanged, his body buried within the precincts of the prison ; and

presently afterwards William Huntley to appear
ıgain alive and well?——

The counsel for the prosecution opened the case
with candor and judgment, giving a clear account
of the facts he expected to be able to establish ; and
in one of his observations the judge subsequently
expressed his anxious concurrence, namely, the necessity there was for the jury to be on their guard
against a certain air of romance, which seemed to
shed over the case, and against a secret notion that
the guilt of a long-hidden murder was destined, by
some sort of special providence, to be brought home
against the person now charged with it.   I shall now
proceed to give a carefully condensed account of all
the material facts proved—the reader keeping his
eye, all the while, on any points of coincidence or
contradiction that may strike him ; and I shall add
such observations on the demeanor and character of
the witnesses, as may possibly enable him the bet·
ter to appreciate the value of their evidence.   He
is already supplied with the key to it, in the brief
narrative which has gone before.

At the instance of the prisoner's counsel, all the
witnesses were ordered out of court before the counsel for the crown opened the case for the prosecution.   The following, then, was the evidence

adduced to prove, first, that William Huntley had been murdered; and secondly, by Robert Goldsborough, the prisoner at the bar.

William Garbutt, an attorney and solicitor, proved the facts stated, at the commencement of the narrative, as to the family, the property, and the person of William Huntley, particularly the prominent tooth; the payment to him of £85, 16s. 4d. on Thursday, the 22d July, 1830. He had examined the skull which had been found, and, from his recollection of the form of Huntley's countenance, believed it to have been his. He had never heard Huntley talk of going to America. A warrant had been issued against Garbutt in 1830, but unsuccessfully, as he had then absconded, and had never since been heard of.

George Farnabay had known both Huntley and Goldsborough well. They were very intimate; and the last time he had seen them together was on Thursday, 29th July, 1830. He saw Goldsborough enter his house (which was in the same yard as the witness's house) about 3 P. M. the next day (Friday), with a sort of sack, but could not guess what it contained, nor whether it was light or heavy. On the next evening (Sunday,) Goldsborough stood at his window, and pressed the witness to accom-

I 2

pany him to Yarm fair the next morning, saying, that a man there owed him £5; which sum Goldsborough offered to lend to the witness. Goldsborough went to the fair, and bought a cow there, and put it into a field belonging to witness. A week afterwards I was at Goldsborough's, when Dalkin called in to inquire after Huntley. Goldsborough said, Huntley had gone to Whitby to sail for America. The witness had himself heard Huntley speak, at different times, of going to America.

Robert Braithwaite, saw Huntley come to Goldsborough's door, knock, and be admitted about five o'clock in the morning of Friday, 30th July, 1830. He had a particular tooth in his under jaw, which pushed his lips out. Witness had seen the skull and jaw-bone; and the tooth in it corresponded exactly with that of Huntley. Just before his disappearance, witness (a tailor) had made him a dark green coat with yellow 'roundish' buttons, raised in the middle; a 'yellowish' striped waistcoat with yellow buttons; and a pair of patent cord trousers, with a yellow sandy cast, and a 'broadish' rib; and he distinctly observed that Huntley wore those trousers when he called at Goldsborough's, at five o'clock on Friday morning. Witness had known Goldsborough all his life. He was always very poor, and unable to pay witness for his clothes without the greatest difficulty.

James Gears was sitting smoking his pipe on the roadside (where he was engaged breaking stones) at Hutton-Rudby, between three and four o'clock in the afternoon of Friday, July 30th, 1830. Huntley, Goldsborough, and Garbutt came up together, lit their pipes at that of the witness, and then went down the lane, northward, towards Middleton. That was the last time he ever saw Huntley. The witness proceeded—"On Wednesday, August 4, 1830, Goldsborough and I were walking together towards some potato fields, and he pulled a quantity of silver out of his left-hand pocket, and four or five £5 bank-notes out of his right-hand pocket. I knew them by the stamp to be £5 notes. He told me they were Bank of England notes. I said, Robert, thou's well off—much better than I : I work hard for my family, and yet never have a penny to call my own." He said he had got the money out of the Stockton-on-Tees bank, where he could draw money whenever he wanted it, for he dealt in poultry. He had always till then been poor; having many times occasion to borrow a little meal and a little flour from the witness. The witness had mentioned the circumstance of the three men lighting their pipes from his, to Bewick the constable, on Monday the 2d August, 1830. [If that were so, he must have then had his suspicions against Goldsborough; and it is rather odd that two days afterwards he should be walking so familiarly with Goldsborough, and should not have challenged him more strictly as to his suddenly acquired wealth. As singular is it, that Goldsborough, if guilty, should have so stupidly exhibited it to one who well knew his previous poverty; and that, too, at the time when everybody was beginning to suspect him as Huntley's murderer.]

James Braithwaite—The last time he ever saw Huntley was about eight o'clock in the evening of Friday, 30th July, 1830, sitting on a box near the fireplace in Goldsborough's house. His face was full towards witness, who saw him quite plainly. Monday, August 2d, 1830, was Yarm fairday; and on witness passing along the highroad, about nine o'clock in the evening, he observed a pool of blood about fifty yards from the bridge, which is a little below Foxton Bank on the road from Yarm to Rudby. He mentioned the circumstance the same day to Brigham the constable. About ten days afterwards, in passing Goldsborough's house, about ten o'clock one night, he

observed a large fire, and went in, and told Goldsborough that there was a strong smell of woollen
burning. He replied that he had been burning
some old rags. The witness soon afterwards
reminded him that it was bed-time, and said, "Aren't
you going to bed?" He replied, "No; I can't
sleep."

James Maw—[This man was by far the most
important witness in the case. A violent attempt
was made to impeach his credit; but, in my opinion, and in that of all whom I conversed with, quite
unsuccessfully. He was about forty years old, very
calm and collected—with a sort of quaint pedantry
of manner, and gave his evidence in a fair, straightforward way.] The last time he had ever seen
Huntley was about nine o'clock on the night of Friday, July 30th, 1830, near the bridle-road leading to
Crathorne Wood, in company with Goldsborough,
who carried a new gun, and Garbutt—all three
of whom the witness had long known well. Huntley
wore a dark green coat, a yellow neckcloth (which
the witness particularly noticed), and darkish trousers and waistcoat. He spoke to witness, and said,
"Where hast thou been, thou caffy dog? [which
was a common expression of Huntley's.] Wilt go
along with us?"—"No," replied the witness; "you'll

be getting into mischief with your poaching!" "Do thou go with us," said Huntley; "we're going to try a new gun, and if we catch a hare, we'll go to Crathorne, have it stewed, and get some ale." He then pulled out of his pocket some notes, showed them to witness, and said, "I've plenty of money; I've been to Mr. Garbutt's and drawn part of my fortune." On this, Goldsborough said, "Put up thy money, thou fool; why art exposing it that way?" And then he added (but the witness was not sure whether to Huntley or Garbutt), "We'll have nobody with us." They then went on through the gate on to Crathorne bridle-road, and the witness went home, which he reached about ten o'clock. [I shall give the remainder of his evidence in his own words.] "On Saturday, August 7th, Bewick the constable and I went to the shop of Hall, a butcher at Hutton-Rudby, and there we had some talk about Huntley's being missing; and we and several others went that night to Goldsborough's house. Bewick said—'Goldy, there are strange reports about Huntley; what hast thou really done with him?' Goldsborough was very much agitated, making no answer for some time; then said he had set Huntley on the Whitby Road as far as Easley Bridge, to take ship for America. But I said that

was very unlikely, for there had been no ship advertised to go to America. Shortly afterwards, he
said he had set Huntley on the Tontine Road, to
take coach for Liverpool—which was in the opposite
direction to Whitby. I asked if Huntley had
booked at the Tontine? Goldsborough said no, he
had got on the coach beyond the Tontine. On this
we all told him these were two opposite tales. I
forget what his answer was, but he seemed very
much agitated—so much so, that he quite shook,
and required to use both his hands to put his hat
on. Bewick and I at another time went to call
on him, and found him walking up and down before
some houses near his own. Bewick said, ' Now
really tell us, what hast thou done with Huntley?'
He answered and said—[that was the formal
style in which much of the witness's evidence was
given]—' I sent him up to Carlton Bank, to go into
Bilsdale, to see some friends of his.' We said that
was again another different story; but I forgot his
answer. The same evening, I and four other men
(some of them constables), who all died of the
cholera when it was here, went to Goldsborough's
house to search it—he not objecting to it. We
found a pair of woollen corded trousers, an old
waistcoat, and an old coat. I could almost have

sworn they were all Huntley's. We also found six new shirts, marked 'W. H. 1,' 'W. H. 2,' 'W. H. 3,' 'W. H. 4,' 'W. H. 5,' 'W. H. 6,' in an old-fashioned piece of furniture, like a box or press, up-stairs; not in the room where one Hannah Best was engaged washing. The shirts had been made by one Hannah Butterwick; she was then there, and is now living, but I know not where. We asked Goldsborough how he explained all these things; and he said that Huntley had given the things to him. We said, 'No, no; he's too greedy a man for that;' on which Goldsborough said he had lent Huntley money, and he had left these things in part payment. There was a watch, seemingly of silver, with 'W. H.' engraved on the back, hanging up over the fireplace. We took it down and examined it. There were two papers inside, one with the name of ' Mr. Needham,' the other ' Mr. Stephenson, watch and clock-maker, Stokesley.' Goldsborough gave the same account of the watch as he had given of the clothes and shirts. There was a gun up the stairs, like the one I had observed in his hand when I last saw him with Huntley: it was new-looking. His sister-in-law pointed to it, crying, and saying, ' Oh, Robert, this is the thing thou'st either killed or hurt Huntley with. He replied, 'Hold thy tongue, thou fool! and was much agitated. I afterwards made one of those who went to search for Huntley's body. About fifty yards from that part of the road where the blood was found, near Foxton Bridge, I recollect seeing a place, in a potato ground, where the earth seemed to have been newly dug. [It certainly seems unaccountable that, if this circumstance really had been observed at that time, a spot so challenging suspicion should not have been instantly examined.] After we had been searching some time, we met Goldsborough, who said, 'Where have you been searching to-day?' Several persons replied, 'In Foxton Beek, Foxton Woods, and Middleton, and Crathorne Woods.' Goldsborough answered, 'He's far more likely to be found in Stokesley Beck.'" [The very place where the skeleton was found; but the obvious question arises—Could the prisoner have been insane enough thus to indicate the spot where he had deposited the body of his victim?] The witness then described Huntley's face, particularly his projecting tooth; and said he had seen the skull and jaw-bone, with the projecting tooth in it, just in the same place as Huntley's was, and projecting in the same way.

John Sanaerson lived in a house 200 yards from Crathorne Wood, and well recollected hearing, about eleven or twelve o'clock on the night of Friday, July 30th, 1830 (the Friday before Yarm fair), a shot fired in the wood; and a second within about a minute afterwards. It seemed about a quarter of a mile off. He got up and listened; but heard nothing more. There was game in the wood, and there were sometimes poachers.

Bartholomew Goldsborough.—On going on Monday morning, 2d August, 1830, to Yarm fair, saw a pool of stale-looking blood, about one and a half feet in diameter, lying on the high-road (which was not much frequented), a little on the Crathorne side of the road, and in a slanting direction towards the gate leading into Crathorne Wood. He had noticed this blood before he had heard that Huntley was missing. The place where the blood lay was from four to six miles' distance from Stokesley Beck, where the skeleton was found.

Thomas Richardson had sold Goldsborough a single-barrelled gun, on Monday, 26th July, 1830, for 8s. It was an old one, but cleaned and polished up so as to look like a new one. He did not pay for it, saying, he would take it on trial. A day or two after Yarm fair (which was on Monday, 2d

August, 1830), the witness called on him for payment. Goldsborough said he would return it—he
did not want it, and had not used it. The witness
thrust his finger down the muzzle, and when he
drew it out it was dirty with the mark of powder.
The witness showed him the finger, and told him
he had used the gun; which the witness then took
away. When the witness entered Goldsborough's
house, the latter was engaged at a chest, in which
were some clothes; he particularly recollected seeing a pair of woollen cord trousers, broad striped,
and a yellow cast with them; a yellow waistcoat
with a dark stripe with gilt buttons. There were
other clothes of a dark color. The trousers and
waistcoat were Huntley's—for the witness had seen
him wear them. He had also seen Huntley wearing
a green coat with brass buttons, having a nob on
them. [This witness gave his evidence in a satisfactory manner; and admitted, on cross-examination,
having been once or twice, some time before,
imprisoned for poaching, and once for having stolen
some goslings; of which, however, he strenuously
declared that he had not been guilty. Mr. Baron
Rolfe, in summing up, seemed justly to attach no
weight to these circumstances as impeaching the
value of his evidence.]

Joseph Dalkin.—Heard on Sunday, 1st August, 1830, of Huntley's disappearance, and went on that day to Goldsborough's, to inquire after him. Goldsborough said he had set Huntley along Stokesley Lane—that he was going to sail for America from Whitby, at four o'clock on the next morning (Monday). Witness said he would go and stop him, for he owed witness £4 for a suit of clothes. Goldsborough said, " Huntley and I have had all that matter talked over about his owing thee money ; he never intends paying thee—and it's of no use thy going after him." The witness, however, did go immediately to Whitby (a distance of thirty miles), and searched the whole town for Huntley, but in vain: nor was there any vessel going to America. When the witness measured Huntley, he wore a pair of patent cord trousers, with broad rib, and yellowish cast. He had pressed Huntley several times, in vain, to pay his bill.

George Bewick, a linen manufacturer, and also, in 1830, a constable. He had known Huntley, and recollected his disappearance. In consequence of hearing of it, he went soon after to Hall's (the butcher's) shop, where were Goldsborough and several others ; but he did not then recollect whether the witness Maw was also there. Huntley's wife also accompanied witness, and he said to Goldsborough, " There's a report that Huntley is missing; and as I hear you were last with him, I thought you the likeliest person to ask about him." He replied, " that Huntley had some relations at Bilsdale, and had gone there to see them." " Why then," asked the witness, " did you tell Joe Dalkin he had gone to Whitby, and thereby give him a sixty miles' journey for nought?" He made some unsatisfactory answer; but what it was the witness did not recollect. He was agitated, and trembled. The witness then said to him, " I understand thou hast Huntley's five shirts: how did'st thou come by them?" He answered that he had bought them of Huntley: to which the witness replied, " I understand you and Huntley bought a web from George Farnabay between you, which made you five shirts each; and it was not likely that either you could buy or he would sell you his five shirts; and here's his wife says he was badly off for shirts—having only a bad one on, and a worse one off?" His answer to this the witness had forgotten. He proceeded to give the same description of Huntley's person which had been given by the other witnesses: adding, " Huntley had something more remarkable about his appearance than most men ;" and that he had seen and examined the skull and jaw-bone, and believed it to be Huntley's. [This was an important witness; of respectable character and appearance; and corroborating the evidence of Maw in several material particulars. No attempt even was made to shake him by cross-examination.]

Maria Richardson had lived at Hutton-Rudby when Huntley was missed. He wore at that time woollen cord trousers, with a broad rib, and yellow cast; and had a yellow waistcoat with a dark-colored stripe in it. These articles of clothes, which witness knew at the time to be Huntley's, together with others, she saw in Goldsborough's house in a sort of old-fashioned chest or press, about a week or fortnight after Huntley was missing. When she went in, Goldsborough was at the chest looking over the clothes, and did not seem agitated. She was confident about having seen the articles in question.

John Kaye was sitting on the step of the house next door to Goldsborough s, on Sunday, 1st August, 1830, and saw the witness Dalkin go to Goldsborough's house, and then come back. Goldsborough followed him out, and then remained standing close to the witness, and said, "That gentleman's been to my house, asking for Huntley;

but I've told him he'll find him neither at my house nor at Whitby, nor anywhere else!" The witness saw Goldsborough the next day (Monday, 2d August, 1830) driving home a red cow from Yarm fair.

Elizabeth Shaw.—On Friday night, 30th July, 1830 (not having then, nor till a week afterwards, heard of Huntley's disappearance), between twelve and one o'clock, was at Mr. Bainbridge's house, which was just opposite to Goldsborough's. She had brought some linen home from the wash-house. While there she observed Goldsborough go out of his yard; then he went up to the public-house of Catchasides (also a constable), and first listened at the door, then at the low window, and then looked up towards the upper window, after which he returned towards his own house. When, about a week afterwards, the witness had heard that Huntley was missing, she went to Goldsborough's house, and found him sitting by a large fire, reading. "Dear me," said the witness to him, "this is a large fire for summer!" He said he had been burning some old rubbish, from under the stairs. There was a strong smell of woolen burning; and while the witness was talking in this way to him, he got up, opened the back window, and above half an hour before he was found suspended by his neckerchief and braces to one of the iron bars of the window, his knees resting on the floor, and quite dead. He had been in good health and spirits, and perfectly sober, up to the last moment of his being seen alive; having observed, in answer to inquiries, that what he had just been swearing to he had mentioned to two or three persons, whom he named, shortly after the facts had happened. An inquest was held on his body, and a verdict returned of *felo de se.*

To return,—Goldsborough, having heard the whole of the evidence thus adduced against him, including, of course, that of Groundy, voluntarily made and signed the following statement, which also I shall present to you *verbatim :*

"On Thursday, the 22d July, 1830, William Huntley came to my house, and stopped and talked awhile, and asked me to take a walk with him. We took a walk down over the bridge, and through Sir William Foulis' plantation. We sat down on the side of the footpath, in the plantation; and he says, ' I want you to look at some papers I have ;' and so he pulled them out of his inside coat-pocket, one a largish paper; which he had got from Mr. Garbutt, and he says—' I have been drawing my money,' and said he had drawn £85, 16s., and he said, 'What is the reason of all this money kept back?' I looked at the paper, and told him what the sums were for. He said he did not want it mentioned to every person, for Dalkin, Robert Moon, and some others, who wanted money of him, would be at him. I told him I had nothing to do with it —I should say nothing about it—so we came home together, and he was backwards and forwards out of our house, and other houses in the town, all the day. He laid with me all night, as he generally used to do when he came to the town. He was backwards and forwards all the next day, and he hired a cart and brought a loom down from Robert Moon's and sold it to George Farnabay that day, and he stopped all night, again, and slept with me, and then he came to Stokesley on the Saturday, and tried me several times to go to America with him. I went with him to Stokesley. We were together awhile at Stokesley on that day, and then we parted, and I never saw him any more until the Thursday following, and he came down to me at Farnabay's shop, at Hutton, and called of me out, and pushed me sadly to go to America with him, and I told him I had two children, and I should not leave them, as I was both father and mother to them. So he stopped awhile, and he said if I would not go, he could not force me; but if I would go, I should share with him as long as he had a half-penny. I refused, and he stopped a while, and we went out, and I set him down a few yards from the door, and left him. We shaked hands and parted; and he said, if Mr. Garbutt did not put it out about his money, he would stop a few days longer, if people did not get to know about it. I have no more to say about it. That was the very last time I clapped my eyes upon him. If it was the last words I had to speak, I never was in Crathorne Woods, nor Weary Bank Woods, with Thomas Groundy. You may think it's a lie; but if it were the last words I had to speak, I never was with him.

"ROBERT GOLDSBOROUGH."

He was then committed to York Castle, to take his trial at the next spring assizes for Yorkshire—an occasion looked forward to with universal interest by the inhabitants of that great county. Accordingly, at nine o'clock on Wednesday morning, the 9th of March, 1842, he made his appearance at the Bar of the Crown Court, before Baron Rolfe—than whom a more firm, patient, acute, and clear-headed judge could not have been selected to try such a case—to meet the fearful charge now made against him, of the " willful murder of William Huntley, by discharging at him a loaded gun, and thereby giving him a mortal wound, of which he instantly died."

" Put up Robert Goldsborough," said the clerk of arraigns to the governor of the castle, as soon as Mr. Baron Rolfe had taken his seat; and in a few moments' time a man was led along to the Bar of the Court, whose appearance instantly excited in me a mixed feeling of pity and suspicion—the latter, however, predominating. He was forty-seven years of age, of average make and height, wearing an old but decent-looking drab great-coat, a printed cotton neckerchief, clean shirt-collar, and a pair of somewhat tarnished doeskin gloves. His hair and whiskers were of a dull sandy color; his face rather long and thin; his eyes gray, heavy and slow in their movements, and with a sad expression ; his upper lip long and heavy; his mouth compressed, with a certain indication of sullenness and determination. In short, his features were altogether of a rigid cast and a phlegmatic character, wearing an expression of great anxiety and depression. Whatever inward emotion he might be experiencing, he preserved an external composure of manner.

stood leaning for some time against it, saying, " I'm
only looking out to get a bit of fresh air."   Two or
three days afterwards, she again saw Goldsborough
at his house, and said, " What a sad thing it was. if
Huntley was murdered!"   But all he said was,
" You'll all see by-and-by whether he's been murdered or not!"   About that time he appeared
greatly troubled in his mind, and not inclined to
speak to any one.   Goldsborough was a poor man,
scarcely able to get a meal of meat, and, in particular, was badly dressed.   She believed she had heard
Goldsborough, and possibly Huntley, talk of going
to America ; and thought she had heard Goldsborough say that Huntley had gone to America, and
had " rued " it.   [This witness gave her evidence
in a plain, straightforward manner, admitting that
she had had two children before marriage, and had
been once in jail for an assault, and once for stealing geese—the truth of which charge she vehemently denied.   She did not vary at all in her
evidence, under cross-examination.]

Hannah Best (mother of the last two female
witnesses), used to wash for Goldsborough once a
week ; and when at his house, on such occasions,
used to put one of his two children to bed.   The
last time she had washed for him was on Friday,

30th July, 1830; and on that occasion he said he would himself put his child to bed, but gave no reason for so doing. During the afternoon of that day, she observed him bring in something in a sack on his back, and take it up-stairs. She could not recollect ever having seen any shirts in Goldsborough's house that were marked, and must have recollected them if there had been such; nor did she recollect seeing Goldsborough looking into a chest, nor with any such clothes as had been described; nor did she recollect seeing the witness Maw in the house. [This was a stupid old woman of the *non miricordo* class; either really recollecting nothing of what had happened, or resolved to say nothing prejudicial to Goldsborough.]

Anthony Wiles, till within the last seven years, had lived next door to his step-sister, who kept a chandler's shop at Hutton-Rudby; and where he had often seen Huntley go in to change his money into half-crown pieces, for which he always seemed to have a peculiar fancy. Witness knew Goldsborough well; and recollected the time of Yarm fair, on Monday, 2d August, 1830. On the Saturday before, recollected seeing Goldsborough, Thomas Groundy, and two others, in a public-house, drinking, in the front kitchen; they came in about twelve

13

o'clock at night, and remained there till four o'clock in the morning. They had at least thirteen pints of ale ; and Goldsborough paid for all—giving half-crowns, and getting change for them every second or third pint. The witness was one of those who had searched for Huntley's body on the Friday or Saturday after he was missing. After having been home to get some refreshment, they returned to their task ; and while at a hay-stack, which was about two miles from the place where the bones were found, Goldsborough came up, anxious and breathless, and said, "What are you doing there?—a lot of fools ! If you'll only wait, I'll bring him forward in a fortnight !"

John Duck was overseer, in 1830, of the parish where Goldsborough then lived ; and gave him and his family parish relief in the fore part of that year —viz. five shillings a-week for four weeks.

Robert Hall, a butcher at Hutton-Rudby, saw Goldsborough at Yarm fair on Monday, 2d August, 1830, buying a red heifer, for which witness saw him pay £7 ; and observed that he had paper money, gold, and silver. Recollected also Bewick, accompanied by Mrs. Huntley, coming to his shop shortly after Huntley was missing, to inquire of

Goldsborough, who was there also, what had become of Huntley.

William Robinson, a weaver at Barnsley.—In the autumn of 1830—towards Martinmas—Goldsborough came to reside with the witness; he took a loom of witness, and called himself "Robert;" when asked his other name, he used to say, "*Touch me lightly !*" He complained at first of being poorly, and did not work for some weeks, but would go ont with a gun to shoot small birds. When he first came, he had on a pair of broadish woollen fawn-colored trousers, and had also a black coat. His box did not arrive till some weeks afterwards; and then he had a green and black plaid coat, a top-coat, two hats, and two watches—one apparently an old and the other a new one, and made of silver. Both had cases when he first came, but he subsequently lost the case of the old one. Witness never saw him with money; but, from his style of living, he must have had it. Once, on witness talking about buying a pig, Goldsborough told him not to be "fast" for want of a pound or two, and lent him two sovereigns. After living with witness a few weeks, he went away—northward, as he said—and after a month's absence, returned with a woman, whom he said he had married. They only took their meals with the witness; sleeping elsewhere. They lived much better than witness and his family could afford to live.

William White.—In the spring of 1831, Goldsborough came to live near witness's mother, at Barnsley, under the name of Robert Towers. He used to have witness to go out with him shooting, to gather his birds—and the first time he paid witness anything, was a shilling, which he took out of a quantity of gold and silver—there must have been as much as £15 or £16, and 30s. worth of silver, or thereabouts. He had a watch, with a scarlet ribbon and two large seals, which he wore—and another with no outer case. He once offered to sell witness the watch he wore; and on his declining, asked him if he would buy the inside of another, which also the witness declined. At this time, he had been about four or five months at Barnsley. Once the witness asked him where he had come from; and he replied, Darlington. Soon after he came he bought a chest of drawers, a corner cupboard, and some chairs. He said he had got £80 from his wife's friends.

Three witnesses were then produced, to speak to the peculiarities of Huntley's personal appearance, and the correspondence of the skull which had been

found with the form of his face and head. One
was a respectable farmer, who had known him for
fourteen years, and said that he had a low nose and
forehead, and his head was largeish behind. The
witness had seen and examined the skull.—" It
was," he said, " similar to Huntley's head, his face,
and everything about it." A second witness was a
hatter at Hutton-Rudby, whose customer Huntley
had been. He required a large hat; and on the
last occasion, the witness had found it difficult to
fit him. He had a particular shaped face, a short
one, a broad flat nose, and was much sunk between
the eyebrows. The low part of his forehead over-
hung much, and then fell back ; and the hinder part
of his head was very large. The third witness had
known Huntley when a boy, and used, with the
other boys, to plague him about his tooth.

Then was adduced the evidence of the discovery
of the bones, and the locality where they were
found, of which I have already given some account.
The "stell" in question seemed to be a sort of
tributary stream to the river Leven, two or three
yards deep, though not broad, and was occasionally
subject to floods, when its water would run rapidly
down, past the spot where the bones were found,
which was in a sort of small bend or curve of the

stream, where the current had in a manner under-
mined the bank, which is left considerably overhanging. As I understood it, this hollowed part
must have been still further excavated, for the purpose of receiving the body, which was supposed to
have been thrust in " backside foremost," leaving
the skull at one angle, and the feet at the opposite
one of the base of the triangle. The soil was, ı
believe, alluvial. The spot in question was a
secluded one, being the property of a Colonel ——,
who had once or twice been seen fishing in it.
There was a foot-bridge, but at a considerable
distance, higher up the stream. The whole of a
human skeleton was found except the feet, the
small bones of which might have been exposed to
the action of the current, and from time to time
washed away. All the bones, and particularly the
skull, were removed most carefully by the hand, so
that no injury might be inflicted by spade or pick-
axe. When first discovered, it would appear certain
that there was a very prominent tooth on the left
side of the lower jaw, which arrested the attention
of all those who saw it; but soon afterwards, owing
to the inconceivable carelessness and stupidity of
those intrusted with the custody of such all-impor
tant articles, and who permitted every idle visitor

to have free access to them, the tooth in question—
alas!—was lost! I confess I have seldom experienced such a rising of indignation as when this
remarkable deficiency of evidence was thus disgrace-
fully accounted for; and had I been the judge, the
very least symptom of my displeasure would have
been the disallowance of the costs of any witness in
whose custody the bones had been placed when
the tooth in question was with them.

To return, however — it was now nearly five
o'clock in the afternoon, and as the case for the
crown must inevitably close shortly, it was properly
determined upon to produce the bones during the
broad daylight, to enable the jury, judge, and the
witnesses, to see them distinctly. As soon as I
heard a whispered suggestion to that effect, I fixed
my eyes closely on the prisoner. As soon as he
heard the order given to produce the bones, I perceived that he slightly changed color; and turning
his head a little towards the witness-box, where he
expected them to be produced, he directed quick,
furtive glances, while a new square deal box was
brought forward, and unlocked. To the eye of a
close observer, the prisoner's countenance now
evidenced the miserable and almost overpowering
agitation he was experiencing—and that, withal,

he was nerving himself up, so to speak, for a great effort. I perceived his breast twice or thrice heave heavily; and though conscious of being watched closely by those around him, he could not keep his eyes for more than a moment away from the box, with whose mysterious contents he was to be so quickly confronted. At length a dark brown skull, the hinder part appearing to have been broken off, was lifted out of the box; the prisoner's under-lip drooped a little, and perceptibly quivered for a moment or two—and after one or two glances at the skull, he looked in another direction, his eyes, if I know anything of human expression, full of suppressed agony and terror. Yet again—and again—he glanced at the dumb but fearful witness produced against him; and from a certain tremulous motion of the ends of his neckerchief, I could perceive that his heart was beating violently. Still he never moved from the position which he had occupied since the morning; though I learnt from one of the turnkeys who stood near him in the dock, that at the period I am mentioning, and also at several other periods of the day, he trembled so violently, and his knees seemed so near giving way, that they almost thought he would have fallen.

In these observations concerning the prisoner's

demeanor, I am happy to find myself corroborated by a very able and learned friend, himself a close observer, who was leading counsel for the prosecution, and made a point of watching the prisoner at the moment which I also had selected for so doing. He tells me that he had also observed another little circumstance—that the prisoner listened with comparative unconcern to those portions of the evidence relating to the blood found on the road, the sound of the gun-shot heard in the wood, his possession of the clothes of Huntley, and his conflicting accounts concerning them, and the movements of Huntley ; but whenever there was any allusion to the disposal of the body, the carrying of it, and depositing it at Stokesley Beck, he became evidently painfully absorbed by what was said—agitated and apprehensive—always, however, striving to conceal his emotion. For what reason I know not, but no other portions of the skeleton were produced in court than the skull, the jaw-bone, the teeth, and a portion of the pelvis. I examined them all carefully. They were of a dark brown color, with no appearance of decay—on the contrary, they seemed strong and compact. Most of the teeth were so loose as to fall out of the sockets, unless held in them while the jaw-bone and skull were being examined. None of the teeth were decayed, but such as might have been expected in a healthy adult, who had at all events never had diseased teeth. I examined minutely the socket which had contained, when the bones were first discovered, the prominent tooth—the first molar tooth on the left side of the lower jaw—subsequently so strangely lost. There was little apparent difference between it and its corresponding socket on the other side of the lower jaw : than which, however, it was a trifle deeper, and the outside edge projected a little, and only a little, more outwards. But even had they both been precisely similar, I conceive it yet quite possible that the tooth might, in life, have been a larger one than usual above the gum, and inclining a little outwards, so as to cause a perceptible protrusion of the under-lip. As far as my own impression goes, I should certainly have felt great difficulty in pronouncing, from the mere appearance of the socket, that the tooth which it had contained must have been such a prominent and projecting one, as to give the living individual a remarkable peculiarity of countenance. Still, however, it must be borne in mind that a very prominent tooth that socket actually did contain, when first removed from the earth, unless all the witnesses who said that they had observed it, Mr. Strother the surgeon included, are perjured, or laboring under an inconceivable delusion on the subject.

The skull was dark, and of compact texture; but the first thing that struck one was, that a great portion—nearly two-thirds—of the lower hinder part was wanting, and seemed to have been broken off. It had no appearance of having decayed or mouldered away, but of having been fractured—broken off; but whether before or after death, I cannot venture to offer an opinion. The edge was rough and abrupt—I mean not smooth and uniform, but strong and well-defined. In short, the missing part must have been broken off. I observed no traces whatever of shot-marks in any part of the skull or jaw. If one may be allowed to speculate in such a matter, I should say that, if a loaded gun or pistol had been discharged during life-time at the person to whom that skull had belonged, say with the muzzle pointed at or near either ear, in a direction parallel, or nearly so, with the other; or if, even, it had been discharged from behind, but in a somewhat upward direction; or if the person had been felled by a heavy blow from behind, and blows subsequently repeated till death ensued; or if,

having been in the first instance shot, the back of
the head had been battered in by blows from any
heavy instrument, whether before or after death ;—
in any of these cases, I should have expected the
skull, after lying ten or twelve years in the ground,
without having ever been in any coffin, to present
the appearance exhibited by the skull in question,
while I was handling and examining it in court.
But I could by no means say that such an appearance could not also have been occasioned by any
violent injury suffered by the skull five, eight, ten,
or twelve years after death.   It will be observed
that the skull in question was found in a tough,
clayey soil, near a stream, where it may have lain
for twelve years or more, without probably having
ever been touched or disturbed since first deposited
there; and, when first discovered, was carefully
removed by the hand only of him who first saw it.
What inference is to be drawn from the fact that
the skull was found full of earth, but not the sockets
of the eyes, nor the mouth, I know not.

As to judging, from the mere skull, of the general
form of the countenance during life, it is obviously
a matter of infinite difficulty.   Who, for instance,
can tell whether the party's face was a fat or a lean
one ?   All I can say is, that having heard the same

account given by so many of the witnesses of Huntley's face and head, and without regarding their further statement that the skull, in their opinion, had belonged to him, I thought it probable that such was the fact. The skull was large, particularly towards the back part; the forehead narrow, and rather retreating; there was some sinking between the eyebrows; and from the bones of the nose, I should think it must have been a flat, spreading nose. The only professional witness called, was a respectable surgeon who lived in the neighborhood where the bones were found. He swore that when he first saw the jaw-bone, a day or two after it had been discovered, it contained the remarkable projecting tooth in question; and from the form of the skull, and of the pelvis, he was confident that they had been those of an adult male. He also said, that from the form of the socket, it must have contained such a tooth as would have given Huntley the appearance described by the witnesses. " It is," said he, holding the skull and jaw-bone together in his hand, " the skull of a person who had a short round face, a low forehead sloping back, a broad flat nose, and a depression at the top of it. The bones," he continued, " appeared to have been in the ground nine or ten years: they might have

lain there as long even as twenty years; and though
certainly much would depend, with reference to
such a point, upon the nature of the soil where they
had lain, he had not made any chemical examination of it. From the broken appearance of the
skull, he pronounced a confident opinion that the
person to whom it had belonged 'had died a violent death.'" In answer to a pointed question from
the judge, the witness repeated that the tooth in
question, when he saw it in the jaw, projected a
good deal more than such a tooth generally did.
So much for the bones.

Then was offered in evidence the deposition of
Thomas Groundy, (*ante,* p. 166), and the prisoner's
counsel strongly urged that it was inadmissible.
The judge, however, received it. Groundy had
been admitted by the magistrates to give evidence,
having been himself, thereby, exonerated from the
charge against him; that evidence had been given
on oath, voluntarily, and in the presence of the
prisoner, who might have put to him any questions
which he might have thought proper; the witness
was since dead; and his deposition fell within the
ordinary rule—being admissible in evidence; but
what credit was due to it, was, of course, quite
another matter. It may, however, admit of great

doubt whether this all-important document was not really inadmissible on a technical ground, which a careful examination of the "caption" may suggest to criminal lawyers. The governor of the castle was then sworn, and he proved the fact of Groundy's having been found dead in the manner already described; and then the deposition was formally read in evidence by the officer of the court.

Mr. Garbutt (the first witness, and who was also the clerk to the magistrate) then proved, that as soon as the above deposition had been made, he, accompanied by a police officer, went to Crathorne Wood, and they found places in it exactly corresponding with those named in the deposition. At the instance of the prisoner's counsel, Gernon, the officer to whose care the bones had been first committed, was recalled, and produced a flat button which had been found near the bones, and which was of a different description from the buttons which had been spoken of by the witnesses as worn by Huntley; this circumstance was adduced for the purpose, of course, of weakening the evidence of identity. The prisoner's own statement, (*ante*, p. 170), on being committed for trial, was then formally put in and read. This closed the case against the prisoner; and it being nearly seven o'clock in the evening, the court adjourned—the jury being accommodated during the night in the castle, so that they might enter into conversation with no persons whatever, on any pretence.

When the prisoner was again placed at the bar, at nine o'clock on the ensuing morning, his countenance bore marks of the anxiety and agitation which he must have endured in the interval, and looked worn and haggard indeed. His counsel then rose, and addressed the jury for three hours, with much eloquence and ingenuity. He impugned the credibility of almost all the witnesses— especially those who had given the strongest evidence. He denied that there was a tittle of evidence to show that Huntley was not at this moment alive and well—and ridiculed the idea of the skull produced being that of Huntley, commenting with just severity on the absence of the tooth—the great point of the pretended identity. His opinion, he said, was, that the bones had belonged to a female ; and his " hypothesis," that some drunken person had fallen from the bridge into the stream, been drowned, and the body carried down by the current and forced into the bend of the stream, where the bones had been found. He proceeded to argue, that the prisoner's possession of Huntley's clothes and property—which he denied to be the fact, for the witnesses "could not be depended upon"—was consistent with a scheme between him and Huntley to enable the latter to go to America. He said the evidence was a tissue of exaggerations, misrepresentations, and perjuries — the legitimate produce of the "blood money"—which had been had recourse to. If Huntley were murdered, again, might it not have been by Garbutt? or Groundy—who had, immediately after his false evidence, gone and hanged himself, like Judas? He sat down, after a powerful appeal, urging on the jury that it was infinitely better that ten guilty persons should escape, than that one innocent person should be condemned; and Baron Rolfe immediately proceeded to discharge his responsible and difficult duty of summing up the whole case to the jury. I took no notes of it; and do not, consequently, feel myself warranted in giving any detailed account of so critical a matter from mere recollection. None of the newspapers have rendered me, in this dilemma, the slightest assistance: for, after giving at great length the speech of the prisoner's counsel (who, of course, must take only one view of the case), the view taken by the judge—the able, experienced, and impartial person, on whose view, in nine cases

14

out of ten, adopted by the jury, the prisoner's fate almost exclusively depends—is thus summarily dismissed :—" Mr. Baron Rolfe then proceeded to sum up, commenting on the evidence as he proceeded, and pointing out such facts as bore for or against the prisoner ; "—but what those facts were, or how dealt with by the judge, the reader of the newspaper has not the slightest glimmering notion afforded him. If anything said by me could have the least weight with the gentlemen who perform the honorable and responsible duties of reporting cases of law—especially in great criminal trials—in the newspapers, I would recommend them to give the evidence fully, and also a careful account of the judge's summing up to the jury. The following is the best account I can present of this important summing up.

Mr. Baron Rolfe was decidedly adverse to a conviction. He first read over to the jury the whole of the evidence which had been adduced in the case ; and then gave a lucid statement of the principles by which the law required them to be governed, in estimating the value of that evidence. He left it fairly to them to judge whether sufficient had been done to satisfy them, beyond all reasonable doubt, that the bones produced were those of Huntley; but accompanied by a strong expression of his own opinion, that the evidence was of an unsatisfactory nature. Unless they were satisfied on that head, there was an end of the case; for the very first step failed, viz., proving that Huntley was dead. If, however, on the whole of the facts, they should feel satisfied in the affirmative, then came the two other great questions in the case—had Huntley been murdered?—and by the prisoner at the bar? Was the evidence strong enough to bring home the charge to him? His lordship advised them to place little or no reliance on the evidence contained in Groundy's deposition; and then proceeded to analyze the *vivâ voce* evidence which had been given. Even if the whole of it were believed by the jury, still it was not absolutely inconsistent with the fact of the prisoner's innocence of having mur-dered Huntley, and with the truth of his story that he had assisted Huntley in going off secretly to America. Without impugning the general character of the witnesses, his lordship pointed out how unconsciously liable persons were, in cases like these, to fit facts to preconceived notions, giving them a complexion and a connection not warrantable by the reality—and all this without intending to state what they believed to be untrue. Many of

the facts spoken to were utterly irreconcilable with
the supposition of the prisoner's conscious guilt;
while others again were certainly difficult to be
accounted for on the supposition of his innocence.
Some were highly improbable, and others inconsistent; while in one or two instances there were
material discrepancies between the witnesses: for
instance, Maw spoke positively to seeing six shirts,
numbered accordingly, up to " W. H. 6; " whereas
Bewick proved that there were only five—that
Huntley and the prisoner had bought a web
sufficient to make them five shirts apiece.

Again, the time and place where the blood was
found—if found it had been—and the two reports of
a gun in the wood, were, especially when coupled
with the great distance from that locality of the spot
where the bones were found, circumstances very
difficult to connect with the death of Huntley, in
the manner suggested by the counsel for the crown.
The case, in fact, was distinguished by many singular circumstances — and the duty which thus de-
volved on the jury was a serious and difficult one,
requiring of them calm and unprejudiced consideration. They were to remember that it was for the
prosecutor to satisfy them of the guilt of the prisoner—beyond all reasonable doubt. If, however,

they did entertain serious doubts, then it was their duty to consider the case as not proved, or—to use a phrase of which his lordship did not approve—" to give the prisoner the benefit of the doubt." Finally, they had sworn to give their verdict according to the evidence, and that only. It was their solemn duty to do so, and entirely to disregard any consequences that might follow their verdict.

The jury then retired from court, attended, as usual, by a sworn bailiff, and taking with them the bones which had been produced in evidence. The prisoner eyed them as they went with deep anxiety, and was then removed from the bar, to await the agitating moment of their return. While he is sitting alone in this frightful suspense, and the jury are engaged in their solemn deliberation, let us endeavor ourselves to deal with this extraordinary case, by considering the principles which our law brings to bear upon such an inquiry—the various solutions of which the facts are susceptible, and which of those solutions we should ourselves be inclined to adopt.

Let us consider, for a moment, what difficulties the law has to contend with in setting about to discover the perpetrator of such an enormous crime as that of murder—that is, of malicious and premedi-

:ated killing.   In such a case the deed is done, not suddenly, openly, recklessly—the criminal, in the frenzy of the moment, avowing his guilt, or, with the sullen feeling of gratified malice, making no attempt to fly from, or conceal it, but secretly, with time and place so carefully pre-arranged, as to leave no trace of his presence or his acts, and thereby secure every chance of impunity.   His success will depend almost entirely, in such a horrid emergency, upon his fore-thought and self-possession before, during, and after the doing of such a " deed of dreadful note."   He will either be alone in his guilt, or select a confed-erate or confederates not likely to betray him.   His object will be entirely to disconnect himself with the transaction, so as to appear equally innocent and ignorant of it ; for which reason he must, to the utmost of his ability, enact, without seeming to do so, the part of a stranger, shocked and horrified with the rest of the world, at the atrocious act. But to do this successfully, how he must be ever on his guard ! for if he be taken one instant unawares, the mortal thrust comes, and all is over.   The law, therefore, has often to grope in the dark after the most atrocious criminals.   To be cold and circum-spect when all mankind are thunderstruck with the appalling discovery—calmly addressing itself to the circumstances then existing, even of apparently the most trivial character, amongst which may be found the faint, vanishing traces of the guilty one—some little oversight of his—something said or done, or omitted to be said or done — which no human sagacity could have anticipated or provided against—some delicate but decisive evidence of inconsistency, between one single circumstance and a particular person's ignorance or innocence of the black transaction, must be seized upon before it shall disappear for ever—observed accurately, and treasured up safely against the proper moment of disclosure.

Still profoundly anxious equally to avoid accusing the innocent, and allowing the guilty to escape—and aware of the cruel tenacity of public suspicion, when once roused, against the individual, or individuals, towards whom its finger is first pointed, it is slow in announcing the result of its earliest inquiries, even its most stringent convictions, its most conclusive evidences. After a minute and accurate survey of localities, the next inquiry, in case of a murder, is, with whom was the deceased last seen? under what circumstances? what account is given of the matter by such a person or persons? can any motive be suggested on the part of any one? Suppose any inconsistency or improbability should be detected in the account given by a suspected person of his last being with the deceased, is it referable fairly to the confusion into which such a startling inquiry might throw the most innocent person, or, the more it is considered, the more of purpose and motive is there discernible—the more of conscious falsehood? Has some answer been spontaneously given, suggestive of a necessity for some further inquiry, the answer to which is at once perceived, by an experienced and acute observer, to be utterly inconsistent with the supposition of the speaker's ignorance of the transaction in question? Here begins to kindle the law's suspicion, but here, at the same moment, appear her forbearance and humanity; she will not suffer a suspected person to answer a single question upon compulsion, but, on the contrary, deliberately apprises him of the use which may be made of his answers. Suppose, however, the next discovery should be, that the missing person was, within the knowledge of the suspected person, possessed of a considerable sum of money at the time of his disappearance: that the suspected person, up to that time in abject poverty, had become suddenly and unaccountably in possession of ample funds, and also, is incontestably possessed of the clothes and other articles of personal property which had belonged to the missing person.

Yet suppose, on the other hand, the suspected person attempts no concealment of these facts; and further, makes a statement, not in itself improbable or inconsistent with the previous circumstances of the missing party, tending to throw strong doubt on the presumed fact of his death, to say nothing of his murder, which is consistent, on reflection, with all the proved facts of the case, and with that of the missing party's having, for instance, quitted the country, to return hereafter; here the law pauses, is staggered, suspects she has taken the first false step, and begins, with increasing anxiety and diffidence, to inquire further into the matter. The suspected person, in the mean time, makes no attempt to escape, though enjoying ample opportunities; and at length the law feels compelled to remove her hand, at least for a while, vehement as may be her suspicions as to his actual guilt. Fresh circumstances are brought to light, tending to the same conclusion, possibly consistent with his innocence, but far more probably with his guilt. Still the suspected party flies not before the darkening features of suspicion, but persists calmly in his original version of the affair.

First, then, said the law in this case, in the autumn of 1830—let me be assured of THE FACT THAT A MURDER HAS BEEN COMMITTED— that the missing person is really dead.　Melancholy experience warrants the anxiety of the law on this score, namely, to obtain evidence that the missing person is actually dead.　The great Sir Matthew Hale would never allow a conviction for murder, unless proof were first given of the death of the party charged to have been murdered, by either direct evidence of the fact, or the actual finding of the body ; "and this," says he (2 *Hale*, 290), "for the sake of two cases—the first one mentioned by my Lord Coke : ' The niece of a gentleman had been heard to cry out, Good uncle, do not kill me ! and soon afterwards disappeared.　He, being presently suspected of having destroyed her for the sake of her property, was required to produce her before the justices of assizes.　She, however, had absconded, whereby he was unable to produce her ; but thinking to avert suspicion, procured another girl resembling his niece, and produced her as his niece.　The fraud was detected, and, together with other circumstances, appeared so strongly to prove the guilt of the uncle, that he was convicted and executed for the supposed murder of his niece, who, as it afterwards turned out, was still living.' The second case," continues Sir Matthew Hale, "happened within my own remembrance, in Staffordshire, where one A was long missing; and upon strong presumptions, B was supposed to have murdered him, and to have consumed him to ashes in an oven, that he might never be found; and upon this, B was indicted for murder, convicted, and executed. Within one year afterwards, A returned, having been indeed sent beyond seas against his will by B, who had thus been innocent of the offence for which he suffered." But by far the most remarkable case of this kind on record is that of Ambrose Gwynnet, who, on evidence, which really appeared conclusive and irresistible, was condemned for murder, hanged, and gibbeted; yet in consequence of a series of singular circumstances, he survived his supposed execution—escaped to a foreign country, and there actually saw and conversed with the very person for the murder of whom he had been condemned to die. Surely the frightful possibility of the recurrence of such cases as these, warrants the law in requiring full and decisive evidence of the death of the party missing. By this, however, is not meant that actual proof of the finding and identifying of the body is absolutely essen-

tial. "To lay down a strict rule to such an extent," justly observes Mr. Starkie, "might be
productive of the most horrible consequences."
Accordingly, in *Hindmarch's case* (2 *Leach*, 571), a
mariner being indicted for the murder of his captain
at sea, and a witness swearing that he saw the
prisoner throw the captain overboard, and proof
having been given that he was never seen or heard
of afterwards, it was left to the jury to say whether
the deceased had not been killed by the prisoner,
before being thrown into the sea. The jury found
him guilty—with the subsequent unanimous appro-
bation of the twelve judges, to whom the case was
referred, and the prisoner was executed. It is
indeed easy to imagine cases in which the bodies
of murdered persons, especially infants, might be
removed at once, and for ever, by the murderers,
beyond the reach of discovery.

In the case before us—where was, in 1830, the
corpus delicti—proof of the fact that a murder had
been actually committed? The grounds of suspicion were extraordinarily strong; but our law will
not convict upon mere suspicion. Then how far
was this essential deficiency supplied in 1841, by
the discovery of the skeleton, coupled with the
additional evidence which that event enabled those

engaged in the investigation to collect? First—
Was that skeleton the skeleton of Huntley? It was
a very singular place for a skeleton to have been
found in; the position of the bones was curious,
to say the least, strongly favoring the notion of the
body to which they had belonged having been hastily doubled up and thrust into the earth in the way
suggested; the prominent tooth was a most signal
token of identity; and as a fact, spoken to by several credible witnesses; the general appearance of
the skull certainly suited the descriptions of Huntley's countenance and head given by many
witnesses; and its battered, broken appearance behind, was, to say the least, a singular circumstance
in the case. But I can add nothing to what I have
already presented to the reader on this part of the
case—and he must judge for himself.

To come next to the testimony of the witnesses.
Let me first advert to the circumstance of the
reward of one hundred pounds offered for the production of such evidence as should lead to a conviction. Whether or not such a procedure be a pol-
itic one? whether calculated to assist or obstruct the
progress of justice? in the one case, stimulating persons who would otherwise be indifferent, into fer-
reting out real facts; in the other case, by tempting

to the fabrication of false evidence for the sake of gain—I shall not stay to inquire. It is in my opinion a question of importance and difficulty ; but one thing is clear—the practice affords a constant topic, under the name of "blood money," for vituperative declamation on behalf of the most guilty prisoner, and is calculated too often to turn the scale the wrong way—to incline a candid, but anxious juryman to a distrust of evidence really of the most satisfactory description. Of course, I can speak for myself only: but I believe that in the case under consideration, all the witnesses intended to speak the truth. I think Baron Rolfe was also of that opinion, though he seemed to suspect that one or two of the witnesses, by long brooding over the matter, had got to put things together which ought not to have been so connected, and even to suppose one or two matters to have happened, which had not. There were certainly discrepancies—but none, as it seemed to me, of a very material description ; and could it be otherwise, when such a large body of witnesses came to speak to so many different circumstances, which had happened so long before? An entire concord, in things great and small, would have been a most palpable badge of fraud and falsehood. The circumstance of Huntley's sudden disappearance only the day but one before a particular day, viz., Monday, 2d August, on which Yarm Fair was held, will account for a tolerably minute recollection of what happened about that period : and above all, the attention of the whole neighborhood was directed, at the time, to the circumstances attending so remarkable and sudden a disappearance of one of their neighbors and companions. Several of the principal witnesses, moreover, answered promptly in the affirmative to questions put by the prisoner's counsel, manifestly for his advantage—for instance, as to their having heard Huntley himself talk of going to America, and the absence of all concealment by the prisoner of the clothes, &c., belonging to Huntley. As to the discrepancy with reference to the six shirts spoken of so distinctly and specifically by Maw, while Bewick, whom he described to have been with him at the time, spoke of there being only five, and gave a decisive reason for it, with very great deference to the judge, who deemed it of importance, I think it deserving of little consideration. Bewick corroborates Maw up to five of the shirts, leaving it plain that Maw is under a *bonâ fide* mistake—after such a lapse of time—as to there having been a sixth. Thus the 'mportant fact of the prisoner's being in possession

of five new shirts belonging to Huntley, is clearly
established; for the mere negative evidence of the
old woman, Hannah Best, is unworthy of notice.

Let me first direct attention to the prisoner's own
statement—a matter which, especially when the
statement is made deliberately, is always worthy of
attention. "In criminal cases,"—observes the distinguished writer on the Law of Evidence, from
whom I have already quoted,—"the statement made
by the accused is of essential importance in some
points of view. Such is the complexity of human
affairs, and so infinite the combinations of circumstances, that the true hypothesis which is capable
of explaining and reuniting all the apparently conflicting circumstances of the case, may escape the
acutest penetration :—but the prisoner, so far as he
alone is concerned, can always afford a clue to
them; and though he may be unable to support his
statement by evidence, his account of the transaction is, for this purpose, always most material and
important. The effect may be, on the one hand, to
suggest a view which consists with the innocence
of the accused, and might otherwise have escaped
observation; while, on the other hand, its effect
may be to narrow the question to the consideration

whether that statement be or be not excluded by the evidence."

Now, in the present case, the prisoner's statement corroborates a considerable portion of the evidence. He admits a full knowledge, on Thursday, 22d July, 1830, of Huntley's possession of £85, 16s. 4d., and that Thursday, 29th July, 1830, was "the very last time he clapped eyes on" Huntley. Nevertheless, four witnesses speak decisively to the fact of their having seen him in Huntley's company at four different periods of the ensuing memorable day, Friday—viz., 5 o'clock, A. M. ; 3 or 4 o'clock, P. M.; 8 o'clock, P. M.; and 9 or 10 o'clock, P. M.—on the last of which occasions, the prisoner (having a gun in his hand), Huntley, and Garbutt being together, and going towards Crathorne Wood, to which they were then very near. Was this a mere error of recollection, or a wilful falsehood of the prisoner's? Or are all the four witnesses contradicting him—each speaking to a different period of the day, and to a different place—in error, or conspirators and perjurers? If they be speaking the truth, it is next to impossible to believe that Goldsborough could have had forgotten the circumstance of his having been so much in Huntley's company, up even to within an hour or two of his being so mysteriously missing—knowing that his movements in connection with Huntley had immediately become the subject of keen inquiry, and most vehement suspicion. If, then, he deliberately falsified the fact, what are we at liberty to infer from that circumstance as to his object and motives for so doing? Again, before he made the statement, he had heard all the evidence against him read over; and an essential part of it was that respecting his having been, so soon after Huntley's disappearance, in possession of his clothes, and also of a large sum of money. Yet he makes no allusion to these matters; neither denies nor accounts for them in any way whatever: and it must not be forgotten that, when arrested by Gernon, in June, 1841, he denied having ever had any of Huntley's clothes, or his watch. He makes no attempt to account for his sudden possession of so much money between the period of Huntley's disappearance and the spring of 1831; though he did state then, that he had married a wife with eighty pounds! Nor does he offer any explanation of the contradictory accounts which he had given as to Huntley's having gone to America, and his—the prisoner's—possession of the clothes, &c.; nor re-affirm any of them. In short, his statement appears as remarkable for what it does not contain, as it is important for what it does. I also consider it characterized— on the supposition of his guilt—by no little tact and circumspection ; for he frankly admits a great deal which he felt he might be contradicted in, if he were to deny it; viz., his knowledge of Huntley's receipt of the exact sum (within a few pence) on the day of his actually receiving it ; suggesting a motive for his absconding to America, and for his having been so frequently in the prisoner's company—asserting that he finally parted openly with Huntley at the shop door of Farnabay, in the town of Hutton-Rudby; and contenting himself with a brief but solemn denial of the truth of Groundy's statement, that the three men had been with Groundy in Crathorne Woods, or Weary Bank Woods.

That statement, and its author's suicide immediately after making it, invests the whole facts of the case with an air of extraordinary mystery. It contains on the face of it surely a glaring improbability—namely, that the prisoner should have been so insane as to commit himself gratuitously and irretrievably to one whom he knew might immediately have caused his apprehension, and secured incontestable proof of his guilt in the

murdered body.   Stranger still, perhaps, is it, that
if Groundy really had no further part in the business than he represents in that statement, he
should not have disclosed the guilt of Goldsborough
at once, instead of continuing ever after burdened
with such a guilty secret, and for no adequate
motive.   It is to be observed that one of the witnesses, Anthony Wiles (*ante*, p. 189), disclosed
incidentally—(for his evidence was called with another view)—a circumstance worthy of attention—
viz., that one of the men with whom the prisoner
was drinking on the Saturday night after Huntley's
disappearance was Groundy : yet the prisoner says,
" if it was the last words I had to speak, I never
was with him."   At all events, a faint ray of light
is thrown on the case, by the fact that Groundy
was actually acquainted with the prisoner, and in
his company about the very time of the transaction
deposed to.   Again, the truth of his description of
the localities is confirmed by those who went to examine them.   The prisoner asked him nothing when
he made that statement, and the prisoner was invited to question him : was it because he dared not ?

Let us now follow the course of events.   I take
it to be proved beyond all reasonable doubt, that,
contrary to the deliberately signed statement of

the prisoner, he was seen with a gun about ten
o'clock at night on Friday, 30th July, 1830, in
company with Huntley and Garbutt, near a lane
or bridle-road leading to Crathorne Wood. That
gun he had purchased only a few days previously,
but after his knowledge of the fact of Huntley's
receipt of his money. The report of a gun is heard
from the wood within an hour or an hour and a
half afterwards; Huntley is never seen or heard of
any more; and between twelve and one o'clock
that night, the prisoner is observed stealing out of
his house, to go and listen at the constable's house,
and, after being so occupied for a minute or two,
return to his own. The next time that he is seen
is when drinking in company with Groundy, late on
Saturday night. But, to return for a moment to
the wood—it is certainly an embarrassing fact that
the witness spoke to having heard two reports
within half a minute of each other; whereas the
prisoner's was a single-barrelled gun. If the
witness's recollections were accurate—which I saw
no reason whatever to doubt—how is this fact to
be accounted for? If the prisoner's were the only
gun there, it is next to impossible that he could
have so rapidly reloaded and fired again, especially
under the horrid circumstances supposed. Was

there, then, a second gun, which had been observed by the witness, and in Garbutt's hand?—or before-hand, concealed, in readiness, in the wood?—or had he or the prisoner a pistol also, with which to repair an ineffectual first shot?—or was one of the shots fired by a poacher in another part of the wood? However wide of the mark may be all these speculations, there was one fact in evidence respecting this gun which I venture, with profound respect to say, that I was surprised at the learned judge's omitting to comment upon to the jury. A day or two after the disappearance of Huntley, Richardson called on the prisoner for payment of this gun, when the prisoner refused, and returned it, saying that he did not want it, and had not used it: on which Richardson put his finger down the muzzle to try it, and drew it back all blackened with discharged powder, and thus convicted him of a falsehood. What inference may we draw from this fact?

Then, as to the blood found on the road—a fact spoken to by two credible witnesses at the trial, one of them having also named it to the constable the same day on which he observed it—was it human blood? If so, it was lying very near the spot where Huntley had last been seen; and if his blood, it must have been lying there, moreover, two days and two nights—*i. e.,* from Friday midnight to nine o'clock, A. M., on Monday morning. The blood was described as "stale looking," and the weather had been fair and dry, but the road was not a much frequented one. It was spoken of by one witness as a "pool;" but if so, it could not have lain there since the Friday night; blood then shed would have become a dark coagulated mass, possibly covered with dust. Again, on the supposition of its having been Huntley's blood, he must have been murdered on the high-road; was that a probable thing, when they were close by the secret shades of Crathorne Wood, to which they were all seen going? May they have gone into the wood? May Huntley have become alarmed at their conduct—made his way out of the wood into the high-road, and there received the murderous fire of his assailants? But the spot where the blood lay was, moreover, from four to six miles' distance from Stokesley Beck, where the bones were found. When and by whom was Huntley's body taken to Stokesley Beck? It could not have been taken the same night,—at least, it is very highly improbable that such could be the fact; for the prisoner was at his own house between twelve and one o'clock that night, if the witness was correct in his recollection as to the hour; and, according to Groundy's account, the body of Huntley was lying in the wood on Wednesday, 4th August. Where then had it lain between the Friday night and the Wednesday following? In a secret part of the wood, covered up? or had it been buried on the Friday night temporarily, in the potato garth, where Maw said he saw some earth that looked newly dug?

I own that I am not satisfied with the last part of Maw's evidence; for it is hard to believe, that had he really witnessed so suspicious an appearance, at such a spot, after such a supposed tragedy, and when actually in quest of the body, he must have called attention to it, and dug it up. I ought to mention, however, that it did not appear that Maw was then aware of the circumstances of the blood on the road. Here let me put together two little circumstances in the case, which may suggest not an unimportant inference. It would appear highly probable, assuming the bones to have been Huntley's, that for obvious reasons his body would have been stripped of its clothing, to lessen any subsequent chances of detection. Now, there were no vestiges of clothing found with the bones, and eleven years was not, I should think, a sufficiently long space of time to admit of woolen clothes decaying or mouldering away so entirely as to leave no trace of them—not even buttons of bone or metal —with the exception of one large flat button, which was found at or near the spot, and not answering to the description of any belonging to Huntley, and possibly there by mere accident. If Huntley had been shot, his clothes must have been stained and steeped in blood, and the safety of the murderer or murderers would require the destruction of such evidences of their guilt. Now, several witnesses speak to the fact of Goldsborough's being seen alone a day or two after Huntley's disappearance, in his house, late at night, with a large fire (in the first week of August) burning something that gave out a strong "smell of woolen burning." May not these have been the bloody clothes of Huntley?

To proceed. The prisoner, seen in Huntley's company up to within a few hours of his sudden and total disappearance, is seen, the day but one afterwards, laying out £7 in the purchase of a cow, and in possession of both bank-notes and gold—having been, up to a very short time before, in the most abject poverty, and even destitution;—and, moreover, in possession of a large quantity of clothes belonging, unquestionably, and admittedly by the prisoner, to the missing man. This, of itself, unexplained, is sufficient to raise a violent presumption of the prisoner's guilt. But here also great caution is necessary. "If a horse be stolen from A," says Sir Matthew Hale, "and the same day B be found on him, it is a strong presumption that B stole him. Yet I do recollect that, before a very learned and wary judge, in such an instance, B was condemned and executed at Oxford assizes: and yet, within two assizes afterwards, C being apprehended for another robbery, upon his judgment and execution, confessed that he had been the man who stole the horse, and that, being closely pursued, he had desired B, a stranger, to walk his horse for him, while he turned aside, as he said, for a necessary occasion, and escaped, and B was apprehended with the horse, and died innocently."

Now, in the present case, here is a man suddenly missing, known to have been possessed of a considerable sum of money—the prisoner to have been aware of it—to have been seen in his company up to almost the last moment before his disappearance—to have become suddenly enriched, having previously been a pauper—and in possession of many articles of clothing belonging to the missing man. All these circumstances point one way; but then, on the other hand, no attempt was made by the prisoner to conceal his possession of either money or clothes, nor to escape or quit the neighborhood during the time when suspicion was hottest. Then he gives certainly contradictory answers concerning the way in which he became possessed of these matters— but all may be reconciled with the story he tells, that the missing man has gone to America, and that he (the prisoner) assisted him, and still seeks to baffle the pursuit of his absent friend. But if the latter story be true, is it probable, is it credible, that Huntley, meditating such an expedition, would first strip himself of all his newly purchased clothes, leave them behind him, and never afterwards come or send to claim them? All the facts of the case, however, as fairly and as accurately stated as I know how to state them, are now laid before the reader; and is not this indeed a striking specimen of the importance of, and the difficulties attending, circumstantial evidence?

I shall proceed to propose several hypotheses for consideration, in order to see whether any of them will reconcile all the circumstances, or which of them will reconcile most of them, and in the most natural manner.

"The force of circumstantial evidence," observes Mr. Starkie, "being exclusive in its nature, and the mere coincidence of the hypothesis with the circumstances being, in the abstract, insufficient, unless they exclude every other supposition, it is essential to inquire, with the most scrupulous attention, what other hypotheses there may be agreeing wholly or partially with the facts in evidence. Those which agree even partially with the circumstances are not unworthy of examination, because they lead to a more accurate examination of those facts with which, at first, they might appear to be inconsistent; and it is possible that on a more accurate examination of these facts, their authenticity may be rendered doubtful, or even altogether disproved." The same able writer from whom this passage is quoted has another observation, which also should be kept in view, while dealing with the facts of this case.

"To acquit, on light, trivial, and fanciful suppositions, and remote conjectures, is a virtual violation of the juror's oath; while, on the other hand, he ought not to condemn, unless the evidence exclude from his mind all reasonable doubt as to the guilt of the accused, and unless he be so convinced by the evidence, that he would venture to act upon that conviction, in matters of the highest concern and importance to his own interest."

First Hypothesis.—Huntley really did go off in the way alleged, to America or elsewhere, to avoid his creditors, and also his wife, from whom he had already separated, and to be relieved from the burden of supporting her. He may have since died a natural—an accidental—or a violent death, under circumstances depriving him of the opportunity of disposing by will of what he knew was coming to him; and this death may have happened very shortly after his departure. He left the more valuable portions of his clothes and property, and a great portion of his money in Goldsborough's hands, to be forwarded to him at the first convenient opportunity; and Goldsborough acted dishonestly by him in disposing of the clothes, and spending the money. Huntley may be now alive, and meditating a return home.

Second Hypothesis.—Huntley is dead, and was murdered by Garbutt, in whose company he had been left by Goldsborough.—Garbutt being also pursued by the officers of justice for other offences, hastily absconded, and may now be dead, or abroad.

Third Hypothesis.—Groundy was the actual

murderer, possibly instigated by Goldsborough ; or
Goldsborough was only subsequently informed by
Groundy of the murder, and insisted on receiving
a great portion ·of the money, as the price of his
silence.—He committed suicide from fear lest his
guilt should come out in court, at the trial—through
his being unable to stand solemn and public questioning upon the subject.   He may have been also
partly influenced by remorse at having wrongfully
sworn away the life of Goldsborough.

Fourth   Hypothesis.--Groundy,   Garbutt,   and
Goldsborough, or Groundy and Goldsborough,
were all concerned as principals in the murder.
The second gun was Groundy's, who joined them
in the wood.

Lastly.—With reference to the prisoner at the
bar, let us inquire more fully, whether his guilt, or
innocence, be more consistent with the proved
facts of the case.

If innocent, he must stand or fall by the story of
Huntley's having left him on his way to America,
after in vain pressing Goldsborough to accompany
him.   It certainly does appear that Huntley had
contemplated such a step, and there are other circumstances favoring the notion that Goldsborough
and Huntley had been busily concerting a scheme

for Huntley's going off privately to America. He was, during the whole of the time between the 22d and 30th July, incessantly coming over to Goldsborough, and remaining in his company. At five o'clock in the morning of the day of his disappearance, he was seen coming to Goldsborough's house, where he was immediately admitted. They may have arranged that Goldsborough should go and fetch Huntley's things, the same day, from Huntley's to Goldsborough's house, to keep for, or send after, Huntley; in pursuance of which arrangement Goldsborough went, and returned with the articles in question in a sack, during the afternoon of the same day. It may have been a part of the arrangement, that Huntley should leave a considerable portion of his money in Goldsborough's hands, for safety's sake--to be remitted as Huntley might want it. Or Goldsborough might have promised and intended to follow him shortly afterwards; but fondness for his children may have kept him back; and he may have determined on playing Huntley false, and appropriating the money and property left with him to his own use, relying on Huntley's not venturing to return, lest he should be saddled with the support of his wife; but if he should return, then resolving to impose on

him as much difficulty as possible in claiming his
own, by converting his money into articles of furni
ture and farming purchases. His contradictory
accounts of Huntley's movements are consistent
with his wish to baffle the pursuers of Huntley,
by putting them on false scents; and this may
serve to explain his light jocular tone in speaking
of Huntley's absence: "You'll all see, by-and-by,
whether he's murdered or not." In this view of
the case, the blood on the road, the gunshot in the
wood, and the burning of clothes soon afterwards,
if such facts really happened, have no true connection with each other; and the skull and bones produced, were not the skull and bones of Huntley.
Let it, moreover, be borne in mind, that Goldsborough did not attempt any concealment of property
or money, or escape—neither after nor before suspicion had settled on him; nor even when set at
liberty, after his arrest in the month of July, 1841.

But if the prisoner be guilty, let us imagine that,
from the time of learning that Huntley had become
possessed of so considerable a sum of money, the
prisoner had conceived the idea of destroying him,
in order to obtain that money, and in such a manner
as to warrant the belief of the neighborhood that
he had only carried into effect his previously ex-

pressed intention of going off to America. That in pursuance of such an intention, Huntley had sent his clothes, &c., on the Friday, to the prisoner's house—that, in short, they formed the contents of the bag or sack, which the prisoner was seen carrying into his house on the Friday afternoon. That either alone or in company with Garbutt or Groundy, he allured Huntley into Crathorne Wood, under the pretext of shooting a hare, and enjoying a pleasant supper together ; which Huntley, who might have become loquacious through previous drinking with the prisoner, and possibly Garbutt and Groundy, or one of them—mentioned to Maw, in a merry humor, on meeting him on the road, as described by Maw. That he may have been shot, either in the wood, or on the high-road, where the blood was found ; and his body buried for a while, or concealed in the wood till it could be permanently disposed of. That the prisoner then returned to his own house, and having been, possibly, alarmed by some noise into the suspicion that his motions had been watched, slipped out, shortly afterwards, to ascertain whether there were any grounds for his fears. That he then cleansed himself from any marks of the deed in which he had been engaged,

15

and resolved on the course he should pursue—
namely, to give out that he had sent Huntley on
his way to America.   That, finding the current of
suspicion setting in more strongly against him than
he had anticipated, he resolved, on due deliberation, distrusting the chance of escaping by flight, to
stay and brave it out by a bold and consistent ad-
herence to the fiction of Huntley's having gone off
secretly to America.   That if neither Garbutt nor
Groundy had been originally parties to the murder,
the prisoner may have taken both, or either, subsequently, into his confidence, to secure his or their
assistance in successfully disposing of the body;
rewarding him or them by a sum of money, which
he might have represented as being the greater
portion of what he had found on the person of
Huntley.   That, the prisoner, either alone or
assisted by one or both of these men, afterwards
disinterred the body, if temporarily buried, or removed it from any place where it had lain hid,
and carried it to Stokesley Beck, at night-time, and
thrust it naked, into a hole which they dug into the
bank of the Beck, as a place distant, secluded, and
likely to escape suspicion — bringing home the
bloody clothes and burning them as soon as possible.   That subsequently, he became agitated,

silent, and reserved—tormented by his own reflections, and terrified by the continued strength of public suspicion, and the search after Huntley's body.

That his object being to divert the searchers, if possible, from proceeding towards Stokesley Beck, he conceived himself likely to attain that end by himself suggesting that the body might be found there—a bold and desperate expedient, founded on the belief that any suggestion of that sort by him, would certainly be disregarded. That, finding the search at length abandoned, and the vehemence of public suspicion to be abating, but yet rendering his continuance at Hutton-Rudby troublesome and dangerous, he resolved to transfer his residence, under a feigned name, to Barnsley. That when, many years afterwards, so abruptly challenged as the murderer of Huntley, he was thrown off his guard, so as to forget the notoriety of his having possessed the clothes and property of Huntley, and deny that fact to the officer who took him into custody. That he was dismayed by the appearance of Groundy against him, and dared not ask him any questions, lest he should thereby reveal more of the transaction; and consequently, felt compelled to content himself with a general denial of Groundy's statement. That he inwardly shrunk from the frightful spectacle of the shattered skull, knowing it to be that of Hunt- ley,—and that HORROR looked up at him from these eyeless sockets.——But stay! A sudden stir an- nounces the return, after a long absence, of the jury; and the crowded court is quickly hushed into agita- ted silence, as the jury enter—the foreman carrying with him the skull and bones ; and the prisoner is replaced at the bar to hear his doom. The judge has in readiness, but concealed, the black cap, should it become, within a few moments, his dreadful duty to pronounce sentence of death upon the prisoner. The names of the jury are called over one by one, and the prisoner eyes them with unut- terable feelings. Then comes the fearful moment.

Clerk of Arraigns.—Gentlemen of the Jury, are you agreed upon your verdict? Do you say that Robert Goldsborough, the prisoner at the bar, is guilty of the murder and felony with which he stands charged, or not guilty?

Foreman.—Not Guilty.

Clerk of Arraigns.—Gentlemen of the Jury, you say that the prisoner at the bar, Robert Goldsbo- rough, is not guilty. That is your verdict; and so you say all?—(To the Governor of the Castle)— " Remove the prisoner from the bar."

The verdict did not seem wholly unexpected by the audience ; and it was received by them in blank silence.

The prisoner exhibited no symptoms of satisfaction or exultation on hearing the verdict pronounced ; but maintained the same phlegmatic, oppressed air which he had exhibited throughout. As soon, however, as he was removed from the bar, and before he had quitted the dock, he whispered, with tremulous eagerness, in the ear of the officer—" Can they try me again, lad ?" " No ; thou's clear of it now, altogether," was the reply : on which Goldsborough heaved a very deep sigh, and said, " If they'd put me on my trial in 1830, I could have got plenty to come forward and clear me." Within half an hour afterwards, he was seen dressed as he had appeared at the bar of the court, only that he had his hat on, and carried a small bundle of clothes tied up in a blue and white cotton handkerchief under his arm, walking quietly out of the frowning gates of York Castle, once more a free man, to go whithersoever he chose. He was quickly joined by two mean-looking men, and spent the next hour or so in walking about the town, and looking into the various shop-windows, occasionally followed by a little crowd of boys and others who had recognized him.

How now say YOU, candid and attentive reader? Had you been upon the jury, should you have said —*Guilty*, or *Not Guilty?*